A
Critique
of
Film
Theory

DATE DUE			
11/8/13			

BRIAN HENDERSON, who is currently Associate Professor in the Center for Media Study at the State University of New York at Buffalo, received a B.A. in Philosophy from Johns Hopkins University, a J.D. from Harvard Law School, and a Ph.D. from the University of California at Santa Cruz, with a dissertation on film theory. He has written extensively on film subjects for such journals as *Film Quarterly*, *Film Comment*, and *Film Heritage*. His writing has also been included in the anthologies *Focus on the Horror Film* (1972), *Movies and Methods* (1976), *Conflict and Control in the Cinema* (1977), and *Film Theory and Criticism* (2d ed. 1979). He is a member of the editorial board of *Film Quarterly*.

A
Critique
of
Film
Theory

by
Brian
Henderson

E. P. Dutton, New York

To Jane DuBach Henderson and Donald A. Henderson

Grateful acknowledgment is made to the following for permission to quote from copyrighted material:

"Two Types of Film Theory." Copyright © 1971 by The Regents of the University of California. Reprinted from *Film Quarterly*, 24, no. 3 (Spring 1971), pp. 33–42, by permission of The Regents. | "The Structure of Bazin's Thought." Copyright © 1972 by The Regents of the University of California. Reprinted from *Film Quarterly*, 25, no. 4 (Summer 1972), pp. 18–27, by permission of The Regents. | "The Long Take." Copyright © 1971 by Film Comment Publishing Corporation. Reprinted from *Film Comment*, 7, no. 2 (Summer 1971), pp. 6–11, by permission of the Film Society of Lincoln Center. | "Toward a Non-Bourgeois Camera Style." Copyright © 1971 by The Regents of the University of California. Reprinted from *Film Quarterly*, 24, no. 2 (Winter 1970/71), pp. 2–14, by permission of The Regents. | "*Godard on Godard:* Notes for a Reading." Copyright © 1974 by The Regents of the University of California. Reprinted from *Film Quarterly*, 27, no. 4 (Summer 1974), pp. 34–46, by permission of The Regents. | "Metz: *Essais I* and Film Theory." Copyright © 1975 by The Regents of the University of California. Reprinted from *Film Quarterly*, 28, no. 3 (Spring 1975), pp. 18–33, by permission of The Regents. | "Segmentation." Copyright © 1977 by The Regents of the University of California. Reprinted from *Film Quarterly*, 31, no. 1 (Fall 1977), pp. 57–65, by permission of The Regents. | "Critique of Cine-Structuralism, I and II." Copyright © 1973, 1974, by The Regents of the University of California. Reprinted from *Film Quarterly*, 26, no. 5 (Fall 1973), pp. 25–34, and 27, no. 2 (Winter 1973/74), pp. 37–46, by permission of The Regents.

For information contact: E. P. Dutton, 2 Park Avenue, New York, N.Y. 10016

Library of Congress Catalog Card Number: 77-73145

ISBN: 0-525-08740-0 (cloth)   0-525-47526-5 (DP)

Published simultaneously in Canada by Clarke, Irwin & Company Limited, Toronto and Vancouver

Designed by Mary Beth Bosco

10 9 8 7 6 5 4 3 2 1

First Edition

Contents

Preface

What is critique? What is film theory? Is a critique of film theory possible, necessary, or desirable? Does this book constitute a critique of film theory? If not, how does it contribute to this goal?

In the dictionary, "critique" is interchangeable with "criticism"; though critique may refer to an entire review, usually of a literary work, whereas criticism is more general: it may be single or multiple, coordinated or not, and may concern anything. There are some technical uses of the term "critique" in philosophy. Kant's critiques of pure reason, of practical reason, and of judgment concern the possibilities and limits of human knowledge in metaphysics, in ethics, and in aesthetics. But Kant's notion of critique cannot be applied to our project because he addresses the faculties of human reason and judgment themselves, not texts that deal with these.

Marx uses the term critique many times, usually to refer to texts and to disciplines rather than to society or to mind. But Marx never defined critique and indeed uses the term differently in different texts, for example, in the 1844 manuscripts ("A Critique of Hegel's *Philosophy of Right*") and in *Capital* (1867) (subtitled "A Critique of Political Economy"). Marx's work as a whole has been of interest to epistemologists, especially recently. A number of contemporary analysts, steeped in Gaston Bachelard's work in the history and philosophy of the sciences, have studied the full course of Marx's work (1840–1883) from an epistemological standpoint.[1] They make periodizations and other distinctions that Marx did not make, arguing that Marx's theoretical practice was not always theorized by Marx himself. These analysts have also attempted to define "critique" in a more rigorous way, though this is not their primary goal.

Jacques Rancière examines "The Concept of 'Critique'" in Marx by comparing Marx's early and late treatments of economic categories. In the 1844 manuscripts Marx resorts to the categories of political economy, but he does not criticize them. He accepts them as adequate description of economic reality, indeed he *equates them with economic reality*.

> The discourse of the economists is taken only as a reflection of the facts. There is no disjunction between economic facts and economic science. There is no disjunction between economic facts and economic science. . . . There is no *placing* of political economy. In fact two things would have had to be placed: the *economic reality* and the *economic discourse*. . . . The problem of the political economy as a discourse with claims to be scientific is not really posed.[2]

It is Marx's later work, and especially *Capital*, that addresses the concepts and categories of political economy as a realm of discourse, not as economic reality. Hence, "A Critique of Political Economy." Marx wrote Ferdinand Lassalle in 1858:

> The first work in question is *critique of the economic categories*, or, if you like, the system of bourgeois economy critically presented. It is a presentation of the system and simultaneously, through this presentation, a criticism of it.[3]

"Presentation of the system and simultaneously, through this presentation, a criticism of it." This phrase describes, as it were, systematic criti-

---

[1] See, for example, Louis Althusser, *For Marx*, trans. Ben Brewster (1965; London: Allen Lane, 1969).

[2] Jacques Rancière, "The Concept of 'Critique' and the 'Critique of Political Economy,'" Part I, *Theoretical Practice* #1 (June 1970), pp. 39–40.

[3] *Ibid.*, Part II, *Theoretical Practice* #2 (April 1971), p. 31.

cism or criticism of a system; but it does not specify critique in the radical, transformative sense claimed for Marx's practice by the epistemologists. For this we turn to Gaston Bachelard and his work on the philosophy of science.

In Gaston Bachelard's work, critique leads to determination of the "problematic" of a position or realm of discourse. (Louis Althusser defines the "epistemological shift" between early Marx and late Marx as a shift in problematics.) The best definition of the notion is found in Bachelard's reflection on the scientific problem. Bachelard disparages the Cartesian "universal doubt," advanced in the *Discourse on Method* as the way to certain knowledge.

> Universal doubt irreversibly pulverizes the given into a heap of heteroclite facts. It corresponds to no real instance of scientific research. Instead of the parade of universal doubt, scientific research demands the setting up of a problematic. Its real starting-point is a *problem*, however ill-posed. The scientific-ego is then a program of experiments; while the scientific non-ego [that is, unconscious] is already a *constituted problematic*.[4]

Ben Brewster and Althusser define problematic in this way:

> A word or concept cannot be considered in isolation; it only exists in the theoretical or ideological framework in which it is used: its problematic. . . . It should be stressed that the problematic is *not* a worldview. It is not the essence of the thought of an individual or epoch which can be deduced from a body of texts by an empirical, generalizing reading; it is centered on the *absence* of problems and concepts within the problematic as much as their presence; it can therefore only be reached by a symptomatic reading (*lecture symptomale*) on the model of the Freudian analyst's reading of his patient's utterances.[5]

An analysis of the problematic of a theoretical text is attempted in chapter 9, "Critique of Cine-Structuralism." It says:

> The problematic of a text is not only the questions that it asks, but the questions that it does not ask. Specifically it is the relationship between these, for a text raises certain questions only at the price of not asking others. The relationship between questions asked and questions suppressed is always ideological. (p. 215n)

It is only at the end of a long, searching analysis of the texts of auteur-structuralism that a statement of their problematic is attempted.

---

[4] Gaston Bachelard, quoted in Dominique Lecourt, *Marxism and Epistemology: Bachelard, Canguilhem, Foucault,* trans. Ben Brewster (1969; London: New Left Books, 1975), p. 80.

[5] Althusser, *For Marx,* pp. 253–254.

The questions Can modes of myth study be applied to film study? and Can structuralism be merged with auteurism? are *not identical.* . . . Auteur-structuralism treats the two questions as one; specifically, it reduces the first question to the second. It thereby makes the study of films as myths dependent upon the fusion of auteurism and structuralism and effectively rules out other modes of study. . . . Having critiqued auteur-structuralism, we are in a position to reconsider this relationship and to disentangle these questions. When auteur-structuralism is destroyed, it is by no means the case that the study of films as myths is destroyed also. Indeed, it would seem that *only* the destruction of auteur-structuralism *liberates* the other question, that is, allows it to be asked and answered.[6] (p. 215)

We have spoken of critique but not of film theory. At least until recently, film theory was not a field and had no "history" that anyone spoke of. There were simply a number of books on the aesthetics and making of films. By now there are more than a few books, and several critical approaches to the field of film theory itself have been taken. Perhaps the existence of critical approaches does not prove the existence of a field, nor their nonexistence its nonexistence; but every approach to a subject necessarily constitutes it as an object, that is, defines it in a certain way and acts on that definition. Perhaps then a first way to answer the question What is film theory? is to survey some of the approaches that have been taken to it, including our own. We shall discuss a few other approaches to film theory, not to agree or disagree with them but to "place" our own approach.

One approach relates film theories to their intellectual contexts and cultural periods. Annette Michelson says of Bazin's work:

> . . . it alone reflects, however incompletely, a writer's acquaintance and involvement with the central esthetic issues and intellectual forces of his time . . . Bazin's career was not only characteristic of a certain period and its intellectual style; it was more or less coextensive with it. His work spanned the period of Sartre's ascendancy.
>
> As a man of the '40's and '50's Bazin's own polished style and extensive intellectual references are innocent of structuralist preoccupations. Continuity in this critical tradition is insured by an uninterrupted

---

[6] Chapter 9 stands apart from the rest of this book because it treats a different topic—cine-structuralism, an extension of structuralism into certain areas of film study—rather than film theory in the sense in which the other chapters use the term. It stands apart also because it alone of all the chapters brings to completion the inquiries it undertakes. This is possible because of its topic: the texts it interrogates are explicitly derived from other texts that they might be checked against. Chapter 9 does not question the problematics of the source texts, only those of the applications. Of course it is far easier to critique a few individual texts, especially those explicitly derived from other texts, than to critique an entire field of study.

permeability to its cultural context. Mr. Gray's editing has, most un-
fortunately however, abstracted Bazin's work from its intellectual
habitat, eliminated its philosophical assumptions and intentions, thereby
attenuating its historical importance and its present critical interest.[7]

(She adds: "All of Bazin's points had been argued from a diametrically
opposed position by Eisenstein in his elaboration of the montage es-
thetic.")

In another piece, Michelson compares Eisenstein and Bazin as film
theorists. After reviewing the rootedness of Bazin's insights in the intellectual movements of his period, Michelson characterizes Bazin's
"viewer participation in the image" as Christian Democrat in orientation
and Eisenstein's model as Marxist.

> Our two major theoreticians—Europeans both—elevated their chosen
> cinematic styles into filmic ontologies, proceeding then to hypostatize
> those filmic ontologies and the experiences afforded by them into para-
> digms of ontological awareness as such—Bazin positing the response to
> the spatio-temporal continuity of neo-realism as that of existential free-
> dom viewed as choosing in ambiguity, Eisenstein offering to his
> spectators the experience of revolutionary consciousness unfolding in
> the apprehension of the dialectic.[8]

One is not inclined to interrogate Michelson's assumptions and method
because they provide perspectives of interest to any approach to film
theory. From our point of view, the chief limitation of her method is
that it evacuates film theory as a site. Film-theoretical writings are
utterly determined by and absorbed by the larger philosophic positions
they express. Note in the passage on Eisenstein and Bazin above that
philosophy is (at) the origin of each film theory and (at) its end.
Film theory is merely a conduit through which ontology speaks to
ontology. This book postulates, on the contrary, that film theory is a site,
a realm of discourse, that it exhibits regularities of structure, assumptions,
propositions, and concepts.

The method of Dudley Andrew's early study of Bazin is close to that
of Michelson's.

> In summarizing and assessing the realism of André Bazin, one must
> take into account the two poles of his thinking, the purely filmic
> interests and the ethical and metaphysical concerns. There are two
> major directions of possible approach. One can work forward from his

---

[7] Annette Michelson, "What Is Cinema?," *Artforum,* 6, no. 10 (Summer
1968), pp. 66–71.

[8] Annette Michelson, "Screen/Surface: The Politics of Illusionism," *Artforum,* 11, no. 1 (September 1972), p. 61.

belief in the special status of the film image as I have done in this dissertation, or one can work back from his overall beliefs about art and experience.[9]

Andrew's study devotes a long chapter to grounding Bazin's "world view" in the intellectual work of his period—Marcel, Leenhardt, Mounier—but he stresses the systematic character of the film theoretician's work in a way that Michelson does not. Andrew's later book, *The Major Film Theories*, pivots on and extends the notion of system in accordance with its comparative project. The book's introduction states its assumptions and method.

> film theory forms a system in which the answer to any one question can be seen to lead easily to the next question, and any one question can be rephrased in terms of another.
>
> So even though two theorists may begin from differing perspectives, we can relate their views by transposing the questions.
>
> To summarize: by transposing questions and by following out their branches of interdependencies, we are able to compare the most diverse theorists, theorists who begin from different perspectives and ask seemingly different questions. If this were not possible, film theory would become a mere collection of unrelated questions randomly answered by various men. But with these two propositions, that is, by seeing film theory as a system, all questions and all perspectives are interconnected.[10]

Andrew assumes that film theory and every particular film theory are systematic, hence one can extrapolate from Eisenstein's explicit positions to implicit ones he never took. We do not assume the systematicity of film theory or of particular film theories; indeed our studies of Bazin indicate a major breach in his system, permitting a critical activity not at all systematic. Eisenstein as theorist is brilliant, but he is hardly the builder of a single system. Godard's writings are not systematic in any sense, yet they manage to be contradictory and paradoxical in important ways. Chapters 6, 7, and 8 explore in great detail the breaks, contradictions, and failures of system in Metzian film semiotics, yet his work is a valuable contribution to film theory. Several pages of chapter 9 discuss the post-structuralist critique of the "unity" of the text as an ideological illusion; but it does not take a Derridean to

---

[9] J. Dudley Andrew, "Realism and Reality in Cinema: The Film Theory of André Bazin and Its Source in Recent French Thought" (Ph.D. diss., University of Iowa, 1972; Ann Arbor, Mich.: University Microfilms, 1972), p. 158.

[10] J. Dudley Andrew, *The Major Film Theories* (New York: Oxford University Press, 1976), pp. 8–10.

realize that film theory consists of fragments of systems (or of fragments posing as systems), themselves riddled with gaps and contradictions, which seem at times to define different objects as well as to assert different standpoints. However, none of these propositions is inconsistent with the assumption that there are discursive regularities in film theory, that problematic, concepts, propositions, even theoretical structures recur in a virtually constant way and are in fact the basis of those controversies that constitute the field and even, perhaps, of the inconsistencies that characterize it.[11]

What is this book's approach to film theory? Unlike Michelson's approach, we take the texts of film theory, and only them, as the sites to be investigated; unlike the Andrew's approach, we do not fill out film theories by extrapolation in order to oppose them on every point according to an a priori conception of the field. We posit film theory as a realm of discourse comprised entirely by the texts of film theory as they stand.

We have also seen that both approaches employ a comparative method. They study film theories by comparing and contrasting them to each other, whether by opposing the philosophies that work through them or by opposing their positions on "the fundamental questions" of film theory. Our study begins in comparison but moves quickly to another mode by way of chapter 1's exposition tactic of switching back and forth on common points: this becomes virtually the presentation of a single model with differences noted. Chapter 1 poses a typology of film theories —part-whole theories *versus* relation-to-reality theories, exemplified by Eisenstein and Bazin; but it discovers that the two theories have underlying similarities of concept and structure, indeed that the two theories may be expressed as functions of a single theoretical plan or model. Both posit the shot as cinema's basic unit and as the index of film's relation to reality, guaranteed by the camera's automatic reproduction of nature. Both posit the sequence as a grouping of shots signifying a narrative segment. (Though it does not say so, chapter 1's finding of a structural similarity between opposing film theories tends to undermine

---

[11] Compare Michel Foucault: "As for the great controversies that occupied men's minds, these are accommodated quite naturally in the folds of this organization (the table). It is quite possible to write a history of thought in the Classical period using these controversies as starting-points or themes. But one would then be writing only a history of opinions, that is, of the choices operated according to individuals, environments, social groups; and a whole method of inquiry is thereby implied. If one wishes to undertake an archeological analysis of knowledge itself, it is not these celebrated controversies that ought to be used as the guidelines and articulation of such a project. One must reconstitute the general system of thought whose network, in its positivity, renders an interplay of simultaneous and apparently contradictory opinions possible. It is this network that defines the conditions that make a controversy or problem possible, and that bears the historicity of knowledge." (*The Order of Things* [1966; London: Tavistock, 1970], p. 75.)

its initial typology; its anaylsis suggests that both part-whole and relation-to-reality aspects are operative in each theory and may be integrated into a single model of film theory.) The principal differences between the two theories concern the aesthetic and historical values with which each invests the model. It is such disputes over values that comprise the principal oppositions among film theories in the usual view. "Eisenstein *versus* Bazin" means a conflict of cinematic values—formal, aesthetic, ideological, historical. Our approach decenters positions on values and conflicts of value by casting them as the variables of an otherwise invariant model.

Because it posits a common structure of film theories, we may call our approach a "structural approach" and chapter 1's analysis of that common structure a "structural model." Our approach differs from the other approaches discussed in two important ways: first, it posits film theory as an autonomous realm of discourse; second, it posits film theory as a single structure capable of various investments rather than as a group of opposing whole theories. These differences are linked, for it is only by positing film theory as an autonomous realm of discourse that it is possible to move from a comparative to a structural method. At the same time, it is only the move from a comparative to a structural method that makes possible study of film theory as a realm of discourse. Neither is possible so long as one links each theory to a distinct philosophic system or fills out each theory until it opposes every other theory on every issue according to an ideal scheme. The word "posit" is used advisedly, for the logical status of the structural model is that of a construct not that of an empirical fact. Epistemologically speaking, our approach does not *find* a common structure among film theories; it constructs a model that makes certain similarities of film theories central and everything else, including their differences, peripheral. To say this is not to diminish our work, it is to acknowledge the nature of all critical activity and model-making. The value of the structural model lies in what it enables us to do: it must be judged by the analytic operations that it makes possible.

In Part I the structural model serves and is subordinate to an overall project for the criticism and revision of film theory. Chapter 4, the first essay of Part I to appear, analyzes Godard's late films and calls for a revision of film theory in light of them. Chapter 1, the next to appear, announces this revision project at its outset, "new theoretical work is needed: the development of cinema since the late 1950s is far beyond the explanatory capacities of the classical film theories." The other essays of Part I bear in one way or another on the reform of film theory, often opening and closing on a reform note. It is not always clear, however, exactly what overall revision of film theory is urged by these texts. Many individual suggestions and some of the general statements imply preservation of the structure of film theory, minus relation-to-reality and aesthetic prescriptions and with other changes made to overcome the defects noted. Other passages suggest a more radical break with film theory. Chapter 1 embodies this ambivalence by concluding "The classical film theories . . . cannot account for and cannot be stretched or amended to account for . . . these works"; yet by concluding also "Comparison with the classical theories is nevertheless useful—partly because they are the only models we currently have, partly because such comparison reveals the shortcomings of the older theories and possibly the outlines of a new theory."

The structural model is developed by chapter 1 specifically to serve the reform project. That it is an appropriate tool for this task follows from the nature of the reform project, which is to concern film theory generally. It is not this or that film theory that fails to describe films adequately but all film theories. It is not a particular film theory that lacks the concepts necessary for film analysis, it is film theory generally, film theory as a realm of discourse. But how is one to formulate criticisms and frame revisions that will improve film theory generally? Part I's solution to these problems is the structural model. It is not too much to say that all the analytic operations of Part I proceed on the basis of the structural model.

The Introduction to Part I summarizes those operations in detail; a glance at a few of them will suffice. Determining the foundational role of ontology in film theory and the influence of aesthetic partisanship on all aspects of film theory would not be possible without the structural model. Neither would the demonstration that ontology and aesthetic partisanship inhibit the descriptive function of film theory, leading it to avoid large areas of film history and style and to fail to develop the concepts necessary to describe them. The reforms urged by Part I in response to its diagnosis also derive from the structural model: the elimination of ontological foundations, the decentering of aesthetic partisanship, the reorientation of film theory from the reality/film interface to that of critic/film, with the attendant responsibility to provide a full set of tools for the critic's task. These measures, plus Part I's many analyses suggesting specific concepts and models of filmic construction, are called by the Introduction a "descriptive rhetoric" project. (Descriptive here opposes prescriptive or normative rhetoric; it studies what figures exist and how they are used in a realm of discourse, not what figures should exist or how they should be used.) This project too rests on the structural model; for it has been generated by reducing film theory to a core of concepts and propositions, then by rebuilding from that core with new concepts and models.

The descriptive rhetoric project, like Part I generally, is unfinished—it was interrupted to meet the challenge of film semiotics. It is therefore difficult to evaluate. But its theoretical status *can* be evaluated because the theoretical apparatus that sets the project in place . is complete. Various tendencies in recent film theory no doubt oppose or disparage the notion of a descriptive rhetoric of filmic figures. Indeed chapter 9 of this book contains enough material to critique the project many times over. The descriptive rhetoric project may be theoretically indefensible today, but I still wish that we had a full version of it on pragmatic grounds. It would be useful to working film criticism and, indeed, to later theoretical initiatives. The field of film study is strewn with uncompleted projects, barely sketched proposals, and undeveloped ideas, with practical work proceeding most often without relation to theory. Thus new film theories have little to work on; they are at best revolutions "at the top." A new literary theory overturns a field already theorized many times and in which practical work has followed theory at every stage. In film theory a succession of systems has left no certain heritage because few jobs have been finished, because practical work is confused by or indifferent to theories, and because a core of film theory has never been defined. Thus the field of film study has been unduly vulnerable to every invading theoretical army; but it has not benefited from its various conquests because it has not defined itself.

In Part II we use the structural model developed by Part I in other theoretical contexts. It is used to evaluate various attempts to theorize film outside of the film-theory tradition, principally the film-semiotic one. The uncompleted analytical engine of Part I is mobilized for defense purposes in Part II; although, as the Introduction to Part II specifies, our study of film theory tells us about the new attempts and the new attempts tell us about film theory. Note that the comparative approaches have nothing distinctive to say about the new theorizations, except to include them as *one more* theory in the comparative derby. They put it on the same level as other theories; there is nothing else to do under the comparative approach.

As its Introduction notes, Part II of this book does not continue the inquiries of Part I. This includes those operations of Part I that contribute to a critique of film theory; but Part II makes its own, quite different contribution to that critique. The Part II essays were undertaken to defend film theory and its study against the challenges of film semiotics, but their interest for critique goes beyond this defensive project. Their close readings of the film-semiotic texts discover important things about the concepts and structure of film theory.

Film semiotics is of interest to any study of film theory, because it is the first systematic attempt to theorize film from a standpoint other than that of film theory. This attempt necessarily raises fundamental questions about the nature of film theory, though film semiotics does not itself raise these questions—it does not pose the problem of its relation to film theory. Chapters 6, 7, and 8 ask them of the film-semiotic texts.

These chapters find the concepts and structure of film theory beneath the apparent newness and rigor of film semiotics. This indicates first that using a new method does not guarantee a break with the concepts and structure of older theory. Critique is necessary: film theory must be explicitly addressed by any new theory, its concepts identified and analyzed, its structure explained, its problematic declared and criticized. This point goes beyond declaring the failures of film semiotics, it posits the need for critique in *any* future work in film theory.

In the evolution of our work, it is the confrontation of chapters 6, 7, and 8 with film semiotics that gives rise to the notion of a critique of film theory. These chapters remain our best argument for the necessity of such critique. They also confirm what is basic to the notion of critique discussed above: that critique is not only a tool of radical theoretical change, it is indispensable to such change.

Thus our first argument against film semiotics is that it fails to critique and therefore fails to change film theory. This leads to a closer examination of its theoretic structure, asking why it fails to do so. Chapter 6 establishes that film semiotics in its first phase does not significantly improve upon or differ from film theory: on this ground alone the need for critique is affirmed. Chapters 7 and 8 extend this conclusion significantly and find out new things. Chapter 7 finds that even new theoretical prescriptions that explicitly reject certain propositions of film theory are rendered ineffective by operation of the film-theoretical concepts retained. This suggests that film theory, its concepts and propositions, are far more persistent and tenacious than anyone has supposed. It suggests that the mutual dependence and other interconnections among the propositions and concepts of film theory are still largely unknown. These points suggest what our other analyses confirm directly: that the operation of film-theoretical concepts in other texts and systems is a process uncontrolled by and unknown to the theorists themselves, even highly self-conscious ones. (Until the critique of film theory is completed, this is true of film-theoretical texts also.) This in turn suggests that the operation of film-theoretical concepts, in whatever context they occur, is partly unconscious.

Chapter 8 advances critique by examining in detail the full process of an argument that employs a rigorous method but that nevertheless admits and even bases itself on propositions of another system (film theory) having no relationship to the method applied and no place in its formal argument. Chapter 8 shows that even a rigorous method does not prevent old concepts and propositions from passing into a new system. More importantly, it shows, in a point-by-point study of its argument, precisely *how* it admits them and builds itself on them. This suggests again that those concepts and propositions operate largely at a level beneath that of conscious discourse.

The full implications of chapters 7 and 8 for the project of a critique of film theory have by no means been fully absorbed by this inquiry. They do suggest that the critique project might profitably resort to what

Bachelard calls "the psychoanalysis of objective knowledge" before its work is done.[12]

Though chapters 6, 7, and 8 began as a defense of film theory against its dismissal by film semiotics, they ended by contributing to our knowledge of film theory. This justifies Part II's long detour from our principal study of film theory—or rather reroutes the principal study so that it now runs through the detour. This may sound like Milton's paradox of the fortunate fall—the evil of Adam's sin brought the greater good of the Redemption—but there is nothing teleological about it. It is a rather ordinary instance of refutation operating as a discovery procedure in research. Imre Lakatos argues that refutation is an integral part of any proof, or process of proof, itself[13] :

> GAMMA: Do you mean that *all* interesting refutations are heuristic?
> PI: Exactly. You cannot separate refutations and proofs on the one hand and changes in the conceptual, taxonomical, linguistic framework on the other. (p. 93)

If our attention to Metz's work were simply in order to dismiss it, we might have stopped at chapter 6 (some readers would have preferred this). To continue refutation/discovery through two more chapters affirms our interest in Metz's work and our sense that more was to be learned from it. Our findings concerning film theory both justify that sense and raise new questions about film semiotics and film theory and their relation.

---

[12] Bachelard says in *The Psychoanalysis of Fire*: "It is really a question of finding how unconscious values affect the very basis of empirical and scientific knowledge . . . Thus we shall be justified in speaking of an *unconscious of the scientific mind*—of the heterogeneous nature of certain concepts, and we shall see converging, in our study of any particular phenomenon, convictions that have been formed in the most varied fields." Bachelard's study of fire may apply to a film-theoretical notion such as the shot: "scientific objectivity is possible only if one has broken first with the immediate object." Bachelard traces the scientific problem of fire, "how a problem which had been a prime concern of scientific research for centuries was suddenly broken down into smaller problems or set aside without ever having been solved." *"Fire is no longer a reality for science."* (Trans. Alan C. M. Ross [1938; Boston: Beacon Press, 1964], pp. 10, 1–2.)

[13] Lakatos also defines the "negative" function of refutation, but this too he insists on placing within the context of the whole of inquiry. "It is well known that *criticism* may cast doubt on, and eventually refute, '*a priori* truths' and so turn *proofs* into mere *explanations*. That *lack of criticism or of refutation* may turn implausible conjectures into '*a priori* truths' and so tentative explanations into proofs is not so well known but just as important." (*Proofs and Reflections, The Logic of Mathematical Discovery,* ed. John Worrall and Elie Zahar [Cambridge: Cambridge University Press, 1976], p. 49). This passage does not put our inquiry in a new light so much as provide another rationale for it.

We have traced our approach to film theory, based upon the structural model, through Parts I and II of this book. We may now ask how the structural approach and the book itself relate to the critique of film theory. Note that the notion of a critique of film theory does not arise in Part I and emerges only in the course of the analyses of Part II. Critique of film theory is not the goal or organizing principle of either Part I or Part II. It is this preface that defines critique, proposes it as a goal, and evaluates this book in light of it. Indeed it is one of the most important functions of this book to formulate the notion of a critique of film theory and to assert its value, and it has taken the book as a whole to do this. The notion of critique also enables us to review the book from an outside perspective, to shape a sense of work to be done in film theory, and to connect this book's work to the work to be done.

Aside from formulating its notion, the most important contribution of this book to a critique of film theory is the structural model itself. The structural model makes possible most of the analyses of this book, as we have seen, but it is not limited to these. There is no way to know in advance all the analytic operations that the structural model makes possible or to which it might lead. What is clear is that we have not exhausted them in this book, neither have we exhausted the contributions of the structural model to critique.

As noted, the great advantage of the structural model is that it enables us to analyze not this or that film theory but film theory itself, film theory as a realm of discourse. By virtue of the structural model, criticisms of film theory—what would be criticisms if addressed to a single theory—become part of the critique process. This happens throughout Part I, in which, as we have seen, critique is already at work. The structural model explains how it is that Part I, with no notion or program of critique, may nevertheless contribute to the critique of film theory. Part I's analysis of the role of ontology and of aesthetic programs in film theory, its showing that they inhibit the descriptive function of film theory, leading it to ignore important areas of film history and style, these operations contribute to critique. So, less evidently, do the operations connected with Part I's reform project, which eliminate the ontology and aesthetic dimensions of film theory and begin the task of filling out film theory's basic concepts with others necessary to perform the task of description. These operations, among other things, test whether critique has gone far enough, whether a workable new synthesis can be built on the pared-down bones of film theory. They also press other questions fundamental to critique, such as the nature and usefulness of film theory's fundamental concepts, whether they may be the basis of a new synthesis, what is *their* theoretical foundation, etc.?

The essays of Part II uncover new problems, quite unglimpsed by Part I. On the one hand they discover the need for critique. A new system that does not critique film theory is virtually certain to repeat it in whole or in part, and to be quite unaware of that fact. The second point is even stranger in relation to the perspective of Part I—that when a new system does later expunge a fundamental aspect of film theory, the earlier absorption of film theory will prevail. Even explicit, external repudiation is not enough; tenets of film theory will enter or persist in the new system anyway. This is far from Part I's confident assumption that any doctrine or feature of film theory may be dismantled and discarded and better ones put in their place, to meet our needs.

In uncovering these problems, Part II uses the structural model of Part I, which provides that definition of film theory that Part II applies to film semiotics to see whether, and how, it differs from film theory. What it finds turns the inquiry back upon the structural model itself and upon the concept structure of film theory that it represents. The next phase of work on film theory should include a deeper investigation of its concepts, propositions, and theoretical structure. Part I eliminates the ontological doctrines of film theory, but the analyses of Part II suggest perhaps an ontological dimension in the very concepts of film theory. This preserve of ontology is not affected by the operations of Part I; analysis of it must proceed in a different way. Perhaps the concept of the shot will be a good place to begin this phase of the inquiry. This is not the time to begin such a phase but our inquiry has made it possible by its emphasis throughout on the concepts of film theory. Film theory borrowed the terms shot, sequence, and others from film industry practice, without subjecting them to critique, criticism, or even examination. In theory and in practice these terms are used transparently: they refer simply and unambiguously to "real objects," with no intervention of mind, culture, or concept structures. Just to call these terms concepts challenges the traditional view. Posing the concepts of film theory as a phenomenon to be accounted for and as a problem to be analyzed is a main theme of this book from its beginning.

Analytic attention should also be devoted to other systematic analyses of film besides that of film theory, including more attention to film semiotics. These systems, though they theorize film from very different standpoints, or precisely because of this, provide an investigative control on film theory as well as specific information about its theoretical status. There should be attention to other classical film theories also, not as a retreat from the structural model but precisely as an illumination of it.

We have discussed very little the base of the structural model. It may be argued that we have not considered a sufficient number of film theories to construct an adequate model of film theory in general. Initially, however, our argument concerned theory types not just the theories discussed. Kracauer and Pudovkin were included by reference, the other classical theorists by implication. A kind of saturation principle is invoked: at the point at which no fundamentally different new theory is found, the corpus to be analyzed is closed and is considered to stand for the entire field. There is no need to examine every film theory to make an analysis, just as there is no need to examine every language to make a linguistic analysis.

Of course, once the structural model is achieved, however it is formulated, a classical film theory that does not fit may be used to challenge it. Damaging omissions come to mind but are not so easily sustained as might appear. It might seem, for instance, that Rudolf Arnheim belongs to a different tradition or logical set of film theory than the one we have discussed. A few passages make clear that he does not.

> As distinguished from the tools of the sculptor and the painter, which by themselves produce nothing resembling nature, the camera starts to turn and a likeness of the real world results mechanically. There is serious danger that the film maker will rest content with such shapeless reproduction. In order that the film artist may create a work of art it is important that he consciously stress the peculiarities of his medium. This, however, should be done in such a manner that the character of the objects represented should not thereby be destroyed but rather strengthened, concentrated, and interpreted.[14]
>
> We have tried to show above how even a single shot is in no sense a simple reproduction of nature; how even in the single shot most important differences exist between nature and the film image; and how seriously artistic formative processes must be considered. (p. 87)

The Arnheimian scenario of "formative processes" and antirealism is enacted over and in relation to the stage of classical film theory and has no meaning outside of it. Arnheim effects a relativization of the values of classical film theory; that is, he takes up a position within it. His constitutive assumptions—relation to reality, shot as basic unit, etc.—are the same.

Some theorists present difficulties, though these might be portals of discovery for future research. One function of the structural model is to make possible new kinds of research on classical film theory. Theories that do not fit the model exactly may suggest concepts or structures of film theory previously overlooked. Even some that do fit may suggest dimensions, implications, or applications of the model not revealed by other theories. Dziga Vertov as theorist seems to lie at least partly outside the classical tradition. He believes in the shot, his stress on the camera as a perfect seeing instrument seems to assert the "relation-to-reality" point, albeit in unique form; but his radical stand against the dramatic film (and therefore against narrative?) is a decided break with classical film theory. What effects this has on his overall position remains to be evaluated. Vachel Lindsay and Hugo Münsterberg wrote before shot and sequence terminology became standard. They speak of

---

[14] Rudolf Arnheim, *Film as Art* (Berkeley, Calif.: University of California Press, 1957), p. 35.

"views," "images," "scenes," and "events." These seem to mean the same thing and otherwise their theories seem to lie within the model, though this remains to be determined. In any case, determining when and how the term "shot" became standardized is a prime task for research —a matter of historical and theoretical importance.

Work to be done includes work on the category of the object of film theory. Film theory and film semiotics have virtually the same object. Film theory's proclaimed object is "film"; this has always meant narrative film. Film semiotics specifies its object as narrative film and avows that it is only one of many possible objects of analysis, but it does this in a way that preserves the centrality of narrative film—it remains the essence of film (see chap. 6). We need not enumerate the other kinds of film; for our purposes the avant-garde cinema alone may stand for the virtual infinity of filmmaking practices and of kinds of filmic texts that lies beyond the narrative film tradition. Some questions for the future: Can film theory make explicit its tacit definition of object and then alter it to include this vast realm? Can it do so and still remain film theory? Or will the attempt to include the avant-garde cinema explode film theory and transform it into something else? Will the attempt hasten the completion of the critique of film theory by inducing in it a kind of nervous breakdown or a catastrophe in the mathematical sense? This is the subject of another book.

The essays of this book are much concerned with the relations of film theory to language and of language to film. These concerns take different forms in different chapters and parts of chapters. Various aspects of language use in film theory are discussed directly in "Two Types of Film Theory," in "The Structure of Bazin's Thought," and in the critiques of Part II. Other chapters, notably "Toward a Non-Bourgeois Camera Style," *enact* certain relations of language to film and perhaps also manage to pose the problem of these relations. A chapter such as "The Long Take" combines both kinds of concerns.

Although concerns with language and film, language and film theory pervade this book, they are not discussed as such at any point in it— chapter, introduction, or preface. We might have written a separate preface on the linguistic aspects of this book but the problem requires more than this. It would be necessary to study all of film theory from this vantage point, a task as difficult as it is worthwhile. Among the difficulties is that of separating linguistic points from doctrinal ones. Just as our study of theoretical issues has entailed linguistic analyses of various kinds, so it is probably not possible to study linguistic issues without venturing into theoretical ones. As Milton Babbitt says of music theory,

> [O]ur concern is not whether music has been, is, can be, will be, or should be a "science," whatever that may be assumed to mean, but simply that statements about music must conform to those verbal and

methodological requirements which attend the possibility of meaningful discourse in any domain.[15]

This book began at the University of California, Santa Cruz. Bert Kaplan made many valuable suggestions and remained at all times encouraging. Albert Hofstadter and Robert Goff helped to clarify my ideas about the relations between film and philosophy. I also benefited from dialogues on film with Tim Hunter, Albert J. LaValley, and Anthony Reveaux.

Work on the book continued at Buffalo. Since well before I arrived there Gerald O'Grady, Director of the Center for Media Study, has been a constant source of bibliographical suggestions, ideas, encouragement, and material supports of various kinds. For extraordinary stimulation on film, video, and other topics, I am grateful to my colleagues in the Center: James Blue, Tony Conrad, Hollis Frampton, Paul Sharits, Steina and Bohuslav Vasulka. Partial support toward the completion of this book was provided by the University Awards Committee of the State University of New York and the Research Foundation through Summer Fellowships and a Grant-in-Aid.

Although they have not read the present manuscript, I've learned much from Lionel Abel, Marshall Blonsky, Marta Braun, Allan Casebier, Seymour Chatman, Daniel Dayan, Umberto Eco, Paul Garvin, Ronald L. Gottesman, Christian Metz, Bill Nichols, Ted Perry, Vladimir Petric, Martin L. Pops, Michael Prokosch, Michael Silverman, Alan Spiegel, Denise Warren, Alan Williams, and Peter Wollen. To my brother, Donald Henderson, Jr., I am indebted for an enriching dialogue of long standing.

Finally, to Ernest Callenbach I owe an inestimable debt. Chapters 1, 2, 4, 5, 6, 7, and 9 originally appeared in *Film Quarterly,* and had the benefit of his expert editorial suggestions and corrections at several stages. I am also indebted for suggestions on these pieces to members of the *Film Quarterly* editorial board, past and present; to Andriess Deinem, John Fell, Hugh Gray, Albert Johnson, Marsha Kinder, Neal Oxenhandler. The late James Kerans was an invaluable reference source for my writing projects during the years that we worked together. I am also grateful to Richard Corliss for his editorial work on chapter 3, which originally appeared in *Film Comment.* To Richard Dyer MacCann, I am indebted for editorial suggestions in early phases of production. And finally, many thanks are due my publishers for patiently and helpfully seeing this book through to fruition.

---

[15] "Past and Present Concepts of the Nature and Limits of Music," in *Perspectives on Contemporary Music Theory,* ed. Benjamin Boretz and Edward T. Cone (New York: W. W. Norton, 1972), p. 3.

Part I:

Classical Film Theory

Introduction

Part I of this book concerns the work of three film theorists: Sergei Eisenstein, André Bazin, and Jean-Luc Godard. It is not a historical study of any or all of these figures; it does not place them within the context of public events, intellectual currents, or biography. Neither is it a comprehensive review of the total theoretical work of any of them. It concerns itself with a number of fundamental issues that recur persistently in the apparently very different theories of each. These issues have dominated film theory (indeed they have comprised it), at least until very recently. They include the relations between film and reality, the relations between film and narrative, and the question whether film is a language and, if so, what kind of language. Related to these questions is the even more fundamental one of determining the basic units of film (and of film analysis) and the rules governing the combination of these units.

The essays below reconstruct the positions of the three theorists on these issues and the arguments that present and support these positions. Each essay also develops criticisms of the positions and arguments presented. These criticisms are not coordinated in advance, that is, they do not derive from a film-theoretical position determined anterior to the process of critique itself. As is said several times, this review and critique were undertaken in order to aid development of "an adequate theory of film." The completion of this project lies beyond the scope of the present study; but critique of the classical film theories promotes this project in several ways. It reveals the weaknesses of the older theories, hence the pitfalls to be avoided and the lacks to be overcome. It reveals also what is irreducibly of value in the older theories, in their insights and specific observations as well as in their fundamental orientations. Subsequent work may dispute particular positions of the classical film theories, may seek to break with their fundamental premises, or both. Any of these operations depends upon the kind of close analysis of the classical theories attempted here.

We shall not summarize the chapters that follow but shall instead indicate some of the principal links among them. These connections are, like the essays themselves, neither linear nor single-leveled. One essay does not simply begin where the last ends. Several strands of theoretical inquiry and criticism interweave and overlap throughout the essays of Part I. One of the main connections is that each of the later essays may be read as an extension of the first, "Two Types of Film Theory." This essay, which analyzes the foundations of classical film theory, is itself the basis of the inquiries that follow it. It is a kind of hub around which the others revolve. Arguably, each subsequent essay of Part I takes one of its aspects and either develops it or identifies it in a new theoretical context.

"Two Types of Film Theory" examines the theories of Eisenstein and Bazin as typical of the principal approaches to the subject in the classical period. The essay traces them from their basic premises, which concern reality and cinema's relation to it, to their conclusions, which concern filmic styles. Both theories ground *film* in some other order, specifically in reality or the nature of things. In so doing, they also ground *film theory* in another order, as do all the classical theorists, in some version of metaphysics. Each theory makes use of its conceptual ground outside of film to judge film in general as well as particular styles within it. A fundamental operation of "Two Types of Film Theory" is to explore and critique this grounding of film theory in an ontology or metaphysics. Each theorist uses his ontological position to justify certain aesthetic preferences among filmic styles. (At times, the ontology of each seems a system of justification for prior, otherwise untheorized tastes and concepts.) Each also uses his ontology to carve up film history in a certain way, to say what kinds of film are valid and invalid, art and non-art, higher and lesser art within it.

This point is no longer controversial. It now seems widely accepted that film theory should not proceed from ontology and metaphysics, or at least that the classical theories proceeded from these bases in a mistaken fashion. "Two Types of Film Theory," however, develops a critique besides the antimetaphysical one. The essay explores and criticizes each theory's analysis of cinematic structures, definition of basic units, and rules for combining these units into intermediate units (at several levels). The intermediate units themselves combine to form the whole film (and perhaps even larger units such as particular shooting styles, schools of filmmaking, etc.). The essay reviews the model of cinematic structures provided by the theories and probes for what might be called descriptive adequacies, inadequacies, omissions, and values in each. In doing so, the essay specifies requirements that film theories should meet: Each should provide a comprehensive model of cinematic units at all levels and of the modes of combination and interaction of units at each level. In short, a film theory should provide concepts, terms, and dynamic models of interaction for the analysis of cinematic parts and wholes of all kinds.

When this standard is applied and is not itself dependent upon the analysis of the ontology or metaphysical base of a theory, then the question of ontology may be resumed in a new context. To what degree and in which ways do the metaphysical bases of each theory impede, inhibit, limit its model-making function? (Beyond this question is another one posed by our inquiry as a whole: To what degree and in which ways does ontology structure, affect, and limit the film-theoretical enterprise generally?)

"Two Types of Film Theory" traces the limiting effect of an initial ontology in the theories of Eisenstein and Bazin: Each got only as far as the visual sequence, due in part to making cinematic units a function of reality. In Bazin's case the connection is obvious: It is only at the local level of shot that the desirable bond with reality is maintained and in the sequence shot is maximized. It is less obvious in the case of Eisenstein, who sought to *break* the film-piece's ontological bond. It may be that his focus on the breaking of a prior bond, stipulated by his initial ontology, kept his attention fixed at the local level throughout his theoretical work. For to Eisenstein it is only here that the ontological bond can be broken— a complex structure of long takes or even one including long takes remains unfilmic because its component units are unfilmic. On the other hand, more complex combinations and permutations at higher levels (that is, beyond the immediate montage figure made up of individual shots) add nothing to the initial bond breaking. They merely mix, combine, and structure figures that are already filmic, that is, genuinely remodeled from nature. His ontologism seems the only explanation of Eisenstein's failure to consider filmic wholes. Given that Eisenstein had before him instances of complex sequential and overall filmic forms, it is puzzling that he failed to theorize these in relation to his own films, and plans for films, which are intricately organized at many simultaneous levels as few films have ever been. (His celebrated analysis of "Organic Unity and Pathos in the Composition of *Potemkin*" treats the whole film, to be sure; but as a tragic whole not a visual one.)

Can the theories of Eisenstein and Bazin be adapted to overcome the limitations discussed? We were concerned above with a familiar criticism in philosophic discourse: that the systemic reach of a position is shorter than it claims or shorter than it must be to accomplish its tasks, with the result that some areas of the problem are not covered and/or that the treatment of other areas does not derive from the premises announced and is therefore without grounding. When such criticisms are made, the question arises: Can the position be revised in such a way that the areas ignored or unsystematically treated may be treated systematically? If the ontology components are dropped, each theory becomes in principle free to overcome its limitations. However, because of these limitations, Bazin developed no account of montage forms and Eisenstein developed no analysis of long-take constructions, etc. For example, experiments with sound-image relations in Godard's late films can be read as extensions and adaptations of Eisenstein's ideas. But Eisenstein's programmatic stand against the long take severely limits the ability of his theory to treat such work. Eisenstein's theory can consider overall filmic constructions only, it seems, in the form of more complex orderings of Eisensteinian montage passages. An example might be a feature-length montage film that orders its main parts and/or sequences according to certain parameters of the whole, and/or bases itself on certain recurring figures—for example, a certain kind of montage trope at the local level. In any case, it seems futile to make such speculative, partial adjustments, when the necessity for major change in each theory seems adequately established.

As noted, "Two Types of Film Theory" may be taken in several directions. One leads to a more comprehensive treatment of the two theory-complexes discussed therein. This direction is pursued in chapter 2, "The Structure of Bazin's Thought," which extends the analysis of one film-theoretical position. It develops a fundamental split or contradiction in Bazin's position and, in so doing, discovers in it a conception of film theory other than the ontological. This side of Bazin's work is concerned with film history and the film critic, specifically with the relation of the film critic to the films of his own period and to film history more generally. In this aspect of his work, Bazin makes a complex theoretical gesture toward making the critical act or some general orientation of the critic the basis or foundation of his film theory, rather than an ontology. This attempt is important and provides a bridge to later approaches, specifically those of Godard and Metz, and of auteurism and semiology more generally. All of these approaches make fundamental the relation between critical discourse and cinema. As the essay makes clear, Bazin does *not* let go of his ontological theory in making this gesture but instead tries to affirm both; this attempt splits his system in two. Other remarks of Bazin may be seen as attempts to overcome or bridge this gap, but these fail for the reasons elaborated in the conclusion of the essay.

Chapters 3, 4, and 5 build on chapters 1 and 2, but each goes off in a different direction. Chapters 1 and 2 are concerned with the structure of the classical film theories themselves. Their criticisms are structural criticisms—how one aspect of each theory connects with other aspects, or fails to do so, etc. They do not question the adequacy of the classical theories—whether they correspond to actual films and whether they are useful to the critical activity. It is this set of questions that is raised by chapters 3, 4, and 5.

"The Long Take" takes from "Two Types of Film Theory" its basic categories, that is, the categories of classical film theory: shot, sequence, montage, long take. It performs two operations in relation to these concepts. First, it divorces them from the ontological, aesthetic/valuational, and historical foundations given them by the classical film theories. Second, it elaborates and combines these concepts and a number of additional, derived concepts, in new ways. These operations point toward, though they hardly begin to achieve, a comprehensive *descriptive rhetoric* of filmic figures. Such a project entails definition of units and rules of their combination at several levels—the various kinds of shots, shot arrangements, sequences, whole filmic structures, and shooting styles. Let us examine these two operations in greater detail.

"The Long Take" shears the ontological foundations from the concepts of classical film theory. No type of shot or sequence is more or less realistic than any other. None has any existential bond with reality. Various kinds of long-take and various kinds of montage sequences are no less and no more than different filmic figures, with different structures and different sets of effects. (Among these, in *both* cases, is the *impression* of reality. Roland Barthes calls this the *effet de réel.*) With the elimination of its ontological foundations, other important dimensions of classical film theory are also eliminated. Without its ontology, the value system attached to classical film theory falls. The descriptive rhetoric outlined in "The Long Take" does not attach a scale of aesthetic values to different kinds of shots and sequences. It is equally interested in *all* filmic figures and in the system that defines and differentiates them. Thus, "The Long Take" does not propose an aesthetic. (The chapter does not criticize the aesthetic positions of Eisenstein and Bazin in order to replace them with its own, but criticizes from another standpoint and for other reasons, discussed below.) The classical film theories are *normative,* as well as descriptive; "The Long Take" is strictly descriptive.

When the valuational operation of classical film theory is discarded, its distinctively narrow and divisive approach to film history gives way also. A normative approach to film, particularly one that assigns different values to different kinds of filmic figures, necessarily takes a normative approach to film history. Certain styles and certain periods in which these flourished are valued more highly than others. Other styles and periods receive less attention or are positively devalued. The descriptive rhetorical approach of "The Long Take" makes no normative divisions within film history. It ranks neither periods, nor films, nor filmic figures. It takes as its province all of film history—the entire extant body of cinema. It regards the entire field and all types of filmic figures as equally interesting and important to study.

Rejecting the ontological foundations of classical film theory entails rejecting its historical and valuational extensions; and leads to a different mode of interpretation. Bazin's use of his theoretical concepts in interpreting filmic styles and figures is not dissociable from the ontological base of his theory. Bazin argues in "The Evolution of the Language of Cinema" that the long take is more realistic, more ambiguous (potentially though not necessarily), and demands more participation of the viewer than other styles. Conversely, montage is unambiguous, diminishes viewer participation, and is unrealistic in its temporal and spatial orderings (although the surface of its images may be realistic).

As critical categories, Bazin's theoretical categories become ontological principles of interpretation. Bazin as theorist begins with reality and moves to the long take; Bazin as interpreter of films begins with the long take (when he comes upon it) and moves to reality. The ontological base of the long take remains with it in all cases so that for Bazin *every* long take embodies a certain relation to reality. (It respects the temporal and spatial integrity of the event.) Bazin associates reality with the long take, but he also associates the long take with reality. There is a reciprocal relationship between them and, even more important, that relationship is fixed, permanent. It is the apriority of this approach that distinguishes Bazin's position. For him the long take is inherently more realistic, participatory, and ambiguous by virtue of its relation to reality. This relation is not dependent upon the content of the shot or its placement in a context; it is fixed, constant, prior to experience or situation.

(It should be noted that Bazin made the long take superior on historical grounds also—it emerges at and as the latest stage of film-historical development. This argument depends upon what we call in Part I Bazin's "history system," which is quite different from his ontology system. It is the long take's late appearance in film history that makes it superior to other modes. Bazin's double adherence to ontology and history systems was possible because of a historical accident. If Bazin had lived through the revival of montage forms in the late 1950s and 1960s, he would have had to choose between his ontological standard, which made the long take superior in all instances, and his historical standard, which made later work in a tradition superior.)

When one drops the ontological baggage (and its aesthetic and historical extensions), the long take is *not* inherently realistic, ambiguous, and participatory. No kind of shot or sequence or whole filmic structure is inherently any of these. Such qualities depend upon the relation of the visual form to the content of the shot and upon the context of the shot, both visual and narrative. Consider Godard's *The Married Woman* (1964): its long montage/collages of lovemaking tend to be ambiguous—spatially, temporally, narratively; its long-shot, long-take sequences rather obvious. An exception is the airport sequence—shot in a single take—in which one must watch the characters carefully to understand what is happening, in the Bazinian manner.

Bazin also tends to identify the long take with composition-in-depth, because historically they arose together and because greater depth means greater ambiguity and participation. But Godard, Jerzy Skolimowski, and others frequently shoot long takes against a flat or shallow background. Thus, none of Bazin's equivalences holds up.

Long take, various kinds of montage, and various combinations of these have no essential or a priori meaning or effect: these latter depend upon the use to which the filmmaker puts them. Hence the interpreting critic must be open to the meaning and effect given filmic figures by context (visual and narrative) and to the relation of visual form to content within the figure itself.

"The Long Take" performs a second operation in relation to the categories of classical film theory. It elaborates the basic concepts of film theory and some new ones in new ways. This involves definition of units and their rules of combination at several levels: shot, shot arrangements, sequences, whole filmic structures, shooting styles. "The Long Take" shares the basic unit of the shot with classical film theory. Furthermore, it agrees that the unit-level of the sequence includes both sequence shots and montage sequences. But it also finds at this level a number of other filmic figures that are not reducible to the simplistic dualism of classical film theory (long take or montage). These other figures include the combination of one or more long takes within a sequence and various combinations of long take(s) and shorter pieces of film within a sequence. Quantitatively, this "mixed stylistic sequence" is far more common than the sequence shot and the unmixed montage sequence. Neither Eisenstein nor Bazin deals with this large domain of filmic figures because both are committed to ontological positions that demote this realm, therefore they do not describe it. This aesthetic and historical devaluing of the mixed stylistic realm is in effect a denial of its existence; the classical theories say nothing about it at all. This denial extends to other levels of filmic figures also: that of shooting styles based on mixed elements and that of whole filmic structures that include mixed sequences. These arguments are made concretely in "The Long Take" sections on Max Ophuls and on Orson Welles, respectively.

We cannot summarize here—let alone fill out—that sketch of a comprehensive rhetoric of filmic figures of all levels suggested by "The Long Take." But we should note the important shift in theoretical perspective implied by the criticisms of "The Long Take." These criticisms are performed from the standpoint of the working film analyst. From this perspective, the omission by the classical theories of long take/montage interaction is a crippling defect: it blinds them to vast areas of narrative cinema (and to parts of other cinemas), indeed to the quantitatively major portion. The working analyst does not wish to divide up film history a priori. The analyst requires a set of concepts and a theoretical framework that will permit one to describe and analyze any and all films. Thus the chief evaluative standard for film theories becomes the pragmatic test of which critical operations a theory permits one to perform and which sets of filmic objects it permits one to work with. Foundational and a prioristic in approach, classical film theories do not pose themselves any such standard. On the other hand, the working analyst is far less concerned with the systematic side of film theories than with their results. The ideal working analyst develops critical concepts from work with films themselves—although, as with "The Long Take," this requires some theoretical capital as a starting point, such as the basic concepts of classical film theory.

"The Long Take" and chapters 4 and 5 analyze and evaluate the theories of Eisenstein and Bazin from a very different perspective from that of "Two Types of Film Theory" and "The Structure of Bazin's Thought." Chapters 3, 4, and 5 judge them by the critical categories that they produce. "The Long Take" makes this explicit at the outset:

> film theory is, after all, a metacriticism or philosophy of criticism. It is pursued to clarify and improve film criticism through the determination of basic film categories and the identification of those assumptions about film on which any criticism is based. . . . film theory itself is the continual improvement and clarification of the principles and assumptions of film criticism. (p. 49)

This is *not* how the classical theories of film define film theory. (In fact they do not define it at all except "in action.") Neither

Eisenstein nor Bazin, except in the latter's "history system," relates film theory to the problems of working film analysis. Neither makes film theory responsible to the needs of working analysis. (Bazin's history system prescriptions are merely another kind of a priori stipulation imposed on the critic.) Thus "The Long Take," unlike "Two Types of Film Theory," does not stay within the theoretical bounds of the classical theories. The essay proposes its own definition of film theory and uses this both to judge the classical theories and to develop revisions and improvements of them.

Chapter 4, "Toward a Non-Bourgeois Camera Style," examines the visual structure of several late films of Jean-Luc Godard. It practices several of the kinds of visual rhetorical analysis proposed in the preceding chapter, "The Long Take." The essay performs analyses at three or more levels of visual units, each with distinct rules of combination. It first examines a particular filmic figure at the level of *shot,* the lateral tracking shot, in several variations (strict 90°, track combined with turning of camera, etc.). Several kinds of sequence construction are analyzed (the sequence shots of *One Plus One* [1968], the sound-track-discourse segmentations of *Pravda* [1970], *Wind from the East* [1971], etc.). The essay also describes and analyzes several kinds of organizational figures at the level of the whole film (the overall montage of *One Plus One,* the bands construction of *Weekend* [1967], etc.). In this the essay goes beyond "The Long Take": it extends the latter's projected system of visual rhetoric to include sound organizaton at all levels and it considers several new kinds of audio-visual configuration at the level of whole filmic construction.

The analyses of visual, sound, and audio-visual organization of the whole film are the most important contribution of "Toward a Non-Bourgeois Camera Style." The essay presents one set of answers to the demands of "Two Types of Film Theory" and of "The Long Take" for analysis of filmic wholes. But its modes of analysis, valid for Godard's very important late films, are not widely applicable. ¨y far, the majority of feature-length films do not exhibit the tight formal organization of Godard's late films at any level—least of all at the level of the whole film. Related to this problem is the question of film and narrative generally. Godard's films since *Weekend* are not narratives in any usual sense. They do not follow characters through a continuous series of actions; indeed most do not have characters at all. (*Wind from the East* is an exception. See chap. 4.) It may be that the rigorous (and conspicuous) overall organization of the late films is in some measure correlated to their absence of narrative. Narrative films generally require the subordination of visual form to framing the actions of the characters and of sound form to recording what they say. In the binding of cinematic expression to narrative, the ambition and potential complexities of filmic form are usually severely limited. The problem of filmic wholes and of local organization in the vast realm of narrative cinema persists.

Chapter 4 extends another point of "The Long Take": the critique of the Bazinian mode of interpretation. Godard's long takes are precisely *not* ambiguous, participatory, and realistic. Neither do his montages correspond to Bazin's interpretation of montage. As the text says, Godard "reinvents" the long take and the tracking shot, as well as montage.

Chapter 5, *"Godard on Godard:* Notes for a Reading," fills a historical and logical gap. *Godard on Godard,* Godard's collected writings, appeared in French in 1968 and in English in 1972. It revealed that Godard had developed in the mid-1950s certain criticisms of the Bazinian position that became widely accepted only later. Not only did these criticisms escape attention at the time they were published, they were not much remarked on when the pieces appeared in collection over a decade later. This is no doubt due in part to the nature of the book—an unreconsidered collection of pieces written very much earlier. Godard wrote the pieces hurriedly, never rewrote them, and never bothered to connect one with another at any time. Godard provides a clue to his method in a 1962 interview:

> But improvisation is tiring. I have always told myself: this is the last time, I can't do it again. It is too exhausting going to bed in the evening and wondering, what am I going to do tomorrow? It's like writing an article in a café at twenty to twelve when the deadline is midday. The curious thing is that you always do manage to write it, but working like that for months on end is killing.[1]

The primary work of *"Godard on Godard:* Notes for a Reading" is to construct a connected argument out of the fragments that comprise the book. Three sets of arguments or motifs are developed.

---

[1] Jean-Luc Godard, *Godard on Godard,* ed. Jean Narboni and Tom Milne, with an introduction by Richard Roud; trans. Tom Milne (New York: The Viking Press, 1972), p. 174.

The first is a critique of Bazin's film theory, particularly its onto-logical base and rigid aesthetic standard that calls for automatic approval of certain filmic figures and automatic disapproval of others. Godard enlists Jean-Paul Sartre and Denis Diderot to criticize Bazin's ontological film theory and criticism. Art must not be given metaphysical pretensions, neither should some figure or other be given astronomical implications. The artist is concerned with morality and perspective. Godard also pointedly disputes Bazin's version of film history. Classical construction—what we have called the mixed stylistic realm—did not give way to long take and com-position-in-depth at some historical point; it still flourishes.

Godard pivots on these two points to make a more fundamental one, which is apparently the foundation of his thinking about film in the early pieces: One should not choose a figure or style for aesthetic praise in the abstract. The effectiveness or beauty of a figure depends entirely upon its appropriateness in the context in which it is used, that is, its relationship to its subject matter. Thus, Godard admires the American cinema, "which makes the subject the motive for the mise-en-scène." Godard's most extended piece of textual examination, his analysis of Hitchcock's *The Wrong Man* (1957), shows in detail that the style of each sequence is appro-priate to the subject matter of the scene.

What is to replace Bazinian ontological film theory? Godard does not take up this question. He never takes upon himself the re-sponsibility to propose a theory, or even to suggest what such a theory should be or do. Neither does Godard speak of a descriptive rhetoric of the cinema; though he does occasionally describe filmic figures at the level of the sequence. In any case, Godard's exclusive emphasis on form-content relations perhaps moves in a different di-rection from the rhetoric suggested by "The Long Take." Godard seems at times to dissolve filmic figures into the content they ex-press. Form is optimal for Godard at this stage when it is a direct emanation of content, when it is entirely justified by its relation to narrative context. Thus, though he sometimes describes them well, filmic figures are never autonomous for Godard. Far from arranging themselves into a system, filmic figures seem to him rather the uniquely right expression of a particular narrative segment or mo-ment, hence unrepeatable.

The second major topic identified by "*Godard on Godard:* Notes for a Reading" centers on Godard's notion that all films are simul-taneously documentary and fiction. Here he flirts with a reversion to Bazinian ontology of the image, despite his own earlier criticisms, but he remains ambivalent on the point. As noted in chapter 5, Godard sometimes speaks of the effect of life*like*ness in a way that suggests "the impression of reality," that is, the effect of an apparatus or figure. But he does not come to a conclusion on this point either way. The third topic is barely a hint—the meta-cinematic possibilities suggested to Godard by films of Jean Rouch and Anthony Mann.

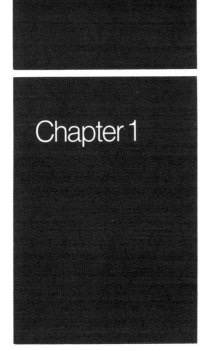

Chapter 1

Two Types of Film Theory (1971)

Philosophers often find it useful to classify theories bearing upon a problem according to some typological scheme. In *Five Types of Ethical Theory* (1930) C. D. Broad treats Spinoza, Butler, Hume, Kant, and Sidgwick not only as moral theorists but also as examples of basic approaches to the subject. In a final chapter Broad includes these and other theories—actual and possible—in a comprehensive classificatory scheme. Similarly, in *The Foundations of Aesthetics* (1948) Ogden, Richards, and Wood advance a schematic outline of the principal approaches to aesthetics. Why such schemes are helpful is not hard to see. For one thing, they bring order to the otherwise unmanageable number of theories in such fields as ethics and aesthetics. In order to be useful, however, classification must also be accurate, and this means that a good typology of theories embodies a good deal of analysis. Before one says that two or more theories are fundamentally—not just apparently—similar or different in this or that respect, one must have penetrated to the base of the theory, to its generative premises and assumptions. One must also know intimately how the theory gets from these to its conclusions and applications, so as not to be misled by them. This analytical work, as well as the classification scheme that is its completion, is helpful, finally, in the criticism and evaluation of the theories themselves, thus preparing the way for new theoretical work.

A classification of film theories stands on different ground from classifications in more developed fields. Whereas typological schemes in ethics and aesthetics grow out of an abundance of theories, a classification of film theories faces a paucity of positions and the fact that most possible approaches to the subject have not yet been explored. Moreover, whereas classifications of philosophic theories usually concern not fragments of theories or attempted theories but only fully complete approaches to the problem, it is possible that there *has not yet been* a comprehensive or complete film theory.

The underdevelopment of film theory, however, may itself be a reason for close analytical work, including a classification scheme of the principal approaches already taken. It is also incontestable that new theoretical work is needed: the development of cinema since the late 1950s is far beyond the explanatory capacities of the classical film theories. Either new developments are seen in old terms or—more often—the attempt at theoretical understanding is not made.

The careful review of older theories is part of the spadework necessary for the formulation of new theories. Just as film art is stimulated by ploughing back the work of the past, so film theory may be stimulated by ploughing back the thought of the past. The limitations and weaknesses of older theories reveal paths to be avoided just as their achievements reveal, cumulatively, the problems and doctrines that a new theory must take into account.

The principal film theories that have been developed are of two types: part-whole theories and theories of relation to the real.[1] Ex-

---

[1] These theory types are neither new nor unique to cinema. Part-whole theories and theories of relation to the real (sometimes called imitation theories) have had a long life in the history of aesthetic thought generally. Through the eighteenth century these were the principal, most widely held approaches. See Monroe C. Beardsley, *Aesthetics from Classical Greece to the Present*

amples of the first are those of Eisenstein and V. I. Pudovkin, which concern the relations between cinematic parts and wholes; examples of the second are those of Bazin and Siegfried Kracauer, which concern the relation of cinema to reality. Our examination of these two theory types will limit itself to Eisenstein and Bazin. Theirs have been the most influential film theories; arguably they are also the best, and, in essential terms, they are probably the most complete. Theirs are also the theories closest to actual films and based on fullest knowledge of cinema history. Closeness to subject does not guarantee a good theory; in the cases of Eisenstein and Bazin, however, it ensured that the theoretical concerns of each were nearly always those of the makers of cinema.

The focus of this essay is less the truth or falsity of the theories discussed than the theories themselves. It examines not the relation of theories to cinema but their operation *as theories*. Thus behind our typology of theories lie larger questions: What is a film theory? What are its necessary features? What does it seek to explain?

The real is the starting point for both Eisenstein and Bazin. One of the principal differences between them is that Eisenstein goes beyond the real (and cinema's relation to it) whereas Bazin does not. It is obviously of primary importance to determine precisely what each means by the real; as this term is the theoretical foundation for each, it determines in some degree everything that comes after it. In fact, however, neither theorist defines the real nor develops any doctrine of the real whatever. To some extent each theory is built upon a foundation that is itself an unknown. Concerning cinema's relation to the real, both Eisenstein and Bazin are far clearer.

For Eisenstein, as for Pudovkin and André Malraux, pieces of unedited films are no more than mechanical reproductions of reality; as such they cannot in themselves be art. Only when these pieces are arranged in montage patterns does film become art. In *Film*

(New York: The Macmillan Company, 1966) and *Aesthetics: Problems in the Philosophy of Criticism* (New York: Harcourt, Brace and Company, 1958). It suggests the backwardness of film theory that they are still the principal approaches in its field. Neither in aesthetics generally nor in film theory are part-whole theories and theories of relation to the real necessarily or always inconsistent. One task of analysis—perhaps the chief task—is to determine where competing theories are inconsistent, where they do not conflict, and where they are positively complementary.

Form ² Eisenstein states this doctrine repeatedly, perhaps most succinctly in the following formulations:

> *Primo:* photo-fragments of nature are recorded; *secundo:* these fragments are combined in various ways. Thus the shot (or frame), and thus, montage.
>
> Photography is a system of reproduction to fix real events and elements of actuality. These reproductions, or photo-reflections, may be combined in various ways. (p. 3)

> The shot, considered as material for the purpose of composition, is more resistant than granite. This resistance is specific to it. The shot's tendency toward complete factual immutability is rooted in its nature. This resistance has largely determined the richness and variety of montage forms and styles—for montage becomes the mightiest means for a really important creative remolding of nature. (p. 5)

Elsewhere Eisenstein speaks of "combining these fragments of reality . . . into montage conceptions" (p. 5). Defining cinematic art in this way requires one to reject uncut pieces of film, what we would call long takes, as non-art; and this Eisenstein does. He refers to:

> . . . [T]hat "prehistoric" period in films (although there are plenty of instances in the present [1929], as well), when entire scenes would be photographed in a single, uncut shot. This, however, is outside the strict jurisdiction of the film-form. (pp. 38–39)

> In 1924–25 I was mulling over the idea of a filmic portrait of *actual* man. At that time, there prevailed a tendency to show actual man in films only in *long* uncut dramatic scenes. It was believed that cutting (montage) would destroy the idea of actual man. Abram Room established something of a record in this respect when he used in *The Death Ship* uncut dramatic shots as long as 40 meters or 135 feet. I considered (and still do) such a concept to be utterly unfilmic. [135 ft. = approx. 2½ min. at silent speed.] (p. 59)

Whereas Eisenstein only mentions the real, then hurries to other matters, Bazin discusses at length cinema's relation to it. Like Eisenstein, however, Bazin neither advances a theory of the real nor defines it. Even his theory of cinema's relation to the real is put not ex-

---

2 Ed. and trans. Jay Leyda (New York: Harcourt Brace Jovanovich, 1969).

plicitly but through a series of metaphors, each suggesting a slightly different theory. Seeing the theory in operation in "The Evolution of the Language of Cinema" [3] gives a surer sense of it than Bazin's metaphoric definitions. Applying his theory to cinema history, Bazin contrasts "directors who believed in the image" with "those who believed in reality." Image directors "add'ed to" the object depicted by editing techniques and/or plastic distortion (lighting, sets, etc.). A "reality" director such as F. W. Murnau "strived to bring out the deeper structure of reality" and "adds nothing to reality, does not deform it." This style exhibits, in Bazin's revealing phrase, "self-effacement before reality." Elsewhere Bazin speaks of the "supplementary reality" of sound and, more generally, of cinema's "vocation for realism."

In "The Ontology of the Photographic Image," [4] the being in question is not that of nature or reality but that of the image itself. Bazin is inquiring into the nature of the image and finds that the image shares in or partakes of the real. The precise nature of this partaking Bazin essays in several formulations:

> the molding of death masks . . . likewise involves a certain automatic process. One might consider photography in this sense as a molding, the taking of an impression, by the manipulation of light. (p. 12)

> [The photographic image resembles] a kind of decal or transfer. (p. 14)

> Let us merely note in passing that the Holy Shroud of Turin combines the features alike of relic and photograph. (p. 14)

> The photograph as such and the object in itself share a common being, after the fashion of a fingerprint. (p. 15)

"The photograph as such and the object in itself share a common being"—Bazin never makes clear what he means by this, though he gives the concept several formulations:

> The photographic image is the object itself, the object freed from the conditions of time and space that govern it. No matter how fuzzy, distorted, or discolored, no matter how lacking in docu-

---

[3] Translated by Peter Graham, in Peter Graham, ed., *The New Wave* (New York: Doubleday & Company, 1968).

[4] André Bazin, "The Ontology of the Photographic Image," in *What Is Cinema?*, vol. I, trans. Hugh Gray (Berkeley, Calif.: University of California Press, 1967), p. 9.

mentary value the image may be, it shares, by virtue of the very process of its becoming, the being of the model of which it is the reproduction; it *is* the model. (p. 14)

In spite of any objections our critical spirit may offer, we are forced to accept as real the existence of the object reproduced, actually *re*-presented, set before us, that is to say, in time and space. Photography enjoys a certain advantage in virtue of this transference of reality from the thing to its reproduction. (pp. 13–14)

Photography affects us like a phenomenon in nature, like a flower or a snowflake whose vegetable or earthly origins are an inseparable part of their beauty. (p. 13)

[Bazin hedges his doctrine here by casting his discussion in terms of the *psychology* of photography (how we react to it) rather than strictly the nature of its image; but Bazin does not stay within these bounds—the essay's title is, finally, controlling.] Though he seems to do so at times, Bazin never does identify object and image. Where Eisenstein seems to merge them (the film-piece *is itself* "a fragment of reality"), Bazin keeps them distinct, though he makes the image dependent upon and inferior to the real—not only at its birth but throughout its existence. For Eisenstein, on the other hand, the film-piece's connection or identity with reality is defeasible: that bond is severed or dissolved when the piece is combined with others in montage sequences.

For Eisenstein, the only way that pieces of film can overcome their "unfilmic" status as mere "fragments of reality" is by combination into montage patterns. Through this nexus alone filmed reality becomes art. Thus much of Eisenstein's theoretical writing is devoted to the various kinds and methods of montage association. He devotes considerably less attention to the kinds of artistic units—greater than the shot, less than the whole film—that these montage associations form or constitute. What sort of unit is the montage combination? The word that Eisenstein usually uses for this intermediate formal entity is the sequence, but he never develops a doctrine of the sequence or discusses the sequence as such, and indeed seems not to acknowledge it as a category of his film theory. It enters through the back door, as it were, for want of a better term/concept, though Eisenstein sometimes uses it as a term of accepted meaning and common usage. It appears thus in an early essay, "The Filmic Fourth Dimension," in which it is italicized as though a technical term and then, without definition, slipped into the discourse and used again and again (in this essay and others). The sequence, that is, the montage sequence, is in fact a central category in Eisenstein's aesthetics, though an unacknowledged and unanalyzed one. At times Eisenstein discusses methods of montage and other association categories without reference to the sequence, as though entire films were built out of them directly. Of course this is not true, as viewing an Eisenstein film makes clear: each of his films proceeds by way of narrative blocks or segments, each of which is composed of one or more montage sequences. Indeed, when Eisenstein discusses his own films he frequently falls into this usage also, referring to the "fog sequence" of *Potemkin* (1925), the sequence of the gods in *October* (1927), etc. Sometimes he uses the alternative phrases "a fully realized montage composition" and "a film fragment" as synonyms for "sequence," but the structural concept and its indeterminacy remain the same.

Eisenstein's short essay "Organic Unity and Pathos in the Composition of *Potemkin*" creates additional puzzles regarding the sequence and the intermediate formal units between shot and whole film generally. Eisenstein proffers an elaborate analysis of *Potemkin* as a tragedy in five acts, including such classical machinery as a caesura, golden-section construction, etc. Eisenstein's breakdown of the acts makes clear that they are composed of several subevents or sequences. It would seem, therefore, that shots—in various montage patterns—make up sequences, and sequences in turn make up larger parts or areas or acts, and these in combination make up the entire film; but to these intermediate formal entities Eisenstein devotes almost no analytical attention at all.

It is of the greatest importance that Bazin's critique of montage is in fact a critique of the montage sequence; and that the alternative to montage that he advances is consequently another kind of sequence. Bazin speaks of montage filmmakers as dissolving "the event" and of substituting for it another, synthetic reality or event. "Kuleshov, Eisenstein, and Gance do not show the event through their editing; they allude to it. . . . The substance of the narrative, whatever the realism of the individual shots, arises essentially from these [editing] relationships; that is to say there is an abstract result whose origins are not to be found in any of the concrete elements." [5] In speaking of Flaherty, Bazin says:

> The camera cannot see everything at once, but at least it tries not to miss anything of what it has chosen to see. For Flaherty, the

---

[5] Graham, *The New Wave,* p. 27.

important thing to show when Nanook hunts the seal is the relationship between the man and the animal and the true proportions of Nanook's lying in wait. Editing could have suggested the passage of time; Flaherty is content to *show* the waiting, and the duration of the hunt becomes the very substance and object of the image. In the film this episode consists of a single shot. Can anyone deny that it is in this way much more moving than "editing by attraction" would have been. (p. 29)

In regard to Welles, too, Bazin defends the substitution of the sequence shot for the montage sequence.

Anyone who can use his eyes must realize that Welles' sequence shots in *The Magnificent Ambersons* are by no means the passive "recording" of an action photographed within a single frame, but that on the contrary this reluctance to break up an event or analyze its dramatic reverberations within time is a positive technique which produces better results than a classical breakdown of shots could ever have done. (p. 39)

In these passages Bazin idealizes the sequence shot but he does not insist on it. The sequence shot is the perfection of the long-take style or tendency, but there are other possibilities. For instance, Bazin defends Wyler's use of a repeated inset shot within a long take (in *The Best Years of Our Lives* [1946]) as a kind of dramatic "underlining." (I disagree: fundamental values of the long take are lost or diminished by such interruptions/insets.) A more common variant of sequence shots Bazin does not discuss—the use of two or more long takes to make up a sequence. How the shots are used, particularly how they are linked, presents interesting theoretical problems. Such considerations belong to a comprehensive aesthetics of the sequence and of the whole film—something neither Eisenstein nor Bazin provides. That is, such problems take us beyond the present, into the realm of a new film theory.

The sequence is as far as either theorist gets in his discussion of cinematic form. The film theory of each is in fact a theory *of the sequence,* though neither Eisenstein nor Bazin nor both of them together contain or achieve a complete aesthetic even of the sequence. The problem of the formal organization of whole films, that is, of complete works of film art, is not taken up by either. This is the most serious limitation of both theories. Both Eisenstein and Bazin contain fleeting references to whole films, and Eisenstein a short essay, but—what is crucial—both discuss the problem of wholes in literary, not cinematic, terms. Thus *Potemkin* is a tragedy. Bazin, more incidentally, speaks of the cinematic genres of the Western, the gangster film, the horror film, etc.: it is these that govern the whole film and hence determine the nature of the sequence, which in turn calls for a certain choice of treatment. It is at this point that Bazin's film theory enters. Bazin has definite ideas concerning how the sequence, so determined or given, might best be treated or realized. These film genres, as well as the older genre of tragedy, of course, have literary origins. Consider the importance of this: after the most technical and detailed discussions of shot and sequence—*in purely cinematic terms*—both theorists veer off into literary models for answers to the ultimate (and arguably most important) question for film theory: the formal organization of the whole film itself, of the film *as film*. In fact, the answers Eisenstein and Bazin give avoid this question rather than answer it. Their solutions in terms of (pre-cinematic) literary models are a failure to take up the problem at all.

The foregoing raises the difficult problem of narrative and film form's relation to it. Put crudely, it is possible to analyze cinema in either perspective, formal or narrative. That is, one can consider each category—shot, sequence, whole film—in terms of narrative (sometimes present) or cinematic form (always present) or both. Eisenstein and Bazin discuss shot and sequence primarily as cinematic form, not narrative. Why narrative should then emerge as the central or sole category of analysis at the level of the whole film—when it has not been an important category at lower levels—is not clear. In fact Eisenstein and Bazin subtly shift ground at this level; they turn to another problem as though it were the continuation of their initial one. They consider shot and sequence in terms of cinematic form and then the whole film in terms of literary models and do so as though treating a single problem from start to finish. They write as though formal parts added up to or constituted a narrative whole. Indeed, this seems not far from the traditional view: cinematic form in shot and sequence serve or realize story or content.

We have been concerned primarily with exposition of the theories under examination; it is now time for analysis of them. Our focus here is the way the theories are put together, how they operate as theories, what their internal dynamics are. Our inquiry will concern, among others, these questions: What is the cause of the failure of Eisenstein and Bazin to consider the formal organization of entire films? Is it internally determined by the premises of each theory? How does each define cinema as an art? What are the relations in each theory between the two essential terms of cinema (as art) and the real? How does the real affect or condition film as art and how does film as art relate to the real?

Both theories start with the real; from this common point the two diverge sharply. The choice or move that each theory makes just beyond this point is crucial for its entire development. As noted, Eisenstein breaks with the real in order that film may become art. It is montage, the arrangement of film-pieces, that transforms them from "fragments of reality" into art. There is a logical or ontological problem or gap here: the real on the one hand and the finished film-work on the other, with only a nexus of arrangement in between. To bridge this gap Eisenstein emphasizes again and again that montage is (or involves) a qualitative alteration of the film-piece itself. "The result is qualitatively distinguishable from each component element viewed separately," "the whole is something else than the sum of its parts." [6] To get the same material from non-art to art, montage had to be given magical, almost alchemical, powers. Eisenstein undoubtedly indulges in mystification here. The problem could be avoided if Eisenstein would admit that unedited film-pieces were already art in some sense, if lesser art, or that they might be in some circumstances. But this is what Eisenstein cannot allow. If the uncut shot could be art, then montage would not be necessary for art—the long take and long-take styles could be art also. Eisenstein must make montage the sole nexus of film art, that is the strategy of his theory. Put another way, Eisenstein is not content to accept montage as his aesthetic preference and to advance reasons for its superiority; instead he must ground his preference for montage in an ontology, in the nature of things, to insure its exclusivity as film art. This leads Eisenstein to certain other distortions also. To emphasize montage he must de-emphasize the shot and its categories of artistry: composition, lighting, actor placement, etc. Eisenstein can hardly deny the importance of these, so he tries to assimilate them to his theory of montage in various ways. Thus the shot is a montage cell; that is, the smaller unit is explained in terms of the larger. At other times Eisenstein emphasizes the unstructured reality of the shot, calling it "more resistant than granite" and referring to its "complete factual immutability." Thus Eisenstein plays down also the careful planning and preparation of shots before shooting and the careful formation and composition of individual shots (evident in his own films).

---

[6] Sergei Eisenstein, *The Film Sense,* ed. and trans. Jay Leyda (New York: Harcourt Brace Jovanovich, 1969), p. 8.

On the positive side, Eisenstein correctly realized that (having begun with the real in the first place) he had to break the connection with the real if cinema was to become an art. For relation to the real, Eisenstein substitutes montage. Montage is a part-whole theory: It concerns the relations of cinematic part and part, and part and whole. Thus, for relation to the real, that is, relation to something else, Eisenstein substitutes relation to self, relations within self, which is the first condition for art. To speak of part-whole relations is to speak of art. Thus Eisenstein's is a genuine aesthetic theory and a genuine film theory because it concerns the conditions and requirements in which film is art. This is indeed the focus of all Eisenstein's theoretical writings: he is continually drawing parallels and differences between cinema and the other arts, theatre, painting, fiction, etc. Thus, Eisenstein's is a two-stage film theory, proceeding from the relations of cinema to the real to the relations of cinema with cinema (part and whole). The theory's chief defect is that it defines this nexus—from first to second stage, from reality to art—too narrowly, limiting it to the doctrine of montage.

There remains the question why Eisenstein did not get beyond the sequence. In principle—concerned as he was with part-whole and with cinema as art—he *should* have. And he certainly recognizes the need in his piece on *Potemkin* as tragedy. (What he does not say there is what the tragic apparatus he describes has to do with film, or with the subject of this film. Neither does he convince us that this is what unifies the film, let alone accounts for its effects.) The answer to the question is perhaps to be found in Eisenstein's intense concern with the *emotional effects* of cinema, specifically of course with the effects of montage, and in his devotion to this factor in his own films. This—the various effects of montage organizations on the viewer— seems at times the central category of Eisenstein's aesthetic. As film-maker and theoretician, Eisenstein is concerned, indeed obsessed, with the closest possible control of the viewer's emotions. His analysis and attention here are literary on a shot-by-shot basis. Now it is obvious that one cannot talk about effects of this precision in regard to whole films. One cannot speak of a single emotion in *Potemkin,* or of a single emotional process. They are too many and too complex, even in regard to any of the film's main parts. The precision and control Eisenstein speaks of occur on the local level. To Eisenstein cinematic form means precise ordering of the viewer's emotions, and this cannot be conceived or spoken of except for relatively short stretches. Eisenstein is weak on formal wholes because of his commitment to the part-complex (the sequence) as aesthetic center and theoretical focus and because of his concern with absolute emotional control at the local level.

Bazin's is a one-stage film theory. Bazin begins with the real but, unlike Eisenstein, does not go beyond it; he never breaks with the real in the name of art. This severely limits Bazin's theory of film, in a very different way than Eisenstein's starting point limits him; but has implications hardly less odd than those that Eisenstein's position has. For in Bazin, film art is complete, is fully achieved in the shot itself. If the shot stands in proper relation to the real, then it is already art. Indeed, there are for Bazin no higher or more inclusive units or categories of film form and film art. The shot depends on no larger unit and on no combination with other shots for its status as art. Bazin does not get beyond the shot (which may also be a sequence): for his theory it is the beginning and the end of film art. Bazin's theory is a theory of shots and what shots ought to be.

Bazin has no theory of part-whole relation, though one could be extrapolated from his discussions of the shot and sequence. One recalls first that simple linkage is the only connection between shots that Bazin approves—he frowns on expressive editing techniques, that is, on explicit shot relation. If the individual shot exhibits fidelity to the real, then it follows that a series of such shots, merely linked, must be faithful to the real also. Bazin is not concerned with this resultant sum and *its* relation to the real at all. His position seems to be: Be true to the real in each shot and the whole will take care of itself (the whole being the mere sum of parts). Or perhaps: True parts linked together add up willy-nilly to a true whole. Bazin has no sense (and certainly no doctrine) of the overall formal organization of films. Indeed, one suspects that in Bazin it is the real that is organic, not art—except that art, in this respect as well as others, may reflect the real in its derivative sense and thus have a reflected organic unity. That is, film art has no overall form of its own, but that of the real itself. Bazin has a theory of the real; he may not have an aesthetic.

There is a sense in which Bazin's theory impinges on previous conceptions and practices of part-whole relation, though it does not have a doctrine of part-whole itself. Bazin critiques the montage sequence and substitutes for it the sequence shot. The long take replaces the montage sequence—a part replaces a whole (or complex of parts). Viewed differently, the long take is itself a whole (at the sequence level) as well as a part (at the overall film level). This part-whole relation Bazin does not consider—the relation or ordering of long takes within the film. In neither Bazin nor Eisenstein is there any carry-over from sequence to sequence or any intersequence relation. Also like Eisenstein, Bazin has no theory of whole films. Bazin said how Flaherty should and did shoot the seal-hunt sequence in *Nanook* (1922), but he could not say how Flaherty or anyone else did or should shoot and construct whole films.

It is easy to see how Bazin's theoretical substitution of the long take for the montage sequence could have led to a new awareness of the formal organization of whole works and to new theoretical formulations thereof. With far *fewer* and more conspicuous parts in the overall work, their relation to each other and to the whole becomes at once a simpler matter to conceive and a more difficult one to ignore. Within the hundreds of montage pieces, Eisenstein could shift ground, suggesting now that the entire film is single, continuous montage, now that it is organized carefully into five separate and distinct acts, now that montage pieces go to make up sequences within whole films and within "acts"; but a relatively small number of long takes call attention to themselves and raise the problem of their mutual relation.

To proceed from the sequence to the whole, however simple a step, is inadmissible for Bazin because the work seen as formal whole rises up against the real, or stands over against it, as a separate and complete totality. To recognize the formal organization of the whole work is to recognize the autonomy of art, its nature as a whole with complex inner relations. The autonomy of the work, its status as a rival totality to the real, is to Bazin literally unthinkable. Hence he downgrades any kind of form except that subservient to the form of the real. Bazin's emphasis on the part, the sequence, serves to keep cinema in a kind of infancy or adolescence, always dependent upon the real, that is, on another order than itself. The real is the only totality Bazin could recognize. His "self-effacement before reality" placed serious limitations on the complexity and ambition of cinematic form.

Our analysis has revealed internal weaknesses in the classical film theories and therefore implicitly criticizes them. This is not, however, a criticism of the theories in relation to their own periods or even "in themselves"; such operations would be irrelevant to present needs and also unhistorical. Our purpose has been instead a critical review of the theories for their usefulness for the present, conducted from the standpoint of the present, with the goal of helping prepare for new theoretical work.

Overall film organization has been stressed because, in the present, Godard has revealed the possibility (and the achievement) of new kinds of formal cinematic wholes, as well as new kinds of organization at the local level. Thus *One Plus One* (1968) is not a tragedy or a Western; it *is* a montage, that is, a purely cinematic being, organized in purely cinematic ways. (Obviously certain of Godard's other late films present more complicated cases—*Wind from the East* [1971] is a Western, as well as a sound-and-visual formal whole.) In these films (as no doubt others do in other films) Godard raises cinema to a more complex, more total organization, and arguably to a higher stage in its evolutionary development. The classical film theories, for the reasons given above, cannot account for and cannot be stretched or amended to account for (or include) these works. Comparison with the classical theories is nevertheless useful—partly because they are the only models we currently have, partly because such comparison reveals the shortcomings of the older theories and possibly the outlines of a new theory. (We noted that Eisenstein slighted overall formal organization because of his interest in close emotional control of viewer response at the local level. Godard's freedom to create new kinds of formal wholes derives partly from his forgoing such control at the local level and perhaps any certain or preplanned emotional effects whatever. Certainly the postulation of a critical rather than a passive audience requires this. Thus Godard's later films are increasingly cerebral, that is, intellectual rather than emotional organizations.)

We began with the need for new theoretical work. Does our analysis of the classical film theories yield any indication of the direction such work should take? Answering such a question goes beyond strict analysis of the theories themselves, that is, how they operate as theories, necessarily bringing in other assumptions, orientations, etc. If our analysis has been accurate, it should be accessible to various aesthetic positions, not just to one. What follows then, our conclusions concerning the classical theories, is separated from what has gone before by the line that divides analysis from preliminary advocacy or synthesis. It seems to me that consideration of reality and relation to reality in Eisenstein and Bazin, and in the senses that they mean, have been a source of serious confusion and even of retardation to theoretical understanding of cinema. It seems to me also that the next period of theoretical effort should concentrate on formulation of better, more complex models and theories of part-whole relations, including sound organizations as well as all visual styles; and only after this is done, or taken as starting point, proceed to relations with "reality," but not in the Bazinian or Eisensteinian sense of an antecedent reality out of which cinema develops. Finally, the focus of inquiry should be shifted from reality-image interaction to image-viewer interaction, as is being done in other critical disciplines, notably in the psychoanalytic approach to art.

To proceed we must return to our typology of film theories, which may be taken to a further level of generality and abstraction. Behind part-whole theory and relation to the real lie relation-to-self and relation-to-other, the two most fundamental categories in which anything may be considered. Thus part-whole relations include all possible relations of cinema with itself, and relation to the real or other includes all relations of cinema with that outside itself. (Our two theory-types are less fortuitously chosen than at first appears or—more correctly—since they are the principal theories that have been developed, their appearance and opposition in the history of film thought are more fundamental than first appears.) We no sooner say this than we realize that there can be no choice between them, that these are the two fundamental categories or aspects of the subject, neither of which can be ignored or suppressed. Rather the question is one of the mode of their interrelation, the answer to which will be different at different times and places. In more usual critical terms this question concerns the relation between intensive criticism and extensive criticism.

In regard to film criticism and film theory (which is, after all, a philosophy *of* criticism or metacriticism) at the present, it seems to us that extensive criticism of cinema has been far more developed than intensive criticism. What this imbalance involves is not merely a "catching up." Because the two categories are correlative, that is, dialectically interrelated, it implies that extensive criticism, where imbalanced in this way, has been falsely based. For what *can* relation-to-other mean when relation-to-self, or part-whole relation, has not been established? We are talking about those critics who hold up a work and read off its social (or moral) meaning at sight, without bothering to reconstruct its formal relations. The place to begin is always with the work itself. Only when the work is comprehended in its complex relations with itself, can relations with anything other be made. If one attempts extensive relations without plumbing the work itself, he is very likely to get the second relation wrong (for works of art, like systems of courts, often reverse themselves at higher levels of organization). At the least, one has no basis to suppose himself right. Much more importantly, and fundamentally, he misses *how* it is that a work of art can mean—or stand in any relation to—something outside itself, and that is only as a totality, that is, as a complex complete in its own terms. Only a totality can sustain relations with a totality. There are two terms to any extensive relation, the work and its other. Concentrating on this relation itself, extensive critics often ignore or slight the first term. Thoroughgoing part-whole analysis ensures that this does not happen.

Eisenstein and Bazin present a special case—one that has not existed in the other arts (and their criticisms) for a long time. They seek to relate cinema to an *antecedent* reality, that is, the reality out of which it develops in becoming art. As we have seen, Eisenstein defines this nexus very narrowly and Bazin never allows cinema to break with the real at all. It is difficult for us to find any value in this approach whatever. Such theories would keep cinema in a state of infancy, dependent upon an order anterior to itself, one to which it can stand in no meaningful relation because of this dependence. We no longer relate a painting by Picasso to the objects he used as models or even a painting by Constable to its original landscape. Why is the art of cinema different? The answer in terms of "mechanical reproduction" assumes an answer rather than argues one. Similarly from an ideological point of view, only when we begin with the work (rather than with the real as Eisenstein and Bazin do) and establish it fully in its internal relations, that is, as a totality, can we turn it toward (or upon) the sociohistorical totality and oppose the two. (Or rather allow the work itself to oppose.) It is clear that nothing less than a totality can oppose or criticize a totality. It is also clear that something still dependent upon reality, indeed still attached to it, can in no sense criticize or oppose it. Only when the work of art is *complete* in its own terms does it break this dependence and take on the capacity for opposition; hence understanding the conditions and kinds of artistic completeness and organization becomes primary for criticism.

Chapter 2

The Structure of Bazin's Thought (1972)

Even before his death, André Bazin's disciples and opponents were "going beyond" him—absorbing what they considered new and important in his work, discarding the rest. Especially since the appearance of *What Is Cinema?* (1967) in English, this process has gone on in England and America also. The project is a healthy and necessary one for film thought, but in the hurry to go beyond Bazin it has not been clearly established who Bazin was. If that which is gone beyond is not fully known, then neither is any subsequent position. We must know who Bazin was to know who we are.

What is needed is a theory of Bazin, which in turn requires a history of film thought in which to place Bazin, that is, a theory of film theory. In "Two Types of Film Theory" we tentatively formulated an analytical theory of film theory. What is needed also is a historical theory of film theory, one that includes the analytical moment. Toward this goal, the present essay addresses the structure of Bazin's thought; a later essay will address the place of that structure in the history of film thought, attempting to relate inner dialectic to outer dialectic. An analytic moment will be followed by a synthetic moment.

It is surprising that no one in Bazin's country of origin has studied the structure of his thought, for it is complex and interesting, with its own problems and laws. Perhaps the fact that Bazin was so clearly "wrong" in his formulation of many questions and answers has prevented serious structural study. Paradoxically it is dialectical thought (notoriously interested in wrong positions) that insists on studying the structure of Bazin's thought, by making that thought as a whole central to its inquiry. Not the least importance of dialectics is its effective deployment of analytic thought; because only dialectics can say what it is important to study and why. Analytic thought has no internal standard of relevance; accounts of its successes invariably bring in hunches and instinct to explain its application here rather than there. But the dialectical reconstruction of a whole, determined by dialectics to be worth study, is itself dependent upon an initial analysis of that whole into its parts, and can only be as true, as precise, and as comprehensive as the analysis on which it builds.

For English readers, the structure of Bazin's thought is reflected in the principal source of Bazin texts available to them. Hugh Gray's translated volumes of 1967 and 1971 collect the principal theoretical pieces and many of the most important critical-historical pieces, respectively. (In addition to Gray's volumes, there are now a number of other Bazin essays or excerpts available in English.[1])

---

[1] Other Bazin writings available in English include the following: "La Politique des Auteurs" (1957), in *The New Wave,* ed. Peter Graham (New York: Doubleday & Company, 1968), also in *Cahiers du Cinéma in English,* no. 1 (1966); "Hitchcock versus Hitchcock" (1954), in *Cahiers du Cinéma in English,* no. 2 (1966), reprinted in *Focus on Hitchcock,* ed. Albert J. LaValley (Englewood Cliffs, N.J.: Prentice-Hall, Inc., 1972). Several brief Bazin pieces appear in the Seghers volumes on Cocteau, Welles, Renoir, and Fellini: *"Les Parents Terribles"* (1948) in *Jean Cocteau* by René Gilson (New York: Crown Publishers, 1969); two brief pieces (1948) in *Orson Welles* by Maurice Bessy (New York: Crown Publishers, 1971); two extracts from a 1952 *Cahiers du Cinéma* article on Renoir in *Jean Renoir* by Pierre Le-

The historical Bazin did not exist in English until the appearance of *What Is Cinema?* (volume II) in 1971. Its immediate effect is to call seriously into question the widely held belief that Bazin's thought is a unified exploration "based on one central idea, an affirmation of the objectivity of the cinema." [2] Upon closer examination, Bazin's ontological work and his historical work appear virtually as separate and opposed systems operating within the same body of thought. As this division is central to the structure of Bazin's thought, it must be established in detail.

Bazin's writings on reality theory, what could be called his "ontology system," consist of: "The Ontology of the Photographic Image" (1945), "The Myth of Total Cinema" (1946), "Theatre and Cinema" (1951), "Cinema and Exploration" (1953, 1956), and "The Virtues and Limitations of Montage" (1953, 1957). These essays concern the relations between cinema and reality, that is, between the camera and its objects. Their treatment of the problems concerned and of the films used as examples or as subjects of critical analysis is ahistorical. For Bazin's purposes in these pieces, it does not matter when these films were made, what their connections with current film styles were, or even who made them. The later essays on this subject connect directly to the "Ontology" essay and its concerns, without any film-historical or individual-stylistic mediation whatever; they occur in the timeless realm of pure aesthetic theory.

Bazin's critical-historical writings, what could be called his "history system" or simply his "history," divide into two continuous groups. There is "The Evolution of the Language of Cinema" (1952, 1955, 1950), Bazin's survey of the development of the cinematic form from 1920 to 1948; and there are Bazin's essays on the cinema of his own period, centering on his neorealist essays from 1948 to

---

prohon (New York: Crown Publishers, 1971); *Federico Fellini* by Gilbert Salachas (New York: Crown Publishers, 1968) contains three extracts from "*Cabiria:* Voyage to the End of Neorealism" (1957), which appears in its entirety in *What Is Cinema?,* vol. II (Berkeley, Calif.: University of California Press, 1971). Substantial extracts from "*Le Jour se lève . . .* Poetic Realism" (1953) appear in *Le Jour se lève* (New York: Simon & Schuster, 1970). *The New Wave* also contains Peter Graham's translation of "The Evolution of the Language of Cinema" (1952, 1955, 1950), which contains five pages (pp. 40–45) on William Wyler not contained in Hugh Gray's translation, *What Is Cinema?,* vol. I (Berkeley, Calif.: University of California Press, 1967); it appears that Graham has interpolated an article on Wyler (1948) into the text of "Evolution." A two-page excerpt from Bazin's *Orson Welles* (Paris: Chavane, 1950) appears in *Focus on Citizen Kane,* ed. Ronald Gottesman (Englewood Cliffs, N.J.: Prentice-Hall, Inc., 1971).

[2] Eric Rohmer's phrase. See Gray's Preface in *What Is Cinema?,* vol. II.

1957. Most of Bazin's other critical work takes its place within and fills out this two-part historical scheme. Thus his books on Renoir and Welles belong (in the main) to the 1920 to 1948 period and fill out his treatment of these two figures in "Evolution." This is true also of his piece on *Le Jour se lève* (1939), his piece on Jean Gabin, his journal articles on Renoir, Welles, etc. Many other pieces fill out the 1948 to 1957 period: the essays on Bresson, Cocteau, Hitchcock, etc. Some of Bazin's other work, particularly the sociological essays and occasional discussions of genre, bear a tangential relation to the more stylistically concerned historical work. Thus his two essays on the Western lie outside of his central historical concerns but are themselves historical in form and treatment. "In Defense of Mixed Cinema" (approximately 1952), concerned with the wave of literary adaptations that appeared from 1940 to 1951, occupies an odd place of its own. The four essays on Chaplin would seem to belong to the historical work but in fact they are largely ahistorical, that is, removed from Bazin's usual concerns with historical period and style. The reason is that Bazin treats Chaplin as his own history: *Monsieur Verdoux* (1947) and *Limelight* (1952) refer back to Chaplin's early films, which Bazin sees as the worldwide myth of cinema itself. No other historical relation is necessary.

Several things should be noted about Bazin's historical work. First, its two historical periods form a single, continuous history. "The Evolution of the Language of Cinema" ends, perhaps self-consciously, with mention of the neorealist films: one of the principal functions of the essay is to serve as formal and historical preface to the neorealist period and to the films of Bazin's time generally. Contrariwise, neorealism is the continuation and fulfillment of the formal movements that Bazin traces in "Evolution." Second, the continuity between these two areas of Bazin's work is methodological as well as historical. The same critical concerns and historical/developmental concerns are found in both. Thus "Evolution" is critical history and the neorealist essays are thoroughly historical criticism. "Evolution" does not collect titles, dates, and disembodied styles as most work that goes by the name of film history does; it is a conceptually coherent, developmental analysis of the films, styles, and movements covered. Its texture is thereby continuous with the neorealist pieces and with Bazin's other critical work. If "Evolution" is critical in this sense, it is also true that the neorealist pieces are historical. Written year by year as the films appeared, these essays constitute a history of the aesthetic peaks of that movement better

than any that has since appeared. Bazin accomplished this un-
paralleled feat by relating the work of each director to his earlier
work, and by comparing the style of each to those of other artists,
all within the framework of the neorealist movement—itself in process of unfolding but clearly set off from other historical periods
and styles. The resulting network of relations is a comprehensive
analysis/synthesis of the most important neorealist work and remains
a model of criticism.

Thus Bazin's critical-historical work constitutes a single history
of cinema, 1920 to 1957. Of course there are many gaps and a great
unevenness in density; much of this history is no more than an outline. The important point is that Bazin makes clear what he believes
are the principal movements, historical tendencies, and achievements of this period.

The opposition between ontology system and history system, and
more generally between ontological thought and historical thought,
is the central feature of Bazin's work. Neither of these systems can
be reduced to the other nor can the gap between them be bridged
in any satisfactory way. Similarly, in our analysis there is no way to
proceed logically from one to the other; we must constitute and
examine each separately, and then the opposition and other relations between them. As we do so, we shall look for links between
them, but this cannot be done in advance. At the phenomenal or
given level, these systems are utterly opposed. If they can be reconciled in any sense, it will be in and through their contrariety.

The ontology system essays stand together by virtue of common
concerns and similar reasoning, not by strict logical connection. "The
Ontology of the Photographic Image" states that photograph and
reality, image and object, share a common being. It sets forth this
relation for all cases; it does not discuss camera style or montage
versus long-take treatment. *All* photography bears a certain relation
to reality; neither reconstructed expeditions nor Soviet montage nor
German expressionism is excluded. Both the ontology system and
the history system are built, as it were, on the silence of "Ontology."
When the ontology criticism judges certain exploration films and
fantasy films to be more faithful to reality than others, and therefore aesthetically superior, it does not apply "Ontology" or even
extend it. These essays invent ontological principles of criticism,
since none is given or implied by "Ontology."

"Cinema and Exploration" and "The Virtues and Limitations of
Montage," dealing with expedition films and fantasy films respec-

tively, attempt to develop critical equivalences for the descriptive propositions of "Ontology." The connective reasoning—implied, not given—seems to be this: in an expedition film or children's adventure, some real event is the object of the image. If the ontological identity of image and object is to be honored (in spirit as in letter), then the image should record the real event (not a reconstruction as in *Scott of the Antarctic* [1948]) as far as possible in its spatial-temporal integrity. (The struggle with the alligator on a fishing line in *Louisiana Story* [1948] fails on both counts because the "event" is synthesized by montage.) This is, strictly speaking, a reinvention of the "Ontology" principle, but a plausible one.

What are the features of this criticism? It is ahistorical: it does not matter when these films were made or what is their relation to movements or styles. The filmmaker is in no sense the subject of inquiry; his is merely the name to which credit or blame is ascribed. The sole category of this criticism is relation of camera and event, the sole judgment that of correct or incorrect relation, the sole logic that of noncontradiction. The ontological principle applied by these essays is not a critical tool at all but a narrow canon of validity. Its results are achieved mechanically and tend to be either trivial or tautological. Immediate documents of expeditions are superior to reconstructed ones. Fantasies and adventures should show dangerous or unusual events in a single shot rather than fake them through montage. If Bazin's ontology criticism eliminates the director, it eliminates the critic also. One who read only these pieces would not meet the viewer who wrote so well on Rossellini, Bresson, etc. It is a damaging critique of the entire ontology side of Bazin's work that it leads only to this. The ontology criticism is a dead end; if he had done only these pieces, Bazin would have small claim on our attention.

"The Evolution of the Language of Cinema" is Bazin's principal historical essay; but it also has an ontological aspect, even a function within the ontology system. We shall consider that function here, as an adjunct to our consideration of the ontology system; and the rest of "Evolution," or rather "Evolution" itself again in discussing the history system. (Because "Evolution" performs several different functions, finely interrelated, within Bazin's system, we come upon it at several stages in the unfolding of that system.)

One of the tasks of "Evolution of the Language of Cinema" is to develop and apply ontological principles for the judgment of film styles, 1920 to 1948. The results are familiar: long take, composition-in-depth style (Welles, Italian neorealism) is the most faithful to reality; American and French "invisible editing" of the 1930s next so; Soviet montage faithful in image style, unfaithful in duration and relation of images; German expressionism completely unfaithful. The critical principles by which Bazin reaches these results—the equivalences he establishes between shooting styles and relation to reality—are not unrelated to those of his ontology criticism. Indeed the latter pieces should be read in conjunction with "Evolution," in which the discussion of reality-stylistic equivalences is fuller. Of course, "Ontology" is as silent on fiction film style as it is on documentary styles; here too, "Evolution" invents ontological principles, it does not just apply them. The reality-relation of fiction films might seem to require different analysis from the documentary/reality relation. Bazin seems to draw this distinction when he speaks in "Evolution" of "the scenario proper" . . . "the ultimate object of the narrative"; but it has no effect on his argument. In "Evolution," as in the ontological criticism, Bazin speaks again and again of "the event" and of the truth or falsity of different camera styles to it. Moreover, the ontological judgments of "Evolution" are hardly less simplistic and broad than those of the ontological criticism. Thus, expressionism and Soviet montage are invalidated (with what final critical consequences is not clear) by a single application of the principle; and Hollywood composition-in-depth and Italian neorealism are validated just as broadly and undifferentiatedly. "Evolution" is not the very limited operation of the ontological criticism, however, because such ontological value judgment is only one of its functions. (Those functions are so thoroughly mixed that the process of ontological judgment also involves, inextricably, superb description and analysis of styles and movements. In establishing ontological-stylistic equivalences, Bazin orders and exposits film-historical data with great clarity and comprehension; the relation could also be put the other way around. The two processes are mixed but not inseparable: We now read "Evolution" as history and discount its value judgments, that is, the rejection or demotion of montage and expressionism.) Thus, it is the historical functions of "Evolution" that survive, not its ontological function.

The ontology system involves very simplistic judgments and is itself simple in structure. The history system involves far more complex, multifaceted judgments; as a structure of thought it is also far more difficult and complex than the ontology system. The first thing to note about the history system is that it is not derivable from the ontology system. The broad, undifferentiated approvals and disapprovals of "Evolution" are as far as Bazin's ontological thought carries into film history and the critical-historical work. As noted, this is not far at all. These validity equivalences tell little or nothing about the subject itself. They are not critical principles and cannot serve as the basis for a criticism. It is noteworthy that nearly all of Bazin's criticism takes place within the approved zones of "Evolution": 1930s composition-in-depth (Renoir), American composition-in-depth (Welles and Wyler), Italian neorealism, and other postwar cinema. This approval, however, is no more illuminating than the disapproval of montage and expressionism. It provides no basis for evaluation or explication. Bazin's ontological principles could judge this exploration film inferior because it reconstructed historical events; it could judge that neorealist films are in some way better than expressionist ones (although Bazin was very hesitant to apply his ontology principles to specific judgments of worth; he preferred to critique movements generally). It could not elucidate the differences between Roberto Rossellini's style and Vittorio de Sica's or between early and later Rossellini, or make evaluations between artists or within the career of one. Bazin might have used relation to reality as a scale of value for individual films: those films coming closest to reality are better or more interesting than others; but he does not do this. He never asks whether Rossellini or Visconti or De Sica is the most realistic; he asks how each approaches reality, sees, understands, shapes it. Putting this question rather than the other shifts emphasis from reality and its valid reproduction to style, temperament, world view of the individual artist. Thus, the entire realm of Bazin's critical history lies beyond that of the ontology system; though, in systematic terms, it rests upon the conceptual foundation of ontology approval.

If we compare the history criticism with the ontology criticism, we note that the former is historical in several senses. The factor of history is introduced on both sides of the original image-reality model, and transforms it. Both object and image are historicized in the historical work: the films addressed (for example, Italian neorealism) concern humans in a historical situation rather than in timeless relations with nature; and they take their place also in a history of cinema—each film may be placed in a history of styles, of the artist, of movements. One may say that it is the interaction between historical object (human subject) and historical image that now becomes the central question of Bazin's criticism: the historical reality of 1951 is different from that of 1945; the film styles of 1951 are (or may be) different from those of 1945. (Of course expedition films can be viewed historically and fiction films ahistorically; it depends on the interests of the critic.)

Because they are concerned with correspondence between image and reality, the ontology pieces employ a logic of noncontradiction and a vocabulary of like and unlike. The historical pieces employ a developmental logic and a historical vocabulary. Bazin's piece on *La Terra Trema* (1948) that appears in *What Is Cinema?* embodies this logic and vocabulary unmistakably:

> Visconti lets us see that the Italian neorealism of 1946 has been left far behind on more than one score. Hierarchies in art are fairly pointless, but cinema is too young an art still, too involved in its own evolution to be able to indulge in repeating itself for any length of time. Five years in cinema is the equivalent of an entire literary generation. It is the merit of Visconti to have managed a dialectical integration of the achievements of recent Italian film with a larger, richer aesthetic, for which the term "realism" has not too much meaning now. I am not saying that *La Terra Trema* is superior to *Paisa* or to *La Caccia tragica* but only that it does, at least, have the merit of having left them behind from an historical standpoint. (vol. II, pp. 44–45)

This is historical analysis, but it is historical evaluation also. Bazin is careful to disown the descriptive bias that makes later works in a tradition richer or better than earlier ones, but he does make historical development itself into a value. *La Terra Trema* is important, and in that sense good, because it constitutes a stylistic development within neorealism and within film history more generally.

As mentioned above, Bazin had to go outside of the ontology system if he was to function as a critic at all, that is, to say more about the films of his period than blanket approval on ontological grounds. The historical work generally, and especially "Evolution" and the neorealist pieces, suggest that he may have drawn his concepts and methods partly from art history. The historical criticism is concerned with distinguishing stylistic movements, relating movements and individual artists, making comparisons and distinctions between individual artists and between the stages of an artist's development—the classical concerns of art history. At times "Evolution" suggests Heinrich Wölfflin, not only in its admirable clarity but also in its strong period-style emphasis that at times approaches an "art history without names," and in its underlying suggestion that "not everything is possible at all times." "Evolution" also contains hints of the Hegelian basis of much art history: given that each period of film history explores only one aspect (or complex of aspects) of cinema, it follows that cinema itself—the idea of cinema in its full-ness—exists only in the aggregate: in the historical totality of cinema. Bazin's entire critical-historical work would be clarified by a thorough-going methodological critique, perhaps along the lines of Arnold Hauser's *The Philosophy of Art History* (1959). It seems likely from its surface that Bazin's historical work shares many of the errors in reasoning, concept, and method to which much art history has been subject. This is not surprising nor does it diminish Bazin's great value, in that he engaged himself in nothing less than inventing an art history of the cinema.

In structural terms, "Evolution" and "An Aesthetic of Reality: Neorealism" (1948) concern the characteristics and relations of periods and movements and their styles, while the other critical pieces concern artists and films within these movements. Both levels of criticism show Bazin at his best, which is not to say that all difficulties and tensions created by the two perspectives are resolved. In comparison to the ontological criticism, the historical work defines as large a role for the critic as it does for the director. It does this by its openness to integral artistic creation, which is not to be hampered by a priori critical rules (see "In Defense of Rossellini" [1955]); it thereby requires a comparably large scope in the critical function. Bazin's own work is generally excellent to the degree that his subject is: his Rossellini, Visconti, Welles, Renoir, and Bresson pieces are perhaps his best individual criticism.

We have argued that "Ontology" is not the logical basis for the ontological equivalences developed and applied in the ontology criticism and "Evolution." Therefore "Ontology" is not, strictly speaking, the *theory of* the ontological work, let alone the theory of Bazin's work as a whole. It may state a theory of the photographic image, but it is not a theory of or governing the operations that go on in Bazin's ontological (or other) work. As said, "Evolution" and the ontological pieces develop their own theory. If theory consists of the assumptions and methods that guide a certain practice (or the formulation of these), then it must be that the critical-historical work contains an implicit theory of its own. We have discussed some of these methods and assumptions without attempting to formulate them. There exists at least a partial formulation of the methods and assumptions of the critical-historical work in Bazin's own words. These passages have the density and self-containment of theoretical formulation, but they occur in an essay devoted to nontheoretical matters and are certainly not presented by Bazin as a theoretical position.

Let us hope, then, to have as often as possible films like *Le Jour se lève, La Règle du jeu,* or *The Best Years of Our Lives.* But these are platonic wishes, attitudes of mind that have no bearing on the actual evolution of the cinema. If the cinema turns more and more to literature—indeed to painting or to drama—it is a fact which we take note of and attempt to understand because it is very likely that we cannot influence it. In such a situation, if fact does not absolutely make right, it requires the critic at least to be favorably predisposed.

If we take another system of reference we must say of the cinema that its existence precedes its essence; even in his most adventurous extrapolations, it is this existence from which the critic must take his point of departure. As in history, and with approximately the same reservations, the verification of a change goes beyond reality and already postulates a value judgment.

Even if this critical pragmatism does not seem to the reader sufficiently well-founded, he must nevertheless admit that it justifies in us a certain humility and thoughtful prudence when faced with any sign of evolution in the cinema.[3]

These passages certainly reflect in part the operative principles of the critical-historical work; whether they theorize that work fully and adequately is another question. The passages formulate Bazin's "favorable disposition" to the unfolding cinema of his period and also that method of historical evaluation that we noted in the piece on *La Terra Trema:* "the verification of a change goes beyond reality and already postulates a value judgment." Here as in most cases, however, formulating or explicating the theory of a practice goes beyond mere reflection and is itself a qualitative change. Thus Bazin may have been favorably predisposed to the films of his period because he liked realistic styles; his formulation *requires* of himself and other critics favorable disposition *in all cases.* In another respect also, the "Mixed Cinema" formulations go beyond the critical-historical work itself: they are entirely free of that ontology standpoint, of the predisposition toward realism in particular, that still colors most of the critical-historical pieces in some degree. These passages do not permit a position of privilege to *any* style or movement.

The "Mixed Cinema" formulations clarify and give definition to the entirety of Bazin's historical work. In so doing, they sharpen the opposition between the ontology system and the history system.

---

[3] André Bazin, "In Defense of Mixed Cinema," in *What Is Cinema?,* vol. I, pp. 71–72.

They may or may not affect the ontology criticism, which lies or seeks to lie outside of history; they certainly destroy the ontological equivalences of "Evolution." "In Defense of Mixed Cinema" requires openness to montage and expressionism and all other styles, regards these changes in film history as valuable, etc. The effect of "Mixed Cinema" on "Evolution" is to destroy its (negative) value judgments and thereby to recover it as film history. This is how we read "Evolution" in any case, for its admirable analysis/synthesis of film styles (1920–1948), not for the information that montage and expressionism are bad because they distort the image. Because the structure of the essay is historical, its value judgments are easily separable. Where Bazin puts minus signs before the disapproved styles, we put plus signs; where he ranks in value and eliminates in order to form an ideal history, a history of realism, we recover all styles mentioned, in equal value, as a dialectical history of the film styles that have been. Bazin's good-bad-good gives way to a dialectical history of the whole. In short, we are abreast of "Mixed Cinema," that is, somewhat beyond Bazin's actual historical work. Put another way, "Mixed Cinema" is something like the implicit theory of our own film-viewing and film-critical work.

Now that ontology system and history system stand opposed in theory and practice, we must consider to some degree the relations between them. The ontology pieces are unhistorical and self-contained; the critical-historical work has no impact on them—except that of overshadowing them in bulk and importance. It is not true, however, that the critical-historical work is free of the ontological strain in Bazin's thought. The nature and extent of this impingement—in the overall and in each essay—is a difficult and complex question. Those who see Bazin's work as the unfolding of a single ontological idea, and therefore as a unity, presumably see the critical-historical work in this light also. It would be illuminating and valuable if someone would study Bazin's work from this point of view, particularly the critical-historical work. Such a study would surely uncover many important relations within Bazin's work, particularly between ontological and historical areas. We shall consider certain aspects of this relation, which we do not at all see as overcoming the division we have argued, but cannot hope to do a complete job.

The issue of the ontological impingement on Bazin's critical-historical work centers on certain uses of language in that work; particularly, of course, the use of "realism" and "reality." This is by no means a simple question, for Bazin uses these terms in a number of different senses, sometimes within the same essay. The only adequate and complete way to study this question is to trace the uses and senses of "realism" and "reality" and related terms in each Bazin piece, both in the middle-level, period-movement pieces, "Evolution" and "Neorealism," and in the individual criticism. We shall have to limit ourselves to some generalizations about Bazin's use of these terms.

We recall first that there is no logical connection or carry-over between "Ontology" and the critical work, ontological or historical. "Ontology" says that photograph and object share a common being; the ontological criticism and "Evolution" concern the relations of different *styles of* photograph to reality; the historical criticism concerns qualities of and differences between styles within very large groupings of styles considered valid in relation to reality by the ontological function of "Evolution." This is the structure of Bazin's work from the ontology standpoint. As we have seen, this structure has no bearing on the historical criticism itself, except to provide a nonoperative ontological validation. That criticism is internally structured by an art-historical division of function between period-style analyses and criticism of individual artists and works within these periods. This structure and the concepts, methods, and working theory of its two-leveled criticism derive in no way from the ontological system or line of thought. This context defines and controls the meaning of all terms used within it. Thus when a critical essay uses the term realism, the word refers first of all to the definitions and classifications worked out by "Evolution" and "Neorealism." When we examine those essays, we find the term used to describe certain families of shooting styles (also script styles, acting styles, etc., in the case of "Neorealism"). These definitions do not concern reality or relation to reality; they describe artistic qualities. In the middle-level essays, realism is an art-historical term that is used to describe and classify. "Evolution" also supplies ontological analysis of the styles discussed, but this does not affect the descriptive function. The function of the term "realism" in the historical-critical essays is, first of all, to place the director or work in relation to a family of styles described by "Evolution" and/or "Neorealism."

The individual essays sometimes use the term "realism" in other ways also, though almost always *in addition to* the art-historical sense described above. Thus Bazin sometimes uses the term to describe the *particular* qualities of a director's style: he speaks of Visconti's "aesthetic realism," Fellini's "poetic realism," etc. In this usage it is not the term "realism" itself, but how Bazin qualifies that term that is the center of the critical act. Realism becomes the name of the problem to be solved, a kind of x. When Bazin has defined the kind of realism a director practices, he has defined his style (and vice versa). In this usage, which pervades the critical pieces, realism is Bazin's touchstone or basic critical concept; but it remains in itself a blank or open term. Moreover, the term becomes less distinct as Bazin applies it to more and more directors and uses it in different ways, it becomes diluted. This is true also in "Evolution," in which Bazin collects a large number of diverse styles under the term realism (Murnau, Stroheim, Welles, Rossellini). What happens here and in the individual criticism also is that the term fills up with diverse and contradictory contents: it becomes historicized as Bazin uses it to apply to his widening historical interests.

Sometimes Bazin uses realism or reality in the historical criticism in a sense that seems ontological, as well as descriptive in the ways discussed above. What operational effect this has on the act of criticism, however, is not clear. It may be no more than a kind of flavoring by which Bazin attempts to retain connection with his ideas concerning reality.

Despite its realist terminology, the history system is not assimilable to the ontology system. The opposition of the two systems remains irreconcilable. Each system, universalized by its theory, presents itself as the entirety of Bazin's work; but each can make itself into the whole only by enforcing certain modifications or mutilations on the other. The history system can take over the whole only by eliminating the ontology system and the ontological dimension of "Evolution," recovering that essay as descriptive history. The ontology system can take over the whole only by dissolving the structure of the critical history and recovering each piece and each film as a serial application or exemplification of the idea of image-object identity.

It might be asked why this conflict of possible structures, and hence of theories, is important at all. The reality or substance of Bazin's work, its bulk as well as that of greatest importance in it, is the critical-historical work itself. The systematic principles that seek to define this work are metaphysical excrescences in regard to it. They are competing ideologies of the whole that seek to turn it this way or that. The chief effect of "In Defense of Mixed Cinema" as ideology is to turn the finite, finished, in-itself of the historical work into project: unfinished, forward-turned aspiration toward a comprehensive art history of the cinema. The ideology of the ontology system turns it into an unstructured series of emanations of a single idea, essentially backward-turned. Arguably the conflict between the two principles has more to do with ourselves, the heirs of this work, than with the work itself. The project of completing an art history of the cinema is one that we take up, or not; Bazin cannot do it. For this reason alone the conflict is important, and also for the related reason that how a body of work understands itself is inextricably part of that work. This self-understanding does not control the understanding or the use of those who use the work; but it must be engaged by them if they are to understand both the work and their own use of it.

We have argued that Bazin's work understands itself in two ways and that these ways are irreconcilable. There is discernible in that work, however, a serious attempt to overcome this conflict; if it is not an intentional "attempt," it is at least a possible ground of its overcoming. Several passages in Bazin have a teleological flavor; "The Myth of Total Cinema" (1946) and "Evolution" are explicitly teleological. "Myth" argues that the idea of a total representation of reality was the inspiration that guided the pioneers of cinematic technology. The essay suggests that this project remains the aspiration of cinema. "Evolution" suggests also that film history exhibits a movement toward greater and greater realism, and supports this theme in several ways. The essay ends on the combined notes of composition-in-depth and neorealism, which have been presented as the highest stages in film history's long progress toward realism that Bazin explicitly calls its "vocation for realism." "Evolution" implies a technological base for this teleology: it traces the elimination of titles, the development of sound, of deep-focus lenses and panchromatic film stock, and the aesthetic alterations that followed each. Bazin sees each of these developments as an increase in realism.

It is easy to see how this teleology provides a ground for the unification of ontology and history. The ideal of total realism is gradually realized by film history; film history is a long progress toward the realization of its essence. Perfect realism will never be achieved, but it will be approximated more and more closely; in any case this progress is the meaning of film history, its unifying pattern and spirit. This teleology or philosophy of film history overcomes the underlying divisions within Bazin's thought—that between ontology and history and, behind these, between value and fact, essence and existence. This attempt fails on several counts. First of all, although film history up to Bazin's day gave his teleological scheme a certain plausibility—neorealism and composition-in-depth *did* integrate the visual continuity of (certain) silent cinema wth the "added realism" of sound—film history since his death has decidedly reversed this pattern: montage and collage forms of many kinds have appeared or reappeared, and many kinds of expressionism also. Neither is Bazin's scheme unexceptionable in relation to his own period. The truth is that every technological and aesthetic development in film history has increased the expressive resources of realism in Bazin's sense, but of every other form and style of cinema also. Finally, as mentioned above, Bazin makes film history into a progress toward realism (in "Evolution" especially) largely by including everything but montage and expressionism within that term. Instead of film history made realistic, "realism" is historicized.

The ontology/history conflict in Bazin's thought remains. In a subsequent essay we shall return to this conflict from the perspective of the history of film thought.

Chapter 3   The Long Take (1971)

This essay concerns stylistic aspects of the work of F. W. Murnau, Max Ophuls, and Orson Welles in the light of the categories of classical film theory. In "Two Types of Film Theory" we suggest reading back the results of stylistic analyses *into* the classical theories, in order to test the latter and correct them where necessary, toward the ultimate goal of formulating a new, entirely adequate theory of film. Of course, it is distinctive personal styles, not abstract categories, that have meaning in the work of individual directors and therefore in actual films themselves. The consideration of distinctive styles, however, can lead to the recognition and analysis of new expressive categories. Indeed, the interaction between actual films and theoretical categories illumines both areas; for film theory is, after all, a metacriticism or philosophy of criticism. It is pursued to clarify and improve film criticism through the determination of basic film categories and the identification of those assumptions about film on which any criticism is based. Thus good criticism—that which follows its subject and its own assumptions to their limits—frequently raises questions for film theory; and film theory itself is the continual improvement and clarification of the principles and assumptions of film criticism. Thus, in our analysis of the directors under consideration we shall also be questioning, by specific reference, the capacity of the classical theories (especially, in this case, of Bazin's theory) to elucidate and account for their work.

Murnau, Ophuls, and Welles are celebrated metteurs-en-scène, that is, practitioners of the art of mise-en-scène. One does not lightly venture a definition of *mise-en-scène,* cinema's grand undefined term, of which each person, when examined, reveals a different sense and meaning. (To the problem "What is *Mise-en-Scène?*," [1] Alexandre Astruc devotes a brilliant essay that nevertheless fails to answer the question.) The term is originally a theatrical one meaning literally (to) put in place. It is, baldly, the art of the image itself—the actors, sets and backgrounds, lighting, and camera movements considered in relation to themselves and to each other. Of course the individual images of montage have or exhibit mise-en-scène. But it is generally thought that the true cultivation and expression of the image as such—as opposed to the *relation between* images, which is the central expressive category of montage—requires the duration of the long take (a single piece of unedited film that may or may not constitute an entire sequence). Opinion aside, it is the long take alone that permits the director to vary and develop the image without switching to another image; it is often this uninterrupted development that is meant by mise-en-scène. Thus the long take makes mise-en-scène possible. The long take is the presupposition or a priori of mise-en-scène, that is, the ground or field in which mise-en-scène can occur. It is the time necessary for mise-en-scène space.

Bazin's position on long take and mise-en-scène is somewhat equivocal. The brief analysis presented above would be too "expressive" for Bazin. Bazin is concerned, of course, with cinema's

---

[1] *Cahiers du Cinéma in English,* no. 1 (January 1966), pp. 53–55.

relation to reality; hence he shies away from any account stressing the independent, expressive possibilities of mise-en-scène or of any other category of cinema. Bazin analyzes and defends the long take on very different grounds. He favors it first of all for its *temporal realism:* the long take's time is the event's time. His example here is Robert Flaherty. Regarding the spatial implications of the long take Bazin is required to be more ingenious. Here he faces Murnau, whom he admits is not primarily interested in dramatic time. Bazin's answer is that Murnau's mise-en-scène does not add to or deform reality, "rather it strives to bring out the deeper structure of reality, to reveal pre-existent relationships which become the constituents of the drama." It is easy to see what Bazin is trying to do here—to eliminate mise-en-scène expressivity (in any independent sense) by equating it with the preexistent structures of reality. The director therefore does not *create* mise-en-scène or use it to express moods or themes or ideas, but only to bring out the structures already present in reality. Other directors force Bazin into more contorted explanations; thus he says of a scene in Wyler: "The real action is overlaid with the action of the mise-en-scène itself . . ."

There are many interesting and difficult problems raised by the long take and mise-en-scène—besides those raised by Bazin's position—but this is not the primary direction in which stylistic consideration of Murnau, Ophuls, and Welles will take us. (Such a study—that of the long take as such—must await separate treatment.) The present essay takes its chief emphasis from the fact that the long take rarely appears in its pure state (as a sequence filmed in one shot), but almost always in combination with some form of editing. One can locate sequence shots in Murnau, Ophuls, and (especially) Welles, but more basic to the art of each (a fair portion of Welles excepted) is the use of the long take *and* cutting within the sequence. This is to say that the long take is not in itself a principle of construction (in them), but is part of a *shooting style,* or characteristic way of shooting and building sequences. (There have been few shooting styles based on the sequence shot—and these mainly in the present. Miklos Jancso, in *Winter Wind* [1970] especially, and perhaps Jerzy Skolimowski are examples; but each also makes use of intrasequence cuts.) It is obvious that any long take short of a sequence shot requires connection with another shot or shots to fill out the sequence. Thus a long-take style necessarily involves long takes and cutting in some combination. Most analyses of long-take directors and styles concentrate on the long take itself and ignore the mode of cutting unique to it—what we call below the intrasequence cut. But such cuts or cutting patterns (one could even speak of cutting styles) are as essential to the long-take sequence as the long take itself. Moreover, as we shall see, there are several *kinds* of cutting within the sequence—several categories or subcategories of the intrasequence cut itself—that may be isolated and identified, in a preliminary way, from the work of the directors under consideration. Finally, as we shall also see (regarding Welles), the mixture or combination of long take and editing techniques can occur not only within the sequence but also at a higher level of organization: in the relation between sequences, within the whole film itself.

The relation between mise-en-scène and long take in Murnau has been put by Alexandre Astruc in a formulation that cannot be improved upon:

[The image in Murnau is] the meeting place for a certain number of lines of force . . . brought to this point of extreme tension so that henceforth only their destruction can be conceived and supported. With Murnau, each image demands annihilation by another image. Every sequence announces its own end.

And this is, I think, the key to all of Murnau's work—this fatality hidden behind the most harmless elements of the frame; this diffuse presence of an irremediable something that will gnaw at and corrupt each image the way it wells up behind each of Kafka's sentences. How will it manifest itself? *By happening in the sequence.* [Astruc clearly means "shot" here; the logic of the passage is incoherent otherwise.] Every frame of Murnau's is the story of a murder. The camera will have the simplest and most shocking of roles: that of being the annunciating and prescient terrain of an assassination. Its task will be aided by all of the elements of the *mise-en-scène.* The shooting angle, the placement of the people within the frame, the distribution of the lights—all serve to construct the lines of a dramatic scene whose unbearable tension will end in annihilation. The story of the sequence is the accomplishment of that promise of death. *Its temporal unraveling is no other than the definitive realization in time of an original plastic fatality in which everything that must play itself out in these few seconds will be given once and for all.* [Emphasis supplied.] This is why montage is practically nonexistent for Murnau, as for all the Germans. Each image is an unstable equilibrium, better still the destruction of a stable equilibrium brought about by its own élan.

So long as this destruction is not accomplished the image remains on the screen. So long as the movement has not resolved itself no other image can be tolerated.[2]

Astruc's analysis gives body and specificity to Bazin's more general formulations concerning Murnau. "Editing plays practically no role at all in their films [Murnau, Stroheim, Flaherty], except in the purely negative sense of eliminating what is superfluous . . . in neither *Nosferatu* [1922] nor *Sunrise* [1927] does editing play a decisive part."[3] Bazin ignores those sequences of *Nosferatu* in which editing, though still essentially connective, establishes *links* between widely separated scenes and places. Most notable here is the sequence in which Ellen (at home) saves Jonathan from Nosferatu's power (at his castle far away) through her spiritual influence. Murnau cuts from Jonathan in peril to Ellen sitting up in bed, then back and forth several times until Ellen's love forces Nosferatu to withdraw.[4]

What we have here is an event at place A and, essentially, a reaction shot to that event at place B, hundreds of miles away. It is not accidental that the link thus expressed through editing is a mystical or spiritual one. Thus Murnau, who would never use a reaction shot normally (preferring to put the parties to an action in the same frame and work out the action within the shot), uses editing solely to express mystical or nonspatial relations; that is, to treat widely spread subjects as though they were in the same frame. This *is* an expressive use of editing, one beyond *mere* connection. This is also something like D. W. Griffith's parallel editing, with spiritual rather than spatial coordinates—and with the additional difference that the conflicts generated are resolved *within* the parallel format, not in a subsequent or culminating scene that brings the parallel strands together into one frame.

This exception is, nevertheless, a trifling one in comparison with the overall truth of the Astruc-Bazin position, for Murnau makes less use of expressive editing techniques than almost any other director. He is the classic case of the Bazinian ideal: the long-take director who uses editing for no other purpose than to link his shots. But

---

[2] Alexandre Astruc, "Fire and Ice," *Cahiers du Cinéma in English,* no. 1 (January 1966), pp. 70–71.

[3] André Bazin, "The Evolution of Film Language," in *The New Wave,* ed. Peter Graham (New York: Doubleday & Company, 1968), pp. 29–30.

[4] Shots 228–255 in the Byrne shot analysis of *Nosferatu,* in *Films of Tyranny* (Madison, Wis.: University of Wisconsin Press, 1966).

here we encounter another difficulty, for Murnau is not typical in this respect, as Bazin frequently suggests he is. Murnau's elimination or renunciation of expressive editing is, even among long-take directors, the exception rather than the rule.

We must be very clear at this point that we are *not* talking about length of shot. Astruc is careful to note that Murnau's shots characteristically last a "few seconds" (which any close viewing of Murnau's films verifies). Astruc does not even use the terms *long take* or *sequence shot* (and indeed in modern terms Murnau's shots do not look like long takes). The operative category here is not length of shot, but quality or structure of shot, and the relations between shots. Murnau's cinema is characterized in Astruc's essay in *relational* terms; that is, in terms of the way that his shots—because of their structure in themselves—relate to other shots. In Murnau, "everything happens within the sequence"; that is, each shot begins anew and does not (plastically, metaphysically) depend on the shot before or carry over to the shot following. In fact, Kenji Mizoguchi's shots are most often far longer than Murnau's and yet they *do* depend upon and relate to each other in ways that Murnau's shots do not. Mizoguchi uses longer shots than Murnau *and* he makes important use of expressive editing, which Murnau does not. Thus the point in question has to do with different ways of relating and ordering shots (which are in turn—or beforehand—conceived and shot in order to be related in different ways); and these do not depend on, or correlate simply and strictly with, length of shot.

Beyond the pure and magnificent case of Murnau, there are only problems. As mentioned, many or most long-take directors make some use of cutting. Ophuls and Mizoguchi *regularly* do so; Welles frequently does. This mixed realm presents problems partly because film theory has largely ignored this area of interaction. Both Eisenstein montage theory and Bazinian long-take theory not only ignore this stylistic area, they deny its existence, both preferring the either/ or mentality that each sees as necessary to its own survival. Thus Bazin contrasts purely connective editing with the expressive editing techniques of montage; he will not admit or address expressive editing relations within long-take sequences and styles. Contrariwise, montage theory will not admit the existence of any expressive or significant cut (or cutting style) outside of the montage sequence. Stylistic combinations of long-take and cutting techniques fall exactly between the two schools, in that they combine elements of the favored style of each; but they are treated as falling outside of each because each prefers not to recognize them. This is a prime instance of serious omission in the classical film theories, indeed of an entire *category* of film expression missing from them. This limitation is compounded in importance by the expressive impact that editing has upon the long-take sequence.

The category of cinematic expression we are discussing, the crucial cut between related long takes, might be called the selective cut or the intrasequence cut or even mise-en-scène cutting. It must be carefully differentiated from montage. Montage is the connection or relation of two or more shots (usually far more than two)—of entire film-pieces—in some overall format. Montage treats or arranges the whole piece, not just the end of one and the beginning of another. The intrasequence cut does not relate, arrange, or govern the whole of the pieces it joins; it merely has a local relationship to the beginnings and ends of the connecting shots, at the place they are joined.

Eisenstein characterizes montage in terms of rhythm. It is obvious that this is the rhythm of whole pieces, of many shots arranged in certain ways; one can hardly speak of a montage rhythm of two. In the long-take sequence rhythm is achieved not by the lengths of the shots themselves (even where multiple), but rather *within* each shot, through movement—or lack of it—by camera, or both. In this context the intrasequence cut acts to break the rhythm of the sequence and then to reconnect it on a new basis. It is a jump or leap in the sequence rhythm, that is, of the disposition/movement of actors and camera. It *is not itself* a rhythmic element, as in the montage sequence, but it does *affect* the rhythmic elements of the sequence, that is, actor placement, camera disposition, and mise-en-scène.

Finally, our inquiry into the intrasequence cut concerns not just the incidental interaction of two cinematic categories—mise-en-scène and montage. There are important senses in which their interaction defines each and in which each defines the other. Thus the odd quality of the intrasequence cut is that it *reflects back* on the scene (and on mise-en-scène) and defines it or qualifies it in retrospect. The cut that ends a long take—how it ends it as well as where—determines or affects the nature of the shot itself. Looked at oppositely, the mise-en-scène requires a certain kind of cut at a certain time. The two categories are strictly correlative. If one begins talking about the one, he ends talking about the other; and vice versa. The cut is the limit or boundary of the shot, and this boundary enters into and determines the nature of the shot itself. Hegel says:

> A thing is what it is, only in and by reason of its limit. We cannot therefore regard the limit as only external to being which is then and there. It rather goes through and through the whole of such existence.[5]

An entire category of long-take or intrasequence cutting concerns the relation of camera to script and dialogue. A director may cut frequently, even on every line, and if he does so the result is a kind of montage, though one bound in its rhythm to the rhythm of the dialogue, not itself an independent rhythm. At the other extreme he may, as Mizoguchi often does, cut only once or twice within a long dialogue sequence. If he does the latter, then his cut must be carefully mediated and placed in relation to the dramatic progress of the scene, coming at just that point at which the relationships at stake in the scene have ripened into qualitative change—a change reflected in the new or altered mise-en-scène. Such cuts are integral to the art of mise-en-scène and to the particular long-take style of the director involved.

Max Ophuls is best known for his sweeping, graceful tracking shots and crane shots; but he also used cutting in expressive and important ways, particularly in regard to dialogue. The latter statement should probably be qualified to read: *at least in his American films.* Ophuls's camera work in his American films is more closely related to and centered on dialogue than on behavior; whereas his European films center more on behavior, manners, movement. In *Caught* (1949) he uses cutting and a highly varied mise-en-scène to integrate his camera with the action, to get his camera into it via the script, that is, via the segments and movement of the dialogue, sometimes cutting line-by-line. Indeed, *Caught* could be used as a teaching vehicle for the ways in which camera may comment on and reflect dialogue and script action. Ophuls relates camera to dialogue and action in a variety of ways. Sometimes he will use an inset close-up, either within a long take or within an exchange of medium shots, in order to underscore an important line. This happens in Barbara Bel Geddes's first ride with Robert Ryan, shot from two setups in medium shot (or medium-close). He presses her to tell what she knows of him; when he asks again, "What else?," there is a tight close-up of Bel Geddes as she says: "You're rich," then back to the original setups.

---

[5] *The Logic of Hegel,* trans. William Wallace (London: Oxford University Press, 1965), p. 173.

Sometimes Ophuls uses the inset close-up for a silent reaction; that is, he cuts in as though for a line and there is only a look. This is used in the psychiatrist scene, after a previous identical shot of the doctor has been used for a line of dialogue; it occurs also in the talk between Bel Geddes and Ryan after the projection-room fight. Ophuls also does some fiendish things to traditional American cross-cutting on lines of dialogue. In the projection-room scene itself, when Ryan challenges Bel Geddes for laughing with one of the guests, Ophuls cuts between the two across the huge room, from Ryan huge in left foreground/Bel Geddes small in right background to Bel Geddes huge in left foreground/Ryan small in right background. To complete the symmetry, each stares off to the right (when in foreground, to left when in background). This is shot-reverse-shot as never done before or since. Ophuls cuts here on each cryptic, dramatic line, as in a tennis match.

Another variant is employed in the scene between the two doctors when Bel Geddes is gone. As each stands in his doorway conversing, the camera tracks slowly between them, pivoting on the empty chair where Bel Geddes sat. Later in the conversation Ophuls resorts to crosscutting between the two terminal positions established by the camera's movement. From these positions Ophuls moves into two stages of successively closer shots of each (for the crucial lines between them), then reverts to the original positions, and then to the original tracking path itself. This is a highly interesting combination of camera movements (long take) and cutting elements.

These are cuts and cutting patterns in relation to speakers and their lines. There are also cuts that entail comprehensive changes of the entire mise-en-scène, either related to dialogue or not. An example of this kind of cut occurs in the scene in which James Mason comes to Ryan's mansion to find Bel Geddes. She and Mason agree to meet outside; Ophuls cuts to an outside view of Mason walking past the garage; Bel Geddes appears inside in the right background; the camera follows Mason as he goes to her, then holds on a two-shot as they converse; she moves to the running board of a car and there is a cut to a different angle on the two of them. Finally Bel Geddes reveals her situation: "I'm pregnant." Just following this line Ophuls cuts to a shot of her through a ladder that appeared in profile in the shot before. This is a somewhat obvious symbol of her imprisonment, but effective just the same for its suddenness and force. The shot itself contains no dialogue and is held for only a few seconds. This cut serves the purpose of transposing the elements of the mise-en-scène at a crucial stage in the scene's dramatic progress. The cut rearranges the mise-en-scène suddenly, just as Bel Geddes's revelation rearranges their lives and relationships, also suddenly. (Later stages of this sequence show Ryan huge in the foreground, back to camera, literally dividing Mason and Bel Geddes who stand in the same plane in the middle ground. In another stage Ophuls follows Bel Geddes with a tracking shot as she paces up and down between the two men.)

In some cases a director cuts just before a crucial line; in some cases he cuts just after a crucial line. It is interesting to consider the implications and possibilities of each type of cut. In the case of the cut following the line, the transposed mise-en-scène represents the result or consequences of the line, the new set of relationships that it deals. In this case the line itself belongs to the old context or set of relationships, whose logic it completes, leading to and making necessary a new qualitative arrangement. In the case of the cut just before the line is spoken, the new situation and the new mise-en-scène and the line itself are permitted to resonate together in the viewer's consciousness. The change of situation before the line is spoken, however, may seem to anticipate, or even to determine, the character's action—unless it signifies his decision to speak in a certain way before he does so. It is possible, however, that the cut after the line, though perhaps logically more appropriate, may blur and confuse the viewer's perceptions at a crucial point. The shock and dislocation of an important change in relationships may be effectively expressed, however, in just this way, as is done in the ladder cut in *Caught*.

(In terms of our theoretical inquiry, Mizoguchi would be the appropriate director to consider next. His films reveal many varieties of long-take relation within the sequence, including several important kinds of intrasequence cuts that we have not yet discussed. These include a mode of dramatic reversal in which all elements of the mise-en-scène are transposed and the two- or three- [or more] part long-take sequence, relating long takes in a continuous or narrative mode rather than in a reversed or transposed one. Consideration of Mizoguchi in this perspective will have to await another occasion.)

One of Bazin's chief objections to montage is that it breaks down or analyzes the event for the viewer. Bazin exempts the American film of the 1930s from this charge on the ground that it broke the event into shots naturally and logically, that is, according to the logic of the event itself. Bazin nevertheless considers composition-in-depth and the sequence shot as improvements on the 1930s manner, because they preserve the event in its own time and space dimensions. Bazin did not consider or admit that long-take styles, short of the pure sequence shot, *also* break down or analyze the event, and that they necessarily do this. It is clear that Ophuls and Mizoguchi do this once they decide to include even a single cut within the sequence and therefore must decide where to put it; that is, how to break down the scene/event. Thus the question is not, as Bazin has it, whether or not to break down the event, but how to do so, according to what style or system. The differences in approach between montage and long-take styles are great enough so that the fact of event breakdown need not be denied by either—as Bazin does in preferring the long take to montage.

Up to now we have remained at the level of the sequence. When we come to Orson Welles we meet another problem—that of the long-take artist who is also a brilliant montage director, who, indeed, uses sequences of both kinds within a single film.

In defending Orson Welles as a long-take director, Bazin could hardly ignore the fact that Welles, in *Citizen Kane* (1941), also used editing techniques, and used them brilliantly. Bazin's response to this problem is ingenious:

> It is not that Welles purposely refrains from using expressionist editing techniques. In fact, their episodic use, in between sequence shots with composition-in-depth, gives them new meaning. Editing had once been the very stuff of cinema, the tissue of a scenario. In *Citizen Kane,* a series of superimpositions stands in contrast to the continuity of a scene taken in a single shot; it is a different, explicitly abstract register of the narrative. Accelerated editing used to distort time and space; Welles' editing, far from attempting to deceive us, offers us a temporal résumé—the equivalent, for example, of the French imperfect tense or the English frequentative. And so "quick editing," "editing by attraction," and the superimpositions which the sound cinema had not resorted to for ten years, found a possible use in conjunction with the temporal realism of cinema with editing.[6]

Bazin's description-analysis clearly fits the newsreel sequence and perhaps also the breakfast table montage, though the latter is not the temporal résumé of any portion of the film outside of itself: it *constitutes* the process it presents, it *is* the tissue of the scenario for

---

[6] Bazin, "The Evolution of Film Language," p. 46.

its duration. One could perhaps make better anti-Bazinian arguments for other sequences. The important point, however, is that Bazin's explanation applies only to the special case of *Kane*. Expressive editing in *The Lady from Shanghai* (1948), *Falstaff* (1967), *The Immortal Story* (1968), and other Welles films has nothing to do with "temporal résumé" (except in the sense in which all montage is this) and quite often constitutes the tissue of the scenario.

Falstaff presents us with a complex of problems, especially rich and interesting, beyond that of the intrasequence cut (though there are these also): that of the overall film construction that includes both montage and long-take (including sequence shot) sequences. Here the combination and balancing of styles take place at a higher level of organization. Arguably, such constructions make possible far greater visual and dramatic (and *visually dramatic*) variety and contrast than more or less homogeneous long-take styles. Indeed, *Falstaff* could serve as a model of sequence construction and of the richness, variety, and imagination of sequence-style choices. Because of the formal diversity of its sequences, the film's construction gives rise to an additional category of filmic expression—that of the *inter-*sequence cut. These cuts, augmented by powerful sound-editing techniques—as in the cuts from raucous tavern (dark on light) to somber castle (light on dark) with heavy chamber door slamming —provide instantaneous and overwhelming changes of mood, tempo, and tone, as well as high dramatic contrast. (These are, by the narrowest definition, brilliant visual-sound equivalents for the highly charged scene and act changes of classical drama. Moreover, these are achieved instantaneously, and often with the transposition of all cinematic-expressive elements: light-dark, angle, texture, mise-en-scène, sound.)

In an otherwise helpful article, "Welles' *Chimes at Midnight*" [*Falstaff*] (*Film Quarterly* [Fall 1970]), Joseph McBride ignores the visual-sound construction of the film and justifies this neglect by speaking of Welles's "breaking the bounds of his tools"; and serving his actors with the camera in contrast to *Citizen Kane's* "trickery" (a term used as though it is self-explanatory). This is wrong and is hardly bettered by those critics who solemnly noted the battle sequence and nothing more. *Falstaff* is a visual-sound masterpiece, one of the greatest stylistic achievements as well as one of the greatest films of the 1960s. In it every category of cinematic expression is used and stretched to carry the burden of Welles's humanism. There are fast outdoor tracking shots in the thieving scene, done in hilarious long shot; there are fast indoor tracks in the tavern scenes, capturing the swirling motions of dance and ribaldry. There is also the remarkable textural and tonal unity of the film—provided in part by the severe Spanish landscape and the matchingly severe tavern set, the rough-textured boards, balconies, supports, and walls of which Welles makes full expressive use (in conjunction with angle and actor placement).

The angles of the film and specifically the *patterning* of angles throughout the film are also extremely important. There is an intricate grading of angles, which are closely tied to the film's dramatic development. Low angle is the royal angle and therefore crucial to a film concerned with royalty, true and false, presumptive and legitimate, parodied and earned. There are somber low angles for the king in his dignity; less extreme, more tentative low angles for Hotspur, aspirant to a future crown; and democratic straight angles for Hal, Poins, and Falstaff—except when Hal and Jack play king and son/son and king. Then the angles become impossibly extreme in accord with the parodic spirit. (The latter, and several other scenes, make use of a high reverse angle—that is, the royal point of view—but these are used less frequently than low angles.) There are also, of course, the final angle shots of Hal and Falstaff, which are equally extreme but now fully serious.

Overlapping these plastic categories are the film's temporal units: its remarkable montages and long takes. The most brilliant montage sequence is Hotspur's departure from Kate. Harry Percy reads a letter, verbally duels with Kate, and at the same time bustles about putting on his armor. He is preparing himself for battle—physically and psychologically—and Welles eloquently accents the scene's rising martial spirit by cutting again and again, and with increasing rapidity, to rows of trumpeters announcing the battle with a strident call to arms. What is created in this manner is a complex visual *and* aural montage, alternating between images of Harry Percy in motion and images of the trumpeters in motion (turning to left or to right in each brief shot), and between the rising inflections of Harry and the stirring sounds of the trumpets, images reinforcing sounds, sounds reinforcing images. The sequence thus has a rising excitement that is remarkably erotic, giving life to the text's implication that, in Harry, eros is deflected from wife to war.

The battle sequence is also a montage, at first chiefly of tracking shots *into* the battle from all sides of the surrounding area, each fresh, high-purposed charge ending, becoming indistinguishable in the muddle at the center. As the center becomes all, the shots become more and more static and interchangeable, as though it does not matter where the camera looks: all is the same.

In the Harry Percy scene the language of the written text enters into the rhythm of the visual and sound texts, and vice versa. This happens also in an early scene with Falstaff, Hal, and Poins, a long-take sequence in which the three in their bantering continually circle one another gracefully—a delightful and precise counterpoint to the lines themselves. Following his characters with a fluid camera, Welles also moves skillfully among three-shots and various combinations of two-shot here, as one character disappears and the other two parry, then all rejoin—all within a single take.

An extremely long take, divisible into four or five stages, occurs late in the film and reveals new possibilities for the long-take format as a mode of sequence construction. The scene (*Henry IV*, Part II, Act V, scene 3) is the one in which Falstaff hears of Henry IV's death and rushes off to greet the new king and thus meet his destiny. In the shot's opening stage Shallow and Silence are dancing and singing in the foreground while Falstaff paces up and down in the middle distance; Shallow and Silence go out right and Falstaff walks far back into the depth of the frame, where he sits and talks with his page for some time; Pistol enters in a gay mood, followed by Shallow and the others, and Falstaff comes forward (all characters are now in one plane); Pistol finally announces his news, Falstaff comes far forward into the frame (the camera tilting to take him in), gives his speech, and goes out, the others following. Each of these stages realizes a different mood, distinct from that of the stage before—the melancholy gaiety of the first dancing; the sadness and solitude of Falstaff, emphasized by his smallness in the frame; the abrupt rising of spirits on Pistol's entry; the genuine gaiety that greets his news; Falstaff's more serious expectations when he considers the implications of the news for him; his nobility and delusion as he totters out under the burden of this high purpose. This is a highly interesting use of the long take in what may be called the theatrical mode, functioning by virtue of the static camera (until the final tilt) almost as a proscenium stage, *in* which a sequence of actions and movements occurs, which in turn realizes a delicate and precise sequence of emotions.

Chapter 4

Toward a Non-Bourgeois Camera Style

(Part-Whole Relations in Godard's Late Films)
(1970–1971)

Godard has developed a new camera style in his later period. Its prime element is a long, slow tracking shot that moves purely laterally —usually in one direction only (left to right or right to left), sometimes doubling back (left to right then right to left, right to left then left to right)—over a scene that does not itself move, or strictly speaking, that does not move in any relation to the camera's movement. Examples of this shot are the automobile trilogy or triptych: the backed-up highway of cars in *Weekend* (1967), the wrecked cars piled up in *One Plus One* (1968), and the auto assembly line in *British Sounds* (1969); most of the studio scenes with the Rolling Stones in *One*

Plus One; several of the guerilla scenes in *Weekend* ("I salute you, old ocean"); and the shot of the University of Nanterre and environs in *La Chinoise* (1967). Before we consider this shot as part of a stylistic complex and in the various contexts in which it appears, we must consider the shot in itself—its structure and implications as shot.

First we must distinguish Godard's tracking shot from other such shots in the history of cinema. It is not, first of all, forward camera movement, proving the depth of space, as in Murnau. Godard's tracking shot moves neither forward nor backward in space, nor in any diagonal or arc, nor at any angle but 90° to the scene it is shooting. That is, Godard's track lies exactly along the 0°/180° line. The scenes or subjects that these shots address lie also along a 0°/180° line, which, furthermore, is exactly parallel to the camera line. This extreme stylization, wherein a plane or planes of subject are paralleled exactly by the plane of art, is unusual in cinema and gives the shot very much the form of a planimetric painting. A partial exception to the rule is the camera's sinuosity in the traffic-jam shot in *Weekend,* its slight "angling" to left and right as it moves laterally, getting slightly behind or ahead of the scene it is filming, a kind of warp in the shot's even, continuous space-time. The base line of the camera's movement remains exactly straight, however, and exactly parallel to the scene. More fundamental departures from the lateral track are the "Action Musicale" sequence shot in *Weekend,* in which the camera remains in the center of the scene and *turns* 360°, and the shot in *One Plus One,* in which the camera *tracks* 360° around the studio in which the Stones are playing. In the first the camera is at the center of a circle, in the second at the periphery, but in both there is the sense of a circular subject rendered flat and linear: these shots look like the lateral tracking shot and fit easily into formats that align them end-to-end with such shots.

The shot, second, is not like Ophuls's tracking shots that—though often lateral and hence formally like Godard's—are essentially following shots. Ophuls tracks in order to follow his characters, to give them movement or to attend their movement. His tracks center on, are filled with, derive life and motion from his characters, that is, from individuals. Godard, like Eisenstein, repudiates "the individualist conception of the bourgeois hero" and his tracking shots reflect this. His camera serves no individual and prefers none to another. It never initiates movement to follow a character and if it picks one up as it moves it leaves him behind as haphazardly (the workers and Wiazemsky in the Action Musicale and the shot with Juliet Berto in and out, in *Weekend*). Also—though some may dispute this—Ophuls's tracks are essentially uncritical of their subjects, whereas the essence of Godard's tracking shot is its critical distance from what it surveys. Finally, Ophuls frequently uses the composition-in-depth technique of interposing objects in the foreground, between character and camera. Godard never does this.

Third, the shot is not like Fellini's pans and short tracks, though the latter also survey persons fixed in space rather than moving ones, that is, "discovers" them in place as the camera moves. There are two chief differences. First, Fellini's camera *affects* his characters, calls them into life or bestows life upon them. Godard's camera does not affect the reality it unfolds and is not affected by it. There is a different camera dialectic in each: Fellini's camera interacts with reality, touches and is touched, causes as well as registers effects; Godard's camera assumes a position over against reality, outside, detached. Second, Fellini's tracks are frequently subjective—in the sense that the camera eye is a character's eye. In 8½ (1962) the reactions of characters to the camera are their reactions to Guido; the pain we feel when we see them is Guido's pain. Because subjective, Fellini's tracks are most often in medium-close or closeup range, sometimes with only faces coming into view; Godard's tracks, which are never subjective, are usually in long shot, taking in as much of an event and its context as possible. Also, Fellini introduces depth by arraying characters and objects in multiple planes, some very close to the camera, others at a distance, making for surprise and variety as the camera moves over them. Godard avoids depth: he arranges his characters in a single plane only—none is ever closer to the camera than another. The resulting flatness of Godard's shots, particularly in *Weekend,* is discussed below.

Godard's tracking shot is a species of long take,[1] very often of sequence shot,[2] but it has few or none of the characteristics in terms

---

[1] A single piece of unedited film; of course "long" is relative to "short"—the cutoff would seem to be a shot used for wholly independent effect rather than as part of a montage pattern. None of Eisenstein's early films contains a single long take—such was the theoretical purity of his practice; no Godard film is without several long takes.

[2] A sequence filmed in one take; a one-shot sequence. A sequence is a series of closely related scenes; a scene is a shot or shots that cover a single and continuous dramatic action. We must bear in mind that Godard's "sequences" are not those of conventional narrative cinema, hence the concepts *sequence shot* and *sequence* lose the reasonably clear meaning they had for Bazin. What meanings will take their place, we do not yet know. See André Bazin, "The

of which André Bazin discussed and defended the shot and cinematic styles based upon it. In Godard's shot there is continuity of dramatic space and time, the irreducibles of the long take (indeed its very definition); but there is strict avoidance of composition-in-depth, for Bazin the essence of the shot—or that of greatest value in its use. As mentioned, Godard's frames are flat, composed in relation to the plane occupied by his characters. Other planes, where present, are used merely as backdrop to this one. Not only composition-in-depth but the *values* that Bazin found in composition-in-depth are missing in Godard's version of the long take (and in late Godard generally): greater realism, greater participation on the part of the viewer, and a reintroduction of ambiguity into the structure of the film image. It is clear that Godard is no realist; in *La Chinoise* he specifically repudiates the realist aesthetic (of Bazin and others): "Art is not the reflection of a reality; it is the reality of that reflection." Godard's later style does require the active participation of the viewer, but not in Bazin's sense of choosing what to see within a multilayered image and, presumably, making his own moral connections within it also. Godard presents instead an admittedly synthetic, single-layered construct, which the viewer must examine critically, accept or reject. The viewer is not drawn *into* the image, neither does he make choices within it; he stands outside the image and judges it *as a whole*. It is clear also that Godard of the later films is not interested in ambiguity—through flatness of frame and transparency of action, he seeks to eliminate ambiguity. Thus Godard uses the long take for none of the traditional reasons; in fact he reinvents the long take, and the tracking shot, for his own purposes.

A camera moves slowly, sideways to the scene it is filming. It tracks. But what is the result when its contents are projected on a screen? It is a band or ribbon of reality that slowly unfolds itself. It is a mural or scroll that unrolls before the viewer and rolls up after him. To understand the nature of this visual band we must go beyond the tracking shot itself. We encounter here the aesthetic problem of parts and wholes: Godard's tracking shot is but one element in a remarkably rich and complete stylistic complex or repertoire. It appears not in isolation, but in formal combinations with other kinds of shots, and with sounds. In short, the tracking shot cannot be understood apart from the varying contexts in which it

Evolution of the Language of Cinema," in *What Is Cinema?*, vol. I, trans. Hugh Gray (Berkeley, Calif.: University of California Press, 1967), p. 23; also contained in *The New Wave*, ed. Peter Graham (New York: Doubleday & Company, 1968), p. 25.

appears—it has a different meaning and formal function in *La Chinoise,* in *Weekend,* in *One Plus One,* and in *British Sounds,* and even at different places within the same film. Moreover, the matter of "context" is not as simple as it may appear. Each of the later films is built upon a complex camera/sound conception or donnée, and no two of these are alike. Our principal concern is the formal construction of *Weekend* and the specific role of the tracking shot in that construction; that is, the relation of formal part and whole. We shall not understand either aspect of *Weekend,* however, until we see that film's characteristic shot in the alternative contexts of the other late films and understand the formal principles of those works themselves. The use of the tracking shot in the other films clarifies its use in *Weekend* and the formal principles of the other films put into perspective the formal principle of *Weekend* itself.

La Chinoise contains some interesting instances of the tracking shot even though the film is in no sense built upon this shot, as both *Weekend* and *One Plus One* are. (In these two films, the whole is chiefly a relation among tracking shots; in *La Chinoise* the whole is a relation among many kinds of shots, relatively few of which are tracking shots.) There are, first, the remarkable shots from the balcony, in which the action within the apartment is carefully orchestrated in relation to the camera's passage, in various mathematical variations, along the apartment's three windows and two walls, and back. There is, second, a usage of the shot as a special kind of documentation. As Véronique describes her awakening to social contradictions at Nanterre, the camera tracks slowly (from right to left) across the shabby, overcrowded dwellings of the Algerian workers who live near the university, coming to rest at last on the modern, efficient buildings of the university complex. The workers' shacks are flat and horizontal, the university buildings high and vertical, but the shot is set up so that the camera does not have to move back to take in the tall, commanding structures—it takes in everything within a single perspective. Eisenstein would have cut from a shot of the one to a shot of the other, making the juxtaposition for the viewer, obliterating time and space relations to make a clear-cut social relation. Godard observes the time and space relations and lets the viewer make the social relation. His shot establishes the true proportions of extreme contrast and close proximity. He does this by virtue of the long take's continuity of dramatic space and time, which this usage reveals as itself a form of argumentation or demonstration; the shot has its own internal relations, its own logic. This instance of the shot seems Bazinian but, far from fidelity to the real, Godard rips this bit of footage from its grounding in the real and puts it down in the midst of a highly abstract film essay. Godard impresses the real into his own service—ignoring the form of the real itself, he subjects it firmly to his own formal construct. Besides the tracking shots, *La Chinoise* also includes several static long takes—the two dialogues between Véronique and Guillaume, the assassination scene—as well as montage (or collage) constructions. (It has become a commonplace that modern filmmakers fall between Eisenstein and Bazin, that they combine editing techniques and long takes in various, distinctive styles.) The overall formal principle of *La Chinoise* would seem to be collage, which is also the formal principle of *The Married Woman* (1964), portions of *Le Gai Savoir* (1968), and, in certain senses, of *Pravda* (1970).

The difference between montage and collage is a complex question. Film critics generally use the term collage without elucidating its meaning or even its difference from montage. There is sometimes the suggestion that the pieces of a collage are shorter or more fragmented than those of a montage, but this does not hold up. Modern filmmakers rarely use any shot shorter than Eisenstein's average shot in *Potemkin*. Moreover, collage as practiced by moderns allows long takes and tracking shots; montage as practiced by Eisenstein did not. It seems clear that the difference between montage and collage is to be found in the divergent ways in which they associate and order images, not in the length or nature of the images themselves. Montage fragments reality in order to reconstitute it in highly organized, synthetic emotional and intellectual patterns. Collage does not do this; it collects or sticks its fragments together in a way that does not entirely overcome their fragmentation. It seeks to recover its fragments *as fragments*. In regard to overall form, it seeks to bring out the internal relations of its pieces, whereas montage imposes a set of relations upon them and indeed collects or creates its pieces to fill out a preexistent plan. (This point is discussed further in the comparison of the collage principle to the visual organization of *Weekend* and *One Plus One* below.)

In *Weekend* the collage principle all but disappears. Intercut titles—showing the day and the hour, the car speedometer, names of sequences such as "Action Musicale," "Scenes from Provincial Life" —serve as breaks within takes and between scenes, but all within the film's single-image continuum. They do not interact with the pictorial images to form montage patterns, as in *La Chinoise*. Conversely, whereas in *La Chinoise* the tracking shot is incidental, in *Weekend* it is the master shot: the entire film aspires to the condition of this shot. The cuts are merely connective; once outside the Paris apartment, the film might as well be a single, fixed-distance traveling shot along the highway and across the provincial landscape. *Weekend* indeed approximates this ideal form by its remarkable adherence to a single camera range—it is filmed almost entirely in long shot. Thus *Weekend* is the film in which the structure of the tracking shot and the formal principle of the whole very nearly coincide. Not just its characteristic shot but the whole of *Weekend* itself is a continuous visual band that unfolds itself along a linear axis. *One Plus One* is an interesting variation on the *Weekend* plan. It consists almost entirely of very long takes, nearly all of them tracking shots of the sort described above—slow, fixed distance, left to right and/or right to left. Here, however, Godard cuts among two primary situations (the Stones in the studio and the black revolutionaries at the autoheap) and several subsidiary ones, each of which is conceived and shot strictly in terms of a single-band construction. Thus Godard erects a montage construction upon a series of long takes—in the aggregate a montage is created, though all of its ingredients, all the local areas of the film, are long takes.

Put another way, *One Plus One* is made up of parallel visual bands, which correspond to the bands of the song the Stones are recording, the bands of revolutionary experience that the blacks at the autoheap are assimilating, etc., all of which correspond to the bands of the viewer's consciousness of contemporary experience. Recording the song and rehearsing the revolution and watching Godard's film all involve a project of integration, necessarily unfinished, as the film is unfinished. The function of Godard's montage construction, switching back and forth among these bands, is perhaps an attempt to hold them in simultaneity and is thus central to the film's integration project.[3]

British Sounds is fundamentally different in form from the bands construction of *Weekend* and *One Plus One*. Aside from the montage of fists punching through the British flag, it consists almost entirely of long takes, including several sequences consisting of a single shot; there are also a few of the tracking shots, notably the

---

[3] It is possible, however, that Godard's editing here fulfills the classical function of montage—that of contrast or opposition: the commercial protest of the Stones versus the authenticity of black revolt, etc.

long opening track along an assembly line and the later, related shot of workers discussing socialism at a meeting. The film as a whole, however, is organized rather conventionally in terms of sequences, each of which is conceived and shot according to its subject. As the film takes up several subjects (factory conditions, worker organization, women's liberation, right-wing attitudes, etc.), it does not have a single stylistic conception. *British Sounds* is signed not only by Godard but by the Dziga-Vertov group with whom he made the film; this may have made stylistic unity difficult but *Pravda,* also signed by the group, does have overall formal coherence.

Collage and organization by bands are contrasting formal principles. Both are visual organizations, but each is a formal principle of the whole in a different sense. The visual conceptions of *Weekend* and *One Plus One* are prescriptive and proscriptive—they require a certain kind of shot and rule out other kinds. The formal principles of these works not only relate parts, though they do that also, they require and hence create certain kinds of parts, in order to realize a preexistent or overall scheme. As a result, camera style for each scene of these films is determined not by the distinctive content of the scene but by the overall formal principle of the work. Thus many different kinds of scenes receive similar camera treatment, which we see clearly in *Weekend* and *One Plus One* (the highway scene and guerilla camp scenes in the first, the auto junkheap scenes and scenes with the Stones in the second). This is formal principle in the strong sense.

Collage, in film as in the other arts, is by contrast the most heterogeneous and permissive of formal principles. Indeed, it is formal principle only after the fact—it does not require certain kinds of parts or rule any out. Polycentric or decentralized, it relates parts primarily toward each other and only secondarily toward a whole, or ideal unity. (*Weekend* relates parts directly to the whole and only indirectly to other parts or local area.) Collage works from inside, seemingly with preexistent parts, and seeks to find within them or in their arrangement some unifying principle; or at least some ground on which they can stand together. The collage principle of *Pravda,* it is true, is far more aggressive than this—it marshals and orders its images in accord with an overall formal principle. This principle, however, is not that of the collage itself but that of the sound track, which criticizes and interprets the images, not only as parts but as an aggregate or totality. The sound track both constitutes a formal totality and criticizes or relates to the image collage as a totality. The formal principle of the whole work is the relation between these totalities, but that relation itself seems to be contained within the sound track and in no sense in the images. Also, the organization of the images is far less intensive and coherent than that of the sound-track discourse, so the latter easily prevails.

The relation to sound is a touchstone of the difference between collage and bands construction generally. As collage is a weak or weaker formal principle, it is not surprising that use of sounds has a greater impact on it than on the stronger organization into bands. *The Married Woman, La Chinoise,* and *Pravda* are all visual collages, but the overall formal organization of each is very different, in large part because the uses of sound are different. *The Married Woman* uses sound conventionally, as direct dialogue or voice-over; *La Chinoise* is frequently a sound as well as a visual collage; and in *Pravda* the autonomous sound track not visual organization is the most important formal principle. This susceptibility to different uses of sound confirms that collage is not in itself a strong formal principle. In *Weekend* and *One Plus One,* both intensive visual organizations, use of sound is subordinate and supplementary to the visual formal principle.

The difference between collage and bands construction can also be expressed as a difference in relation to subject matter. As we have seen, in collage formal treatment of each part is based upon the subject matter of the part itself. In *Weekend* and *One Plus One* formal treatment of each scene relates to the overall visual conception and *this* in turn relates to the film's subject as a whole. In collage there is an immediate or local relation to subject; in bands construction only an overall or total relation. So also in *Pravda* the sound track criticizes not this and this shot, but the totality of the film's images. The sound track is an overall formal principle in the sense that the bands construction is and as collage probably cannot be.

In *Le Gai Savoir, Pravda,* and *Wind from the East* (1971), the relation of sound and image becomes the central subject of inquiry as well as the central formal problem. Sound/image relation is also important, however, in the other late films and, predictably, is different in each. Sound collage and visual collage are sometimes synchronized in *La Chinoise,* sometimes not. Two characters recite a slogan one word at a time as the camera cuts rapidly between them, U.S. comic-book images are flashed to the sound of a machine gun, etc. At other times sound elements are arranged independently: a Maoist rock song, passages from Schubert, etc. Sound is important in *One Plus One,* but principally as a supplement to image, very much according to the conventions of screen realism: the sound the Stones are recording, the readings of the black revolutionaries, etc. An important exception are the readings from a pornographic-political novel that are cut into the sound track at several points. Sound seems less important in *Weekend* than in any of the other late films; or at least more conventional in usage and straightforward in meaning, as in the orchestration of motor horns in the traffic-jam scene. This usage is paralleled in the first shot of *British Sounds,* with its deafening factory noise that, far more than the image itself, establishes the work conditions in question. Both of these scenes make highly expressive use of more or less realistic sound. A later sequence in *British Sounds* prefigures the sound/image constructions of *Pravda* and *Wind from the East.* A spoken analysis of contradictions faced by the female in capitalist society is run over the static shot of a staircase and landing, through which walks a nude woman. We hear an analysis of concrete conditions; we see the subject under discussion. In a filmed interview, Richard Mordaunt's *Voices* (1968), Godard criticizes American Newsreel films for showing political events without commentary and interpretation. Godard's position is clear: events/images do *not* speak for themselves.

Le Gai Savoir, made between *Weekend* and *One Plus One,* is something of a puzzle. Its subject is the relation of sound to image but, aside from some intercut photos with writing on them, the style and formal organization of the film have nothing to do with this problem. Several factors link the film to *La Chinoise:* its focus on middle-class young people in an enclosed space working out problems of revolutionary theory; its passages of intellectual collage linking its characters to the outside world and to the problems they are studying; its marking their growth through three stages, which are also the movements or parts of the film. In visual style, however, the films are not similar. Most of the character shots in *La Chinoise* are head-on long takes and each of the film's long conversations— two between Véronique and Guillaume, one between Véronique and Jeanson—is done in a single long take. *Le Gai Savoir,* devoted almost entirely to conversations about image/sound, consists of dozens of close-ups of Jean-Pierre Léaud and of Juliet Berto and of both of them. As the two converse, the camera cuts around them: from one to the other, from one to both or both to one, from both to a different angle of both, often a reverse angle. This is something like conventional dialogue cutting (which Godard has almost never used), except that the cuts have nothing to do with the dialogue itself. Perhaps parody is the intention. Or, since the action takes place in a TV studio and the film was made for television, perhaps it is TV style that is parodied. Godard's cutting establishes the pair in 360° depth and in multiple angles and viewpoints, but to what purpose? This is formal variation without evident coherence.[4] Godard also varies plastic elements, particularly the shadows on his characters' faces, again seemingly without principle.

In *Pravda* and *Wind from the East* the problem of sound/image relation is realized in the formal principle itself. Whereas the sound track of *Le Gai Savoir* consists mainly of the speech of the characters before us (or just off-camera), in *Pravda* and *Wind* realistic or synchronized sound disappears altogether. Sound track and image track are absolutely separate and independent. It now becomes a struggle, and specifically a struggle of sound or voice, to make a connection between them. In both films the images are those of the imperialist world (in which Godard includes "Western-contaminated" Czechoslovakia) and the sounds are those of dialectical theory seeking to understand and transform that world. Sounds criticize and negate images, and frequently themselves also. The autonomy of sound vis-à-vis image is never questioned but previous sounds are criticized and corrected by later sounds: "We have made many mistakes. We must go back and correct mistakes." In *Pravda* footage of Prague is run over a dialogue in which two Marxist-Leninists analyze the sickness of revisionism that infects these images and the proper cure for the sickness. The shots seem hurriedly taken and even their arrangement somewhat haphazard; it is the sounds of dialectical theory that must provide coherence and order, even in an aesthetic sense. This they do, as mentioned, by developing a comprehensive analysis, not of this or that shot, but of the image track as a totality.

In *Wind from the East* it is the film's theatrical action—an ideological Western—that is questioned again and again (seemingly every five minutes) by the sound-track voice. Here it is not images of the imperialist world directly but the film's own conceit for that world that is addressed and questioned. Thus self-criticism is taken a step further. Arguably, the divorce between images and sounds is even more extreme in *Wind* than in *Pravda* in that the sound track does not really discuss the images themselves but the imperialist world that the images symbolize. Thus sounds and images are two

---

[4] An interesting variation Godard introduces is to cut away from the person who is about to speak, then to hold on the person who is listening. One character says: "In movies we see people talking but never listening."

sets of symbols dealing with, trying to get at, the imperialist world. In *Pravda* the sounds are tied to the images, in *Wind*—aside from the passages of self-criticism—this is not so. It is possible, however, to turn the question inside out and to see the images of *Wind* as tied to, as an illustration of, the sound-track discourse. If so, this is not a part-by-part, shot-by-shot illustration but a relation of totalities. In either case—sound and image separation or image as illustration —sounds and images are locally independent totalities or symbol structures, dealing with each other only as totalities.

We may draw two tentative conclusions regarding the formal principles of the late films. One is that intensive visual organization and intensive sound organization are probably not possible within the same films. That is, either one or the other must be the dominant formal principle; one will tend to organize and dominate not only itself but the other also. It may be argued that not either sounds or images but precisely their relation is the formal principle of some or all of the late films. Such a balance as this suggests may be possible, but it has not yet been achieved. Perhaps when we understand *Wind from the East* better it will be seen to come closest. Second, visual and sound organizations represent important ideological differences as well as aesthetic ones. Visual organization is as fully an interpretation and critique as sound organization, though it stands on different ground and has certain different emphases. Indeed, regarding *Pravda* and *Wind,* some dialecticians would question the disembodied critical autonomy assumed by the sound-track voices. Others would demand that these anonymous voices identify themselves and place themselves within the sociohistorical totality they are analyzing. Such questions concern the nature, scope, and autonomy of revolutionary theory and other dialectical problems that cannot be pursued here. These questions, however, are central to the understanding and analysis of the later films.

We have found that *Weekend* is the one film among the later works in which the structure of the tracking shot and the formal principle of the whole are nearly identical. Because the shots of *Weekend* deal with a single situation (rather than two or more), they are not juxtaposed (as in *One Plus One*), but merely linked —as though to form one long composite tracking shot. This continuity is emphasized by the near-constant camera range of long shot, which renders the entire film, even static shots, into a single band of reality. In our discussion of the tracking shot as long take we distinguished it from composition-in-depth shots and thereby characterized the tracking shot in terms of a certain kind of flatness. If the overall structure of *Weekend* parallels that of the tracking shot, then the film as a whole must exhibit flatness also. In light of our distinction between parts and wholes, it must also be that flatness of the whole is something different from flatness of the part; and in *Weekend* this is found to be true. Nevertheless, flatness seems an odd category in which to discuss the formal organization of a work, partly because it seems a negative concept, partly because *flatness* has no meaning except in relation to *depth*. In fact, however, *Weekend* itself is negative—regarding its subject, the bourgeoisie—in several important respects. And, as we shall see also, the flatness of *Weekend* has specific relation to a previous depth—composition-in-depth, the principal mode of bourgeois self-presentment in cinema.

If we now propose to discuss the formal organization of *Weekend*, part and whole, in terms of flatness, the effect may well be one of anticlimax and disappointment. If this is so, it is due in large measure to the imprecision that such terms, and especially this term, carry in film analysis. What this means, for the category of flatness comes up inescapably here and elsewhere, is that some theoretical clarification needs to be done. This task cannot be undertaken here but minimal clarification must be done to permit our analysis of *Weekend*. There is no single sense of flatness in cinema but in fact several senses, not only in regard to different films but often in regard to the same film. A single work may be flat in several senses, or now in one sense and now in another; so we must ask not simply which films and scenes are "more flat" than others but in precisely which senses they are flat. An equally great problem area is how critics use the judgment of flatness—the correlations they make between flatness and other matters, particularly those of subject and meaning. Clearly an undifferentiated judgment of flatness cannot be the basis for an adequate interpretation or discussion of subject. A correlation between the "flatness" of *Made in U.S.A.* (1966) or *Weekend* and Herbert Marcuse's theory of a one-dimensional society is too general—in regard to both elements—to be of much use. Criticism must cut finer than this or it is not helpful. Rather we must ask in each case which of several kinds of flatness has/have been achieved and what is its/their specific relation to the subject of the part and/or whole to which it relates.

Cinema, like painting, is a two-dimensional art that creates the illusion of a third dimension. Painting is limited to its two dimensions; cinema is not. Cinema escapes the limits of two dimensions through its own third dimension, time. It does this by varying its range and perspective, by taking different views of its subject (through montage and/or camera movement). Cinema overcomes two-dimensionality through its "walk-around" capability, which is also a prime feature of ordinary human perception. E. H. Gombrich says: "While [one] turns, in other words, he is aware of a succession of aspects which swing round with him. What we call 'appearance' is always composed of such a succession of aspects, a melody, as it were, which allows us to estimate distance and size; it is obvious that this melody can be imitated by the movie camera but not by the painter with his easel." [5] Cinema can take several views of a subject, go from one camera angle to a reverse angle or other angle, from long shot to close-up, etc. It can take the measure of a character or object from many sides, in short, in three dimensions. Both montage and composition-in-depth accomplish this walk-around project, both create and explore three dimensions, though in two-dimensional steps or segments, so to speak. It is obvious how montage accomplishes this—through a succession of shots from different angles and at different ranges. It is equally clear that a moving camera can accomplish the same succession of aspects within a single shot. Even in those long takes that do not involve a moving camera, the actors themselves may move with respect to the camera; that is, they walk back and forth, or at diagonals, changing in relative size, etc. In short, the actors *turn themselves* around for us, creating different angles and perspectives on themselves. Instead of the camera walking around, they walk around in relation to the camera. This also is well beyond the two dimensions of painting, whereby we see only one side of a figure, which must stand for and suggest his entirety.

It is precisely cinema's capacity for depth that Godard excludes in *Weekend*. His moving camera, by adhering rigidly to the single-perspective, one-sided view of painting, eliminates the succession of aspects. The tracking shot's lateral motion *extends* this single perspective rather than alters it, very much as a mural does. The movement of Godard's camera creates not a succession of aspects, but a single aspect upon an unfolding subject matter. Both montage and the usual moving camera multiply aspects or the perspectives *in regard to a single subject*. To borrow a term from music, the succession of aspects is a kind of *elaboration*. The subject in question is put through multiple variations (or views), toward some *exhaus-*

---

[5] *Art and Illusion, A Study in the Psychology of Pictorial Representation* (London: Phaidon Press, 1960), pp. 256–257.

tion of its nature, meaning, or appearance. Godard's tracking shot does not elaborate in this sense. Its variations through time open up ever new subject matter; they do not elaborate or take multiple views of the same subject, as both montage and composition-in-depth (nearly) always do. Throughout the duration of a tracking shot, a one-to-one relation is maintained: a single perspective per stretch or segment of subject matter, with never a doubling or curving of perspective on a single subject.

It should be emphasized that this flatness of the single aspect is a formal quality of the whole, not of the part. We cannot judge aspect succession or constancy on the basis of the part alone because the succession of aspects is often a succession *of shots*. It is true that each tracking shot in *Weekend* is flat in this sense of singleness of perspective, but what is done in one shot may be undone, or complemented, by another. This is the method of montage, whereby the angle and range of one shot give way to those of another and another, until a totality of aspects is accumulated. Even with lateral long takes, a subsequent tracking shot may provide a different view of the subject of a previous tracking shot. Thus, we do not know until a film is over whether a given subject is elaborated multiply or not. We must look at *all* the shots of a sequence or film before we can say whether they present a succession of aspects on a single subject or, as in *Weekend,* a single aspect on a single, unfolding subject. Thus the flatness of the mural effect is an attribute or quality of the whole.

We have argued that *Weekend* is flat in an overall or structural sense because it eliminates the succession of aspects by which cinema approximates the third dimension. This is an absolute flatness, a sequence—a film either varies aspects or it does not. Generally speaking, the frames of *Weekend* are also relatively flat in several painterly respects, and this is always a relative flatness, a question of more or less. The clearest case of this kind of flatness is achieved by posing a character or characters against a short wall or background, as Godard does in *Masculin-Féminin* (1966), *Made in U.S.A.,* and other films, and as Skolimowski does in all his films. *Weekend* has certain of these shots, but it also has others with considerable depth—the camera follows its subject, the bourgeois couple, across a continuous background/landscape that is sometimes flat (thick foliage behind the pair), sometimes deep (the highway backup).

But there are other kinds of flatness. The shallow wall shot achieves flatness simply by eliminating the long-shot range, and perhaps also the medium-shot range. Godard's tracking shot achieves a converse flatness by eliminating the closeup, medium-close, and often medium-shot ranges—by arranging his subject(s) and background all within the long-shot range. The point may be clarified by a comparison with composition-in-depth, which aims for maximum visual and expressive depth, in that both a close-up and a long shot can be included within the same shot. Composition-in-depth achieves its illusion of great depth by arranging its subject through all possible ranges of the deep-focus shot and, of course, by making dramatic relations among these subject ranges. Godard achieves flatness by using only a portion of the depth that deep-focus lenses permit—he uses the long-shot range and leaves the shorter ranges "blank," so to speak. Thus, even where there are several planes in a *Weekend* shot—highway, countryside, tree-line, etc.—they are all relatively flattened together, because all lie within the long-shot range. (Moreover, Godard does not achieve this flattening by using telephoto lenses, as Kurosawa did in *Red Beard* [1968].)

Second, Godard's planes, even where multiple, are strictly parallel—they do not intersect or interrelate. Consequently the eye is not led back into the depth of the frame or forward to its surfaces. How we have to "read" a painting or frame is one aspect of its depth; to read the frames of *Weekend,* the eyes moves strictly from left to right (sometimes from right to left), never from front to back or back to front. What is true in a compositional sense is also true of the subject of these frames: the film's action. The characters, their movements and activities, never take us into or out of the frame but always from side to side. Neither in a compositional sense nor in a narrative sense are we ever required to relate foreground and background in *Weekend.* Strictly speaking, there is no foreground and background, only background, just as in the shallow wall shot there is only foreground. In another sense, foreground and background are here merged into a single plane. Again, composition-in-depth provides a definitive contrast. Like the baroque in painting, composition-in-depth makes a great deal of foreground/background relations, of foreshortening, of huge objects in the foreground, etc. It is not too much to say that foreground/background relation is the axis of composition-in-depth expressivity. As we have seen, it is its moral base also.

Third, the nonintersection of planes in *Weekend* is the result not only of their strict parallelism but also of the fixed, 90° camera angle, which arranges all planes in parallel to the borders of the frame itself. Of these planes, all are inert or nonoperative in both a narrative and a compositional sense, except that occupied by the characters. All interest and movement reside in the characters and they occupy (or constitute) always the same plane; they do not move between planes. *Weekend* is single-planed in the sense that the camera and the viewer's eye fix upon only one plane, that occupied by the characters, and follow it out, in one direction only, at infinite length. The frame may contain several planes, but the film as a whole is constructed in relation to only one of these.

Weekend's single-plane construction sets it apart from either school of film aesthetics, montage or composition-in-depth; comparing *Weekend* to them will help us understand the various senses of the film's flatness historically. It is clear that montage editing (and overall film construction) involves or results in a series of planes or planar perspectives. Cutting among close-ups, medium close-ups, medium shots, and long shots, in any order or combination, is obviously an alteration of the planes of a scene, and the result when assembled a sequence of planes.[6] The scene or event is broken into its component parts or planes, then these are reconstructed in various patterns, in accord with a structural montage principle—rhythmic, emotional, or intellectual. Besides changes of camera range, there are also changes of angle, which can alternate planar perspectives rather than particular planes. Cutting to a different angle on the same scene, however, is also a rearrangement or reordering of the planes bearing upon the action. This ordering or sequence of planes is the very texture of Eisenstein's art. Composition-in-depth is not fundamentally different in principle and overall purpose. Composition-in-depth internalizes the sequence of planes within the shot; its ideal, as Bazin presents it, is the inclusion of all planes bearing upon an action within a single camera setup. With all the planes of a situation before or available to the camera, the entire action of the scene

---

[6] As it happens, this phrase also appears in Stuart Gilbert's translation of André Malraux's *Museum Without Walls* (Garden City, N.Y.: Doubleday & Company, 1967, p. 75): "The means of reproduction in the cinema is the moving photograph, but its means of expression is the sequence of planes. (The planes change when the camera is moved; it is their sequence that constitutes cutting.)" A similar mistranslation of the French *plan* (shot) as plane occurs in Gilbert's translations of Malraux's variants of this passage in *The Psychology of Art: I: Museum Without Walls* (New York: Pantheon Books, 1949–1951, p. 112) and in *The Voices of Silence* (New York: Doubleday & Company, 1953, p. 122), in which Malraux is made to assert that "the average duration of each [plane] is ten seconds." But Malraux was simply expounding the classical view that cutting, the sequence of shots, is the source of expressivity in cinema.

may be worked out within a single shot. As with montage cinema, dramatic action is advanced by way of the alternation and inter-action of planes, but now this is done by camera movement and/or by the movement of actors, themselves planes or parts of planes, through or in relation to the planes of the scene. At the same time the camera must organize these planes in terms of importance, dramatic interest, etc. By composition-in-depth the succession of planes is greatly fluidized, proceeding in a smooth flow rather than in jumps, but the right solution to a given scene becomes more difficult and complex. Implicit in the shot's first image, or accessible to it, must be all the scene's action and the full exploitability of its planes. Shots must be worked out carefully and carefully rehearsed. An example of the way that composition-in-depth orders planes within the frame is given by Bazin—the scene in *The Little Foxes* (1941) in which the steel box sought by several characters oc-cupies the extreme foreground of the frame while its seekers are arrayed in multiple planes behind it. A more extreme case is the scene in *Citizen Kane* (1941) in which Mrs. Kane learns about her son's inheritance. Shot with a static camera, the shot is very nar-row and very deep, virtually a visual corridor. Within the squeezed cabin room we see the mother huge in the foreground, the banker from the East behind her, the window in the wall of the cabin behind them, and in the far distance, young Kane playing with his sled. Not only the composition of the shot but its dramatic action require the eye to move continually back and forth. It is clear that Godard's treatment of planes in *Weekend* is directly opposite to that of this shot, an extreme in the opposite direction. Godard's visual field has little or no depth and has—or aspires to—infinite length; that is, it exists in a single lateral plane.

Consideration of *Weekend* points up underlying similarities be-tween montage and composition-in-depth and serves to set Godard's film apart from either school of film aesthetics: both montage and composition-in-depth define cinema in terms of a multiplicity of planes and both see the problem of form or technique as the inclu-sion or relation of planes in a meaningful format. Godard in *Week-end* renounces the multiplicity of planes as a project of cinema and hence rejects both schools.

What are the implications of these shifts from three dimensions to two, from depth to flatness? An ideological interpretation suggests itself—composition-in-depth projects a bourgeois world infinitely deep, rich, complex, ambiguous, mysterious. Godard's flat frames collapse this world into two-dimensional actuality; thus reversion to a cinema of one plane is a demystification, an assault on the bourgeois world view and self-image.[7] *Weekend*'s bourgeois figures scurry along without mystery toward mundane goals of money and pornographic fulfillment. There is no ambiguity and no moral complexity. That space in which the viewer could lose himself, make distinctions and alliances, comparisons and judgments, has been abrogated—the viewer is presented with a single flat picture of the world that he must examine, criticize, accept or reject. Thus the flatness of *Weekend* must not be analyzed only in itself but in regard to the previous modes of bourgeois self-presentment, particularly of composition-in-depth. The subject of *Weekend* is the historical bourgeoisie, the bourgeoisie in history; the film's flatness must not be seen statistically, as a single moment, but dialectically, as a *flattening*. Given this overall correlation, the specific correlations of the several senses of flatness fall into place. The succession of aspects not only multiplies viewpoints on the bourgeois world so that final judgment and any kind of certainty become impossible, it projects a bourgeois world infinitely inexhaustible and elaborable. Godard's tracking-shot format insists on a single perspective and on the sufficiency of a single comprehensive survey for understanding of the transparent, easy-to-understand bourgeois world. Whereas in montage and composition-in-depth, complex form works on simple material, working it up as complex also, in Godard simple form works on simple material. The tracking-shot and single-plane construction suggest an infinitely thin, absolutely flat bourgeois substance that cannot be elaborated but only surveyed. Finally, the single camera range represents not only a refusal to participate in bourgeois space, through forward camera movement, intercutting camera ranges, etc., it also has to do with the maintenance of critical perspective. Given that the film's subject

---

[7] This transition is more than a formal one. The practitioners and advocates of composition-in-depth genuinely believed in this moral depth and ambiguity. Bazin points out that the conception and interpretation of *Citizen Kane* depend on the composition of the image. It could hardly be otherwise in a great masterpiece. William Wyler's composition-in-depth films, which (as Bazin says) have little or no ambiguity, are not masterpieces. In such a case composition-in-depth becomes merely an imposed format, a style without internal correlates. (Wyler's better films, such as *The Letter* [1940], are not structured around composition-in-depth.) Welles, the greatest composition-in-depth director, is also the director who has made the most of the theme of inexhaustible mystery. Not only *Kane* but many or most of Welles's other films center on impenetrable mystery and several, also like *Kane,* proceed through a multiplicity of viewpoints and perspectives that nevertheless fail to yield certainty concerning the underlying questions.

is the historical bourgeoisie, Godard keeps his subject before him at all times. He refuses to pick and choose within the bourgeois world or to prefer any part of it to any other—even for a moment— because that involves partial eclipse of the whole. The nature of the bourgeois totality and the project of criticizing it require that it never be lost from view, or broken up into parts and aspects, but always be kept before the viewer as single and whole. Obviously the long-shot range is the range of the totality and the tracking shot the instrument of its critical survey. For this reason also Godard does not allow the closeup and medium-close ranges to be filled, for a face or figure huge in the foreground literally obstructs the whole and distracts attention from it in an emotional and intellectual sense also. Flatness in *Weekend,* in its various senses, is in fact the result of a formal totality that refuses to relinquish total perspective on the sociohistorical totality that is its subject.

Chapter 5 *Godard on Godard: Notes for a Reading (1974)*

Godard on Godard [1] contains 116 pieces written or spoken by Godard between June 1950 and August 1967. Items 1 to 85 comprise Godard's output as a film critic through July 1959. In August–Septem-

---

[1] Jean-Luc Godard, *Godard on Godard,* ed. Jean Narboni and Tom Milne, with an introduction by Richard Roud; trans. Tom Milne (New York: The Viking Press, 1972). French edition: *Jean-Luc Godard par Jean-Luc Godard,* ed. Jean Narboni (Paris: Jean Belfond, 1968). Milne's English-language edition, with notes, film and name indexes, and paired stills, much improves on the French original.

ber 1959 Godard dropped regular criticism and shot *Breathless.* He
wrote about films after this, but much less frequently. The book collects thirty-one of these occasional pieces under the heading
"Marginal Notes While Filming"—memorials, statements on his
own films, defenses of neglected films, a speech, a protest letter,
contributions to a dictionary of American filmmakers, and four interviews. Among the last are two long *Cahiers* interviews edited
and revised by Godard himself, dated December 1962 (*Breathless*
to *Vivre Sa Vie*) and October 1965 (*Les Carabiniers* to *Pierrot le
Fou*).

The following notes concern items 1 to 85, Godard's film criticism
written before August 1959. The distribution of these pieces in time
is interesting. Godard wrote eleven pieces between June 1950 and
October 1952, then published nothing for almost four years. In
August 1956 he returned to criticism and turned out seventy-four
pieces in the three years before he made *Breathless.* His most productive period was the last six months, February to July 1959, in
which he wrote thirty one pieces.

"Defense and Illustration of Classical Construction" (9) was
written in 1952, when Godard was twenty-one. It is his longest
theoretical piece and arguably his most important. It is a direct attack
upon the Bazinian position, itself in process of formation at this time
but settled in its main outlines. The specific object of Godard's critique is Bazin's account of classical construction ("decoupage") in
cinema. According to Bazin, a standard mode of shot breakdown
dominated world cinema during the 1930–1939 period. In the 1940s,
the composition-in-depth technique of Welles and Wyler and Italian
neorealism constituted a "revolution in expression." Their avoidance
of editing effects and of frame manipulations was "a positive technique that produces better results than a classical breakdown of shots
could ever have done." These styles showed "the event" in its physical unity, hence tended strongly toward the long take (temporal
verisimilitude) and the long shot (spatial verisimilitude) rather than
the arranged series of closer and shorter shots dictated by classical
construction.

Godard rejects this analysis on all counts—historical, theoretical,
and aesthetic. The historical point should be mentioned here as it
will help make Godard's argument clearer. Godard denies Bazin's
suggestion that classical construction ended or suffered an aesthetic
eclipse after 1939. Godard's favorite directors of this period—Otto
Preminger, Joseph L. Mankiewicz, Mark Robson, and Alfred Hitch-

cock—all use classical construction in some form. A close reading of his critique will be useful. Godard begins by recalling Sartre's denunciation of François Mauriac for playing God with his characters; that is, for failing to endow them with that freedom in which Sartre himself believes. Godard comments:

> But what vanity, too, to insist at all costs on crediting language with a certain metaphysical quality, when it could only rise to the level of the sublime in very special circumstances. Consider, rather, with Diderot, that morality and perspective are the two qualities essential to the artist . . . (*Godard on Godard*, p. 26)

Godard is drawing a parallel between Sartre's criticism and Bazin's; both impose a metaphysical preconception upon art, praising works that fit the preconception, criticizing works that do not. This is vain because art has rarely to do with metaphysics. The workaday tools of the artist are morality and perspective; these should be the concern of the critic as well. Godard restates the argument pungently in the concluding paragraph of the article.

> I think I have said enough about the error of critics in falling under the influence of contemporary philosophy, in elevating figures of style into a vision of the world, in investing some technical process or other with astrological pretensions it cannot possibly have. . . . (p. 30)

The middle portions of the article develop the argument in several directions. Generally they attempt to clarify Godard's opting for morality and perspective as the proper concerns of film and his conception of classical construction as the formal expression of these concerns. He first invokes the French eighteenth century in arguing that the polished speeches and precise mise-en-scène of the American cinema are not inconsistent with serious moral themes. His target here seems to be Bazin's discovery of a new seriousness of theme and subject in Welles and neorealism, "a renewal of subject-matter" in the postwar cinema, and Bazin's connecting this phenomenon integrally with realism and composition-in-depth, "a film like *Paisa* proves that the cinema was twenty years behind the contemporary novel." [2]

---

[2] André Bazin, *What Is Cinema?*, vol. II, trans. Hugh Gray (Berkeley, Calif.: University of California Press, 1971), p. 40.

Have we forgotten that this facility is nothing new, that the ease of the transatlantic film-makers once found its echo in our own amiable and unfortunate eighteenth century?

Everyone wrote well in those days (consider the circumstances under which *La Religieuse* was written), yet serious events were taking place.

My purpose is not paradox. I would like to note certain points common to the art of the eighteenth century and the *mise en scène* of recent years. Firstly, in the attitude of the artist to nature: he acknowledges nature as art's principal model. And then in the fact that it was not the cinema which inherited a narrative technique from the novel, but the novel which inherited an art of dialogue—lost, should one add, since Corneille? (pp. 26–27)

Godard's praise of theatre and his comparison of cinema to theatre throughout the article are partly a response to Bazin's equation of cinema with the novel at several places. The last sentence of Bazin's "The Evolution of Film Language" equates different stages of film history with different arts and makes novelistic cinema the object of a teleology. "The film-maker is no longer simply the competitor of the painter or the playwright; he is at last the equal of the novelist." [3]

The paragraphs that follow interweave several themes rather subtly or disconnectedly, depending upon how they are read. Godard leaps from Corneille to a fear that harmony, however beautiful, will not suffice this most virtuous of the arts. Cinema also needs truth:

to correct—in Delacroix's fine phrase—the reality of that perspective in which the eye takes too much pleasure not to want to falsify it. By this I mean it will not be content with imitating a reality "seized at random" (Jean Renoir). In fact, if the cinema were no more than the art of narration which some would make its proud boast, then instead of being bored, one would take pleasure in those interminable efforts which are concerned above all with exposing in meticulous detail the secret motivations of a murderer or a coquette. But there is a look, posed so afresh on things at each instant that it pierces rather than solicits them, that it seizes in them what abstraction lies in wait for. (p. 27)

He takes an example from Renoir, who he says owes less to Impressionism than to Henri David.

---

[3] In *The New Wave,* ed. Peter Graham (New York: Doubleday & Company, 1968), p. 50.

> Renoir's *mise-en-scène* has the same quality of revealing detail without detaching it from its context. If Renoir uses a deep-focus style in *Madame Bovary*, it is to imitate the subtle way in which nature conceals the relationship between its effects; if he prepares events, it is not in order to make them connect better, for he is more concerned with the impact of emotions than with the contagion they create. (p. 27)

The nature of dialectic in cinema is that one must live rather than last. It is pointless to kill one's feelings in order to live longer. American comedy (sound) is vastly important because it brings back "swiftness of action" and allows the moment to be savored to the full. Our mode of seeing films is important here also—when we concentrate on *plot* rather than on the manner of its exposition, we reduce complex and subtle gestures to dull signals.

What is Godard saying here? It seems to be that cinema, like theatre, is a realm of *heightened* emotions. Its effectiveness depends upon rhythm, pacing, and intensity. This model opposes Bazin's model of cinema as novelistic, as the realist description of relationships existent elsewhere. No, the director *constructs* his film, dialogue, and mise-en-scène, at every point. Even Renoir, the trump card of Bazinism, is more like David than an Impressionist: a careful *arranger* who "prepares events," who may reproduce "the look" of things, but in doing so subjects them to an abstraction or schema that he brings to them. He prepares events not novelistically so that they connect well, but *theatrically*, so as to obtain the desired effect of impact. Godard suggests that the relationship Renoir/nature is less important than the relationship Renoir/audience. The preparations, the emotional effects, the "living not lasting," which Godard values so highly—all depend upon the precise pacing of the decoupage, which is the necessary form of cinema as theatre. Emotions and gestures are defined and sharpened, presented and analyzed, by decoupage. This heightening, which is necessarily quick-perishing, is the true nature of cinema. Novelistic cinema, with its long shots and long takes, *deadens* emotions and gestures in its misguided attempt to narrate and describe them in exhaustive detail and thereby to make them last longer than their nature permits.

Several additional passages give the flavor of Godard's admiration for decoupage and fill out a rudimentary inventory of its rhetorical figures, effects, and possibilities.

> I would like to contend with those who seek to lay down absolute rules. . . . All I mean to claim is that the *mise en scène* of *To*

Have and Have Not is better suited than that of *The Best Years of Our Lives* to convey aberrations of heart and mind, that this is its purpose, whereas the object of the latter is rather the external relationships between people. (p. 28)

I would go so far as to defy anyone to capture in a medium long shot the extreme disquiet, the inner agitation, in a word, the confusion which the waist shot (*plan américain*), through its very inexpressiveness, conveys so powerfully . . . (pp. 28–29)

Abandoning even the habit of placing one of the interlocutors in the foreground, . . . the classical construction sticks even closer to psychological reality, by which I mean that of the emotions; there are, in effect, no spiritual storms, no troubles of the heart which remain unmarked by physical causes, a rush of blood to the brain, a nervous weakness, whose intensity would not be lessened by frequent comings and goings. If this manner is the most classical, it is also because rarely has such contempt been shown for photographing a world seized by accident, and because here language is only the reflection of passions, which they may therefore dominate. (p. 29)

From the art of *Only Angels Have Wings* to that of *His Girl Friday, The Big Sleep* and indeed, of *To Have and Have Not,* what does one see? An increasingly precise taste for analysis, a love for this artificial grandeur connected to movements of the eyes, to a way of walking, in short, a greater awareness than anyone else of what the cinema can glory in, and a refusal to profit from this [like Bresson and Welles] to create anti-cinema, but instead, through a more rigorous knowledge of its limits, fixing its basic laws. (pp. 29–30)

Godard moves from these points to a related one made frequently in his later essays—classical construction is not a system mechanically imposed upon a scene or external to its content; camera and editing treatment derive in each case from the scene itself. Thus Bazin's argument that classical construction reached its peak in the 1930s is doubly wrong, historically and theoretically. It ignores Preminger and many other directors of the present who continue to use it integrally to their art. Even worse, it suggests that classical construction was more or less the same for everyone. In Bazin's version, it merely "presents the event," neutrally and objectively. "The change in camera angles does not add anything, it simply presents reality in the most effective manner." Bazin reduces classical construction to a single format or style. Godard, on the contrary, sees in it a large area of choice and differentiation, within which many and varied styles may define themselves.

Where Preminger uses a crane, Hawks is apt to use an axial cut: the means of expression change only because the subjects change, and the sign draws its signification not from itself but from what it represents, from the scene enacted. Nothing could be more wrong than to talk of classical construction as a language which had reached its peak of perfection before the Second World War with Lubitsch in America and Marcel Carné in France, and which would therefore be tantamount to an autonomous thought-process, applicable with equal success to any subject whatsoever. What I admire in Gance, Murnau, Dreyer or Eisenstein, is the gift these artists possess for seizing in reality what the cinema is best suited to glorify. Classical construction has long existed, and it would be insulting to Lubitsch to suggest that he was anxious to break with the theories of his elders. . . . (p. 28)

One of the article's most interesting arguments is developed only in the final paragraph. Long-shot, long-take cinema

strip[s] classical psychology of that part of it which the cinema could make use of, render explicit, by not reducing man to "the succession of appearances by which he is manifest" (Jean-Paul Sartre), and, paradoxically, by restoring to the monism of the phenomenon only the plurality of interpretation which it lacks. (p. 30)

Godard's paradox is that long-take shooting does *not* after all preserve the ambiguity of a character or actress, as Bazin contended. It merely reduces her to a surface, it identifies her with her appearance. It thereby *flattens* that realm in which ambiguity might reside, the interior, or more precisely, that space, gap, or discrepancy *between* the interior and the appearance, the essence and the phenomenon. Godard has his intellectual coordinates right; he *is* reacting against phenomenology in the name of that classical (dualistic) psychology that phenomenology critiqued. He cleverly suggests, however, that classical psychology provides the more interesting model for cinema:

The eye, since it can say everything, then deny everything because it is merely casual, is the key piece in the film actor's game. One looks what one feels, and what one does not wish to reveal as one's secret. Consider the method of Otto Preminger, the cunning and precise paraphrase this Viennese makes of reality, and you will soon notice that the use of shot and reaction shot, the preference for medium rather than long shots, reveals a desire to reduce the drama to the immobility of the face, for the face is not only part of the body, it is the prolongation of an idea which one must capture and reveal. (pp. 27–28)

The concluding lines of the article state:

> In the cinema, beauty is merely the avowal of personality, it offers us indications about an actress which are not in her performance. The cinema does not query the beauty of a woman, it only doubts her heart, records her perfidy (it is an art, La Bruyère says, of the entire person to place a word or an action so that it puts one off the scent), sees only her movements. Do not smile at such passion fired by logic; one can clearly see that what ensures its worth is that at each instant it is a question of loving or dying. (p. 30)

Something should be said about the numerous references to the French eighteenth century in "Defense" and other early Godard articles. These constitute an extended metaphor that the texts concerned have the integrity to take literally. As with any metaphor, the question is What is it being used to think?—for "the eighteenth century" means what any writer wants it to mean. A reading of these texts must answer this question. We shall merely venture a few notes. There is the historical point that eighteenth-century aesthetics waged a gradually victorious battle against the rationalist aesthetics of the seventeenth century. The latter sought and found a priori rules in the realm of art as in other realms of knowledge. Critically, this was the age of neoclassicism, wherein tragedy was required to meet certain prescriptions such as the unities of space and time, etc. Eighteenth-century aestheticians brought empirical modes of thought to their discipline and sought to free art and criticism from a priori rules. Godard's running battle against Bazin also centers upon the charge of applying a priori standards to art, thereby stifling it and distorting it; Godard too most often proceeds by empirical analysis of works of art he experiences as effective. Godard's invocation of Diderot is likewise well considered. His "the natural order corresponds to that of the heart and mind" is not far from Diderot's later aesthetic theories, wherein the beautiful is dependent upon certain *rapports* that inhere in the object and that must also be perceived as such by the contemplating mind. Diderot's theory is that the artist cannot hope to capture the existential reality of the external world. What he can do is convey to the spectator his own particular and unique way of seeing things. He is not a passive imitator of reality, he must be able to construct a whole universe that has its own laws of harmony paralleling those of external reality.

What the eighteenth century did *not* change in relation to its predecessors was the focus upon rules of discourse in all discussions of art and communication. The appropriate discipline for such studies was rhetoric, its concerns were the organization and the effects of various kinds of discourse. This is where Godard places his emphasis also; we have noted the tendency of "Defense" toward an inventory of rhetorical figures and effects in classical cinema. Of course, Godard's emphasis on discourse is very different from that of the eighteenth century. The interventions of romanticism, realism, phenomenology, and many other movements would define his position very differently even if it were formally identical to some eighteenth-century theory. *In context,* Godard's emphasis on discourse is a break with Bazinism, which resolutely denies or minimizes the organizational and audience-effect operations of discourse. It has far more in common with the semiological positions of Metz and others. If a teleology were being constructed (from the present backward, of course), one would say that Godard "anticipated" Metz in some ways.[4]

---

[4] Roland Barthes defines discourse in relation to speech. "*Speech* [parole]: In contrast to the language, which is both institution and system, *speech* is essentially an individual act of selection and actualization; it is made in the first place of the 'combination thanks to which the speaking subject can use the code of the language with a view to expressing his personal thought' (this extended speech could be called *discourse*) . . ." (*Elements of Semiology,* trans. Annette Lavers and Colin Smith [New York: Hill and Wang, 1964, 1967], pp. 14–15).

Metz defines discourse in "Notes Toward a Phenomenology of the Narrative": "A closed sequence, a temporal sequence: Every narrative is, therefore, a discourse (the converse is not true; many discourses are not narratives—the lyric poem, the educational film, etc.).

"What distinguishes a discourse from the rest of the world, and by the same token contrasts it with the 'real' world, is the fact that a discourse must necessarily be made by someone (for discourse is not language), whereas one of the characteristics of the world is that it is uttered by no one.

"In Jakobsonian terms, one would say that a discourse, being a statement or sequence of statements, refers necessarily to a subject of the statement. But one should not hastily assume an author, for the notion of authorship is simply one of the forms, culturally bound and conditioned, of a far more universal process, which, for that reason, should be called the 'narrative process.'

"Narratives without authors, but not without narrators. The impression that *someone is speaking* is bound not to the empirical presence of a definite, known, or knowable speaker but to the listener's spontaneous perception of the linguistic nature of the object to which he is listening; because it is speech, someone must be speaking.

"Albert Laffey, in *Logique du cinéma,* has shown this to be true of film

There is also the consideration that the empiricism, quasi atheism, and antisuperstition of the French eighteenth century provide a good foil to Bazin's religious, reverential approach to cinema. "Defense" sees in its favored directors "a reaction, maybe unconscious, against the religious tendency of the modern cinema." The chosen language of Godard's texts is perhaps a reaction against a comparable tendency of contemporary film criticism. An ideological analysis might suggest that Godard's texts, unwilling to speak the language of Marxism, yet unwilling to speak the language of revived religion or other current ideology, chose to retreat into a language of the past, in this case that of the safely removed progressivism of the Enlightenment.

Godard continued the attack on Bazin in several pieces subsequent to "Defense," but none of these is as comprehensive or systematic as the earlier text. There is a slight but distinct change of emphasis. Many of the later pieces elaborate a point developed in "Defense"—the responsiveness of form to content in classical cinema, particularly in the great directors like Hitchcock. "The means of expression change only because the subjects change." Godard uses this point, supported by many examples, to critique the Bazinian position, though he is also interested in exploring this cinema for its own sake.

"What Is Cinema?" (10) and "Montage My Fine Care" (4) are generalized critiques in this mode, tending to repeat "Defense." From the former:

> [Contemporary art] has rejected what for centuries was the pride of the great masters, and indeed of humbler craftsmen: the portrait of the individual . . . Metaphysical pretensions are the rage in the salons. This is the fashion . . . This absurd opposition between the artist and nature is the more absurd, the more vain, in

---

narrative. The spectator perceives images which have obviously been selected (they could have been other images) and arranged (their order could have been different). In a sense, he is leafing through an album of predetermined pictures, and it is not he who is turning the pages but some 'grand image-maker' (*grand imagier*) who . . . is first and foremost the film itself as a linguistic object (since the spectator always knows that what he is seeing is a film), or more precisely a sort of 'potential linguistic focus' ('*foyer linguistique virtuel*') situated somewhere behind the film, and representing the basis that makes the film possible. That is the filmic form of the narrative instance, which is necessarily present, and is necessarily perceived, in any narrative" (*Film Language: A Semiotics of the Cinema,* trans. Michael Taylor [New York: Oxford University Press, 1974], pp. 20–21).

that nothing, neither Manet nor Schumann nor Dostoievsky, pre-
figured it. . . . Yet the fact that a landscape may be a state of
mind does not necessarily mean that poetry is only captured by
chance, as our too clever documentarists would have us believe,
but that the natural order corresponds to that of the heart and
mind. Flaherty's genius, after all, is not so far removed from that
of Hitchcock—Nanook hunting his prey is like a killer stalking his
victims—and lies in identifying time with the desire which con-
sumes it, guilt with suffering, fear and remorse with pleasure, and
in making of space the tangible terrain of one's uneasiness. Art
attracts us only by what it reveals of our most secret self. This is
the sort of depth I mean. Obviously it assumes an idea of man
which is hardly revolutionary, and which the great film-makers
from Griffith to Renoir were too conservative to dare to deny. So,
to the question "What Is Cinema?," I would reply: the expression
of lofty sentiments. (pp. 30–31)

This article affirms Godard's human-centered cinema—"the portrait
of the individual," "art attracts by what it reveals of our most secret
self." This opposes Bazin's nature-centered cinema. The second
paragraph implies a man/nature opposition at the center of Bazin;
without it, the urged self-effacement of the director before reality
makes no sense.

"Montage My Fine Care" is clearer and crisper than "Classical
Construction," but whether it adds much to the earlier piece is
doubtful. It argues in favor of montage and hence, at least implicitly,
against Bazin; it also says that editing and mise-en-scène are correlative and interdependent. "Talking of *mise-en-scène* automatically implies montage. When montage effects surpass those of *mise-en-scène*
in efficacity, the beauty of the latter is doubled" (p. 39). As in the
earlier piece, Godard associates montage with "making the look a
key piece in the game":

> Cutting on a look is almost the definition of montage, its supreme
> ambition as well as its submission to *mise-en-scène*. It is, in effect,
> to bring out the soul under the spirit, the passion behind the in-
> trigue, to make the heart prevail over the intelligence by destroy-
> ing the notion of space in favor of that of time. (p. 39)

In a passage suggesting his later film work, Godard says that one
invents and improvises in front of the moviola just as much as on
the set. Cutting a camera movement in four may prove more effective than keeping it as shot. An exchange of glances can only be
expressed with sufficient force, when necessary, by editing. Godard

concludes: to say that a director should supervise the editing of his film comes to the same thing as saying that the editor should move to the set and himself direct. The operations are so interwoven and equal in importance that no sort of subordination is possible between them.

Hitchcock's films exist in a mixed stylistic realm, they contain both long takes and montage sequences, both long shots and close-ups. Godard's recurring point about Hitchcock is that he always makes style dependent upon subject matter: different scenes call for different camera treatments. Hitchcock is not really "classical construction," but Godard nevertheless uses him against Bazin because the responsiveness of his camera to subject matter at any particular moment effectively denies the superiority of any one camera treatment for all subjects. Thus Godard's anti-Bazin polemic continues, but his arguments are now somewhat different and therefore so is his theoretical position. Classical construction gives way to form-content relativism. In the early *"Strangers on a Train"* piece (8), he says: "I find in [Hitchcock and Griffith] the same admirable ease in the use of figures of speech or technical processes; in other words they make the best use of the means available to their art form" (p. 25). "The point is simply that all the freshness and invention of American films springs from the fact that they make the subject the motive for the *mise-en-scène*" (p. 25).

The piece on *"The Man Who Knew Too Much"* (13) does not return to this issue, but that on *"The Wrong Man"* (19) is Godard's most thorough critical treatment of the theme.

Throughout his entire career, Hitchcock has never used an unnecessary shot. Even the most anodyne of them invariably serve the plot, which they enrich, rather as the "touch" beloved of the Impressionists enriched their paintings. They acquire their particular meaning only when seen in the context of the whole. (pp. 48–49)

Even more than a moral lesson, *The Wrong Man* is a lesson in *mise-en-scène* every foot of the way. In the example I have just cited, Hitchcock was able to assemble the equivalent of several close-ups in a single shot, giving them a force they would not have had individually. Above all—and this is the important thing—he did it deliberately and at precisely the right moment. When necessary, he will also do the reverse, using a series of rapid close-ups as the equivalent of a master shot. (p. 50)

Hitch never repeats a device without being perfectly aware of cause and effect. Today he uses his great discoveries as aesthetic conclusion rather than postulate. Thus, the treatment of a scene in a single shot has never been better justified[5] than during the second imprisonment when Manny, seen from the back, enters his cell . . . (p. 52)

Hitchcock shows us that a technical discovery is pointless unless it is accompanied by a formal conquest in whose crucible it can shape the mold which is called "style." To the question "What is art?," Malraux has already given a precise reply: "that by which forms become style." (p. 54)

Godard occasionally makes this point again, as in the piece on Vadim following that on *The Wrong Man*: "Once the characters' motivations are clearly established, *mise-en-scène* becomes a simple matter of logic. Vadim will become a great director because his scenes are never occasioned by a purely abstract or theoretical idea for a shot; rather it is the *idea of a scene,* in other words a dramatic idea, which occasions the *idea of a shot"* (p. 57). By and large, however, *"The Wrong Man"* piece seems to have exhausted this point or line of argument for Godard. There he made the case conclusively, or at least at length.

"The Wrong Man" and *"Sait-on jamais?"* (Vadim) pieces take Godard through the first year of his return to criticism. They seem to have exhausted not only the subject-treatment point but Godard's anti-Bazin impulse also. This central theme of the early criticism drops from Godard's criticism following *"Sait-on jamais?"* (20). Oddly, Godard's concern with this issue was not affected by his lapses from critical activity. After four years away from criticism, he picked it up again almost immediately, "Montage My Fine Care" reformulating the earlier "Classical Construction" in clearer and simpler terms. This issue occupied Godard's critical activity spanning five years, from the *"Strangers on a Train"* piece (8) in March 1952 to the *"Sait-on jamais?"* piece in July 1957, suggesting that its resolution was logical not chronological.

In the year that follows, July 1957 to June 1958, Godard's critical work (sixteen pieces) does not reveal a central theme or focus. Godard pursues a number of critical interests, among them Frank Tashlin, Nicholas Ray, and Kenji Mizoguchi; but he seems to deal with each on different grounds. An exception is his praising both

---

[5] Long takes, like other shots, must be justified contextually, *not* in the a priori Bazin manner.

Tashlin and Ray for developing modern cinematic styles, a point that we consider below.

It was in Godard's third, highly active year of writing criticism that he produced the bulk of his critical texts, forty-nine pieces between July 1958 and July 1959. Located here are a second and third group of themes or ideas that we wish to explore. The second group, unlike the first, exhibits changes and significant development. This group requires especially close attention to the texts concerned.

In "Bergmanorama" (37), Godard argues that Ingmar Bergman is the most original filmmaker of the European cinema. He proposes a comparison between Bergman and Visconti.

> But when talent comes so close to genius that the result is *Summer Interlude* or *White Nights,* is there any point in endlessly arguing as to which is ultimately greater than the other, the complete *auteur* or the pure *metteur en scène?* Maybe there is, because to do so is to analyze two conceptions of cinema, one of which may be more valid than the other.
>
> Broadly speaking, there are two kinds of filmmakers. Those who walk along the streets with their heads down, and those who walk with their heads up. In order to see what is going on around them, the former are obliged to raise their heads suddenly and often, turning to the left and then to the right, embracing the field of vision in a series of glances. They *see.* The latter see nothing, they *look,* fixing their attention on the precise point which interests them. When the former are shooting a film, their framing is roomy and fluid (Rossellini), whereas with the latter it is narrowed down to the last millimetre (Hitchcock). With the former (Welles), one finds a script construction which may be loose but is remarkably open to the temptations of chance; with the latter (Lang), camera movements not only of incredible precision in the set but possessing their own abstract value as movements in space. Bergman, on the whole, belongs to the first group; Visconti to the second, the cinema of rigor. Personally I prefer *Summer with Monika* to *Senso,* and the *politique des auteurs* to the *politique des metteurs en scène.* (p. 79)
>
> No one would deny that *The Seventh Seal* is less skillfully directed than *White Nights,* its compositions less precise, its angles less rigorous; but—and herein lies the essential difference—for a man so enormously talented as Visconti, making a *very good film* is ultimately a matter of *very good taste.* He is sure of making no mistakes, and to a certain extent it is *easy. . . .* [But] for an artist, to know oneself too well is to yield a little to facility.

> What is difficult, on the other hand, is to advance into unknown lands, to be aware of the danger, to take risks, to be afraid. (p. 80)

Godard shares certain of his critical terms with his contemporaries—auteur versus metteur-en-scène, politique des auteurs versus politique de metteur-en-scène. But Godard conjoins these to other oppositions: looseness versus precision of direction, spontaneity versus planning, etc. He seems more interested in the latter concepts than in the former, though this article persistently overlays the two. This conjunction itself does not seem to hold up. Why can't a roomy and fluid mise-en-scène define a metteur-en-scène as well as a precise one? Why can't a genuine auteur have a narrowed rather than fluid visual style? The logic of Godard's conjunction would disqualify Hitchcock and Lang as auteurs. Their visual rigor characterizes the metteur-en-scène. Of course Godard does not accept the consequences of this logic, though in this article Hitchcock and Lang constitute somewhat negative examples. Godard seems to be seeking a model or paradigm of cinema or of direction. He continues the search in several other articles of this period.

Godard's preference in "Bergmanorama" for chance and spontaneity over rigor and precision seems to mark an important change in his work as a whole. We recall his extolling in "Defense" a cinema of "artificial grandeur" in which "nothing is left to chance." This change is confirmed by the other articles of this period. To what degree does Godard break with his former position? Does his new praise of chance constitute in any way a capitulation to the Bazinian system formerly criticized?

A reversal of values is evident in *"The Quiet American"* piece (39), in which Godard reconsiders his admiration for Mankiewicz. He still admires the wit and precision of the latter's scripts, but sees Mankiewicz as perhaps too perfect a writer to be a perfect director as well. What is missing from *The Quiet American* (1958) is cinema. Despite brilliant acting and sparkling dialogue, the result on the screen is slightly academic in shooting and editing.

"The Pajama Game" (1957) (42) provided Godard with the opportunity to work out his ideas of spontaneity versus planning, chance versus precision, in relation to dance. Whereas classical dance fails to get across the screen footlights, "modern ballet is as happy there as a fish in water because it is a stylization of real everyday movements" (p. 87). Classical dance seeks the immobility in movement, which is by definition the opposite of cinema. Rather than a

goal, repose in the cinema is on the contrary the starting point for movement. This is even more true of the musical, which is in a way the idealization of cinema: a balustrade is no longer something to lean on but an obstacle to clear—everything becomes simply a pretext for the "lines which displace movement":

> So hooray for Robert Fosse and Stanley Donen, who have managed to push this aesthetic almost to its furthest limits in *The Pajama Game*. The arabesques of their dance movements reveal an unfamiliar grace, that of actuality, which is completely absent from, for example, the purely mathematical choreography of Michael Kidd. (p. 87)

The originality of this style might be defined by saying that when the actor dances, he is neither transformed into a dancer doing his act, nor is he a dancer playing a role; he still remains in character, but suddenly feels the need to dance.

In a slightly earlier article on *"L'Eau Vive"* (38), Godard discusses a related but quite distinct idea. His subject is the director's ability "to give to romance the lure of reality, as is right and proper in any shotgun marriage between fiction and reality. . . . Here fiction rejoins the reality which had overtaken it . . . The art of the film-maker is, precisely, to be able to seize this artificial beauty, giving the impression that it is entirely natural" (p. 81). The critical tendency of these pieces (from "Bergmanorama" forward) remains consistent, but there is an important conceptual shift here. In the first three articles discussed, spontaneity and chance are opposed to planning and design, imprecision to precision, joy to perfection. Here the opposing terms are reality and fiction. Spontaneity versus planning, etc., enter in, but now in a different way. The director uses or simulates spontaneity in order to naturalize the artifact, to make the fiction *seem* natural and real. Godard's use of the concept of spontaneity in the earlier three articles *can* be read as naturalism not naturalization, that is, as a genuine contact of cinema with the real, with life, with "what is going on around," with "the temptations of chance," etc. In short, Bazinism: some notion of the ontological transfer of living things or objects onto the filmic image. In *L'Eau Vive* (1960), spontaneity is no longer celebrated simply and directly as a thing or quality existing in the world, which is seized or copied by cinema. It is no longer the natural. Godard now situates spontaneity decisively within discourse. This utterly changes it. No longer of the real, it is an effect of discourse, a trick of rhetoric, a quality achieved by the skillful director in order to naturalize his discourse, that is, make it more effective. It is an event, change, or effect occurring entirely within discourse—and therein and thereafter on audiences.

This transition—from a naturalism of the image, from reality itself *caught* by cinema to a specifiable operation within discourse, leading to a certain effect—is of great theoretical importance. The notes that follow trace this idea, that is, this new concept, in its new form, through several subsequent Godard texts.

A long piece on a festival of short films, "Take Your Own Tours" (56—February 1959), contains this note:

> *Blue Jeans* belongs to a category of short film which is false in principle, being half-way between documentary and narrative fiction. Art is difficult here, for as we have seen, one must on the one hand introduce a plot to lend it the suspense natural to the full-length film, while on the other one has not enough time to develop this plot with the necessary care. Therefore, since one *must* tell a story, one must take only the beginning and the end—in other words, schematize—which involves the aesthetic risk of making something seem theoretic when one is trying to make it seem living. So one must make sure that the dramatic structure constitutes a simple emotion, simple enough to allow one time to analyze it in depth, and also strong enough to justify the enterprise. . . . Rozier has staked everything on lucidity within improvisation . . . Here the truth of the document makes common cause with the grace of the narration. (p. 114)

A piece on *"Les Rendez-vous du Diable"* (64—March 1959) makes clear what the passages quoted suggest, that Godard was reconsidering certain of Bazin's ideas during this period.

> What is remarkable, therefore, is this overweening desire to record, this fierce purpose which Tazieff shares with a Cartier-Bresson or the Sucksdorff of *The Great Adventure,* this deep inner need which forces them to try, against all odds, to authenticate fiction through the reality of the photographic image. Let us now replace the word fiction by fantasy. One then comes back to one of André Bazin's key thoughts in the first chapter of *Qu'est-ce que le cinéma?,* thoughts concerning the "Ontology of the photographic image," and of which one is constantly reminded in analyzing any

shot from *Les Rendez-vous du Diable.* Haroun Tazieff does not know, but proves that Bazin did know, that "the camera alone possesses a sesame for this universe where supreme beauty is identified at one and the same time with nature and with chance." (p. 126)

In a piece on *"La Ligne de Mire"* (66–March 1959), Godard says:

Pollet allows his actors complete freedom. Taking advantage of a carefully worked out scenario, he allows them in effect to improvise their scenes almost entirely. Again, why? Quite simply, once again, to upset Diderot's theory [that the actor is more effective when distanced from his role] and turn the paradox of the actor into the more cinematographic, and therefore more moving, one of the character. For faced by this world large or small vibrating before him, Pollet is content to be, at the viewfinder, on the lookout for poetry. (p. 128)

There is a major statement on these questions in April 1959, "Africa Speaks of the End and the Means" (72), a piece on *Moi, un Noir* (1958) by Jean Rouch. Godard first mentions Rouch in two notes written in December 1958 (51, 53). In one he calls Rouch's *Moi, un Noir,* the greatest French film since the Liberation, in the other he says of it: "Everything, in effect is completely new . . . script, shooting and sound recording" (p. 104). *"Moi, un Noir* is a paving stone in the marsh of French cinema, as *Rome, Open City* in its day was in world cinema" (p. 104).

Godard published a short piece on *Moi, un Noir* in *Arts* in March 1959 (69), then the longer one in *Cahiers* in April 1959 (72).

Rouch's originality lies in having made characters out of his actors —who are actors in the simplest sense of the term, moreover, being filmed *in action,* while Rouch contents himself with filming this action after having, as far as possible, organized it logically in the manner of Rossellini. (p. 131)

For, after all, there are no half-measures. Either it is reality or it is fiction. Either one stages something or one does reportage. Either one opts completely for art or for chance. For construction or for actuality. Why is this so? Because in choosing one, you automatically come round to the other.

To be more precise. You make *Alexander Nevsky* or *India '58.* You have an aesthetic obligation to film one, a moral obligation to film the other. But you have no right to film, say, *Nanook of the North,* as though you were filming *Sunrise.* [Malraux's error in *L'Espoir* lay in not committing himself fully to one direction or the other.] In other words, his *mise-en-scène* yields a priori to actuality, and his actuality yields to *mise-en-scène.* I repeat, a priori. For it is here that one feels a certain awkwardness, as one never does with Flaherty, but which one finds in *Lost Continent.* (p. 132)

Once again let us dot a few i's. All great fiction films tend towards documentary, just as all great documentaries tend toward fiction. *Ivan the Terrible* tends toward *Que Viva Mexico!,* and vice versa; *Mr. Arkadin* towards *It's All True,* and conversely. One must choose between ethic and aesthetic. That is understood. But it is no less understood that each word implies a part of the other. And he who opts wholeheartedly for one, necessarily finds the other at the end of his journey. (pp. 132–133)

[*Moi, un Noir*] contains the answer, the answer to the great question: can art be consonant with chance? Yes, Rouch shows, more and more clearly (or getting better and better) . . . All is now clear. To trust to chance is to *hear voices.* Like Jeanne d'Arc of old, our friend Jean set out with a camera to save, if not France, French cinema at least. A door opens on a new cinema, says the poster for *Moi, un Noir.* How right it is. . . . Of course, *Moi, un Noir* is still far from rivaling *India '58.* There is a jokey side to Rouch which sometimes undermines his purpose. Not that the inhabitants of Treichville haven't the right to poke fun at everything, but there is a certain facility about his acceptance of it. A joker can get to the bottom of things as well as another, but this should not prevent him from self-discipline. (p. 133)

In April 1959 and June 1959, Godard published an interview (75) and a brief note (83) on Rossellini's *India '58.*

India runs counter to all normal cinema: the image merely complements the idea which provokes it. *India* is a film of absolute logic, more Socratic than Socrates. Each image is beautiful, not because it is beautiful in itself, like a shot from *Que Viva Mexico!,* but because it has the splendor of the true, and Rossellini starts from truth. He has already gone on from the point which others may perhaps reach in twenty years time. *India* embraces the cinema of the whole world, as the theories of Riemann and Planck embraced geometry and classical physics. In a future issue, I shall show why *India* is the creation of the world. (p. 150)

Godard's theorizing about the relations between fiction and documentary continue into his filmmaking period. The December 1962 *Cahiers* interview (93) contains a good deal of discussion on this point, now from the perspective of Godard's first four feature films. The October 1965 (171) interview has some also, though less. Even in looking back upon his own experience, Godard is unable to define or resolve the question with any more precision than he had brought to bear as critic. That he continued to talk about this problem in the same terms itself suggests that he did not resolve it.

The passages quoted make clear that the conceptual displacement analyzed above is not as firm and clear-cut as suggested. Godard's earlier vacillations resolved themselves into a concept of cinema as permanently, inherently divided between two poles, fiction and reality. That is, a vacillation became a paradox, which is something quite different. Moving between two alternative solutions to a problem is not at all the same thing as recognizing a bipolarity as itself the solution. The latter involves a positive acquisition of knowledge, the former involves a lack of knowledge. A paradox may well be a superior form of knowledge to what preceded it. Still, it is perhaps inherently unsatisfactory.

Once he had attained this paradox, Godard did not retreat from it into a fallacious simplification of explanation. Rather, he explored film theory and various particular films through the paradox itself, by inflecting its two terms and their relations within the narrow maneuvering space permitted by the model. Thus, the citation of Bazin and a few remarks suggesting a naturalism do not deny or dissolve the fiction or discursive pole of the model. Rather, they assume it and venture forth in attempted explanation only by virtue of its anchoring force. (The reverse may be true as well.)

Here too there is an important parallel with Metz. For the latter, films are made up of nonarticulated or analogue materials (footage), which are then articulated into a discourse (digitalized) by the operation of laws or rules whose study is Metz's principal work. Thus, in Metz too (as perhaps in most theories of film to date), film is described by a bipolar model. The difference between Godard and Metz is that Godard arrived at his model at the end of his explorations, whereas Metz takes it as a point of departure and works from there. Also, Godard put his model in the form of a paradox, that is, in a form in which it was unsolvable. Metz's analysis is not paradoxical.

There is a third complex of ideas in *Godard on Godard* that is worthy of examination. This is Godard's nascent concept of the meta-film, the film made out of knowledge of film history and/or the film about film. It is less conspicuous than the other complexes of ideas discussed: it is only touched upon in a few articles. It is also far less developed theoretically than the other two, indeed little more than broached in one article and not returned to again.

In February 1959 Godard published an article on *Man of the West* (1958) by Anthony Mann (57). He calls the film a super-Western, in the sense that *Shane* (1953) and *High Noon* (1952) are; but does not find this to be the defect that it is in those films. After *The Tin Star* (1957), Mann's art seemed to be evolving toward "a purely theoretic schematism of *mise-en-scène*, directly opposed to that of *The Naked Spur, The Far Country, The Last Frontier,* or even *The Man from Laramie*," Mann's classical Westerns employing classical mise-en-scène.

> If one looks again at *The Man from Laramie, The Tin Star* and *Man of the West* in sequence, it may perhaps be that this extreme simplification is an endeavor, and the systematically more and more linear dramatic construction is a search: in which case the endeavor and the search would in themselves be, as *Man of the West* now reveals, a step forward . . . But a step forward in what direction? Towards a Western style which will remind some of Conrad, others of Simenon, but reminds me of nothing whatsoever, for I have seen nothing so completely new since—why not?—Griffith. Just as the director of *Birth of a Nation* gave one the impression that he was inventing the cinema with every shot, each shot of *Man of the West* gives one the impression that Anthony Mann is reinventing the Western . . . It is, moreover, more than an impression. *He does reinvent.* I repeat, reinvent; in other words, he both shows and demonstrates, innovates and copies, criticizes and creates. *Man of the West,* in short, is both course and discourse, or both beautiful landscapes and the explanation of this beauty, both the mystery of firearms and the secret of this mystery, both art and theory of art . . . of the Western, the most cinematographic genre in the cinema, if I may so put it. The result is that *Man of the West* is quite simply an admirable lesson in cinema—in modern cinema. (pp. 116–117)

The reference to Griffith is perhaps a passkey to exploring Godard's thinking here. Griffith's name comes up a few times in this period of Godard's writings, and in each case it is used to suggest a return to origins and a re-beginning, or, in other words, a metareflection on film. Godard wrote in his piece on the short film:

> Today a short film must be intelligent in that it can no longer afford to be naive like, for instance, Griffith's *The New York Hat* or Chaplin's *The Fireman.* By this I mean that in Sennett's day, cinematographic invention was based on spontaneity; this was, so to speak, the starting-point of all aesthetic effort, whereas today it is the end. Growing more elaborate as the footage increased, it has become less and less natural and more and more deliberate. So much so that, looking at it from an historical point of view, I conclude this: to make a short film today is in a way to return to the cinema's beginnings . . . For this instinctive spontaneity can now be replaced only by its opposite, purposeful intelligence. And it is because this inner contradiction is also its sole aesthetic trump that the short film has for long and by definition been a false genre. To make short films has become synonymous with attempting the impossible.
>
> Let us suppose, for example, that you are commissioned to make a film about railways. Now, as we have just seen, at the time of *L'Arrivée en gare de la Ciotat* a train was a subject for a film: the proof, I would almost add, is that Lumière made the film. But today a train, as such, is no longer an original film-subject, but simply a theme which can be exploited. So you will be faced by the extraordinarily difficult task of having to shoot, not a subject, but the reverse or shadow of this subject; and of attempting to create cinema while knowing beforehand that you are venturing into anti-cinema. (p. 112)

He says in "A Time to Love and a Time to Die" (73—April 1959), "I think one should mention Griffith in all articles about the cinema: everyone agrees, but everyone forgets none the less. Griffith, therefore, and André Bazin too, for the same reasons; and now that is done, I can get back to my . . ." (p. 135).

In the December 1962 *Cahiers* interview (93), Godard says: "A young author writing today knows that Molière and Shakespeare exist. We were the first directors to know that Griffith exists." If Griffith equals the mythic origins of cinema, the founding of narrative film conventions and the narrative film tradition, then making films with knowledge of Griffith leads to a new kind of film, a film that is a reflection on itself, on what narrative film is, as well as itself a narrative. "I have seen nothing so completely new since Griffith."

Godard suggests other meta-filmic possibilities also. In both his pieces on *Moi, un Noir,* Godard mentions a crane shot taken by Rouch that is formally identical to an Anthony Mann crane shot, except that it is hand-held by Rouch. The shots are parallel because their relationship to the subject is identical, hence their meaning and emotional effect are the same. *Scale* here means nothing. In a sense, to know this, and to make films in this knowledge—to remake the great films or subjects with hand-held camera—is to make a meta-film. The fact that a filmmaker can paraphrase an action or camera movement by shooting it hand-held and thereby obtaining the same formal relations perhaps makes it impossible to make naïve or traditional films again, as Godard suggests in the piece on short films. Does this make meta-filming possible? Inevitable?

Godard's few passages on what we (not he) call the meta-film are ambivalent. He is optimistic in the Mann piece—"I've seen nothing so completely new since Griffith"—and jubilant in welcoming Rouch as bringer of a new cinema, but the paragraph on the impossibility of the short film is pessimistic. He speaks of "the extraordinarily difficult task of having to shoot, not a subject, but the reverse or shadow of this subject" and of "venturing into anti-cinema." He suggests a certain defeatism in attempting to make films now. Cinema has suddenly become problematic to itself. (Cf. Roland Barthes, *Writing Degree Zero,* trans. Annette Lavers and Colin Smith [New York: Hill and Wang, 1968].)

In eight years, Godard's texts go from a celebration of classical construction, in which nothing is left to chance, through the celebration of chance filming in "Bergmanorama" to the necessity of documentary and fiction in every film and from there to modernism. In eight years, Godard goes from naïve confidence in a classical cinema to discovery of a new cinema that alters the balance and relations between fiction and documentary to the problematics of filming anything at all, wherein the impulse to create is displaced into negativity or anticinema. It is tempting to make out of these facts an itinerary, indeed a teleology, such that Godard progresses from one stage to the next, each absorbing the one before, ultimately arriving at the last, whereupon he is fully prepared to make *Breathless,* acquiring his theoretical baggage just in time to make his rendezvous with history.

Teleologies are inadmissible in principle. Besides, it appears that the three groups of theoretical work we have isolated did not absorb each other. Traces of all three may be located in Godard's later statements and perhaps in his films, at least until May 1968.

These notes are not designed to answer questions but to raise them, and hopefully to put this book on the agenda for serious consideration. Our dividing Godard's writings into three groups according to theme is no more than a working construct. Of course it is possible to divide the book up in any number of other ways.

Part II:

Film Semiotics and Cine-Structuralism

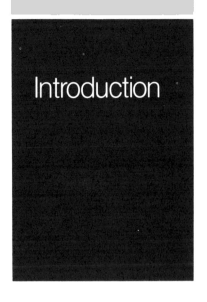

Introduction

The essays of Part I call for further work along several axes. Among these are continuation of the foundational inquiry of "Two Types of Film Theory" and "The Structure of Bazin's Thought"; and realization of the project of a descriptive rhetoric of filmic figures suggested in various ways by "The Long Take," "Toward a Non-Bourgeois Camera Style," and *"Godard on Godard*: Notes for a Reading." In fact, the essays of Part II do not continue any of the inquiries of Part I, at least not directly. For while the essays of Part I were appearing (1970–1974), the very notion of "film theory" was strenuously challenged by a new approach to many of the issues they dealt with—"film semiotics." It seemed necessary to meet this challenge in order to continue to work on film theory, and this is what the essays of Part II do. Strictly considered, these essays seek no more than to relegitimate the work of Part I in the face of attack and to win the right to continue its inquiries.

The film-semiotic position is most fully presented in the work of Christian Metz, particularly in *Essais sur la signification au cinéma*, volume I (1968) and volume II (1972), and in *Langage et cinéma* (1971). (Essays from these books began to appear in English around 1972; the first two books were translated in 1974.) Film semiotics directly challenged film theory in several respects, first in its claim to be itself a full and adequate theory of film, or to be on the way to achieving this; second in its claim that no other approach can attain an adequate theorization, certainly not the approaches already tried. In many passages, film semiotics specifically disparages the classical texts of film theory as, in various ways, failed theorization, but these are often no more than passing remarks. The odd fact is that film semiotics does not accompany its disparagements with a systematic critique of film theory. This omission has various implications that deserve discussion.

We expect a new theory to review and critique previous theories, usually as its first order of business: to say what is wrong or incomplete in earlier work and how it remedies these defects. By not making a sustained review-critique, film semiotics in effect dismisses film theory out of hand. On the one hand, this is a measure of contempt—its sense of its superiority to previous efforts is so great that it need not be demonstrated. Metz does not often come down hard on the word *science,* but the gap implied by his dismissal without critique resembles the disdain of "scientific" analyses for "prescientific" ones, such as the disdain of structural linguistics for nineteenth-century philology.

On the other hand, a failure to critique previous theories makes a new theory vulnerable in several respects. That a new work review and critique its predecessors is more than an academic habit. It demonstrates not only the faults of earlier work and its overcoming of them but also that it has developed, at least partly, out of a reflection on those defects. It thereby demonstrates that it understands previous theories; that it has taken their strengths as well as weaknesses into account in working out its own position; and that it is indeed fundamentally different from them. Among the commonest criticisms in theoretical discourse are that a theory misunderstands previous work and/or that it repeats it in fundamental respects. Critique allows a new theory the opportunity to speak to these questions before outside criticism makes its evaluation. Finally, the critique apparatus aids the reader in understanding and evaluating the new theory: it makes available the materials necessary to formulate an intelligent initial response to it.

To say that it is also not necessary to critique film theory in constructing and presenting a new theory is to say, even more strongly than by saying it, that it is not worthwhile to study film theory. Work on film theory has no relevance to present theoretical work, it has at most an antiquarian interest.

Our work on film semiotics probes the relations between film semiotics and film theory, particularly the dismissal of film theory without critique. (We do *not* consider film semiotics in general, in itself, or in its totality.) It focuses on these questions: Does film semiotics supplant film theory? If so, how? Can film semiotics legitimately dismiss film theory without a critique? On what grounds does it do so? If it may not legitimately do so, what are the consequences of this failure to critique? Is it true that it is no longer worthwhile to study film theory? Can a new, adequate theory of film be constructed without such study?

The essays of Part II, "Critique of Cine-Structuralism" aside, are far more integrated than those of Part I. Its three principal essays, "Metz: *Essais I* and Film Theory," "Segmentation," and "Film Semiotics as Semiotics," treat complementary aspects of a single subject—the relations between film semiotics and film theory. The ties that link essay to essay and that unite all three are clarified by this topological scheme; but, at the same time, each essay is distinct, each discusses these relations from its own standpoint. The material of Part II may be difficult but each essay contains a detailed exposition of all texts and problems necessary to understand it on its own. For all these reasons the Introduction to Part II has less to do than the Introduction to Part I, though there are a number of particulars to fill in.

In a sense, "Metz: *Essais I* and Film Theory" and "Segmentation" comprise a survey of Metz's principal work and of some of the work of his followers. In this respect they fit end-to-end as parts of a single account, though in other respects the two essays are not continuous and are quite unalike. "Film Semiotics as Semiotics" adds to this survey, incidentally to its main purpose, by considering in its course portions of *Essais II* and of *Language and Cinema* untouched by the other essays. Mainly, however, "Film Semiotics as Semiotics" pursues further issues treated in "Metz: *Essais I* and Film Theory," specifically the relations between film semiotics and film theory in Metz's first book, proceeding now from the standpoint of film semiotics rather than that of film theory, as in the earlier essay. (The titles of the two essays reflect these relations of contrariety and complementarity.) In these senses "Metz: *Essais I* and Film Theory" is to the other two essays as "Two Types of Film Theory" is to "The Structure of Bazin's Thought," "The Long Take," and "Toward a Non-Bourgeois Camera Style" in Part I: a hub.

"Metz: *Essais I* and Film Theory" considers Metz's first book not as a series of positions on various topics in film theory, for example, analogy; but as a single, overall argument culminating in the presentation of the *grande syntagmatique* of the image track in (classical) narrative cinema. This presentation focuses the various positions and lines of argument of the book and constitutes its claim to inaugurate a semiotics of cinema and thereby to break decisively with previous theoretical discourses on film. The essay proceeds by examining Metz's treatment of three topics—the centrality of the narrative film in the semiotics of cinema, analogy, and the question whether cinema is a language or like a language—and his weaving of several discourses—phenomenology, linguistics, semiotics, the structural analysis of the narrative—in arriving at and producing the *grande syntagmatique* analysis.

From these analyses the essay concludes that film semiotics is not a complete, adequate theorization of film, hence that it does not supplant or preempt film theory. It concludes also that the book as a whole, and particularly the presentation of the *grande syntagmatique,* reproduces the essential concepts, propositions, and analyses of film theory, in slightly altered form. Film semiotics does not, after all, dismiss film theory, as it claims to do; it absorbs the core of film theory and presents it in a new guise. (Precisely the nature of this new guise and precisely how it is arrived at are the questions of "Film Semiotics as Semiotics.")

Thus "Metz: *Essais I* and Film Theory" answers the challenges of film semiotics to film theory and its study, summarized by the questions posed earlier in this Introduction. Its answers justify our return to the inquiries of Part I and our work on film theory more generally. However, though the essay answers the questions it poses and closes the limited inquiry it initiates, it remains unfinished in other respects, raising new questions and opening new inquiries initially unforeseen by it. These are treated in the remaining essays of Part II, "Segmentation" and "Film Semiotics as Semiotics."

Essais I is not the whole of Metz's work. By the time "Metz: *Essais I* and Film Theory" was published, two other books by him had appeared. Until we examined these, it remained possible that our criticisms were answered in whole or in part by them. Perhaps the later work does attain a comprehensive theorization of film and thereby makes good its earlier claim to supplant film theory. Perhaps it supplies the missing critique of film theory or discusses film theory in important ways. Perhaps it alters the relations between film semiotics and film theory, either by direct discussion or indirectly by redefining film semiotics and thereby changing its relations to film theory. Perhaps it redefines the *grande syntagmatique* and in doing so alters the relations between film semiotics and film theory embodied in it. These questions had to be asked of Metz's later work as well as of his earlier work. "Segmentation" asks them of *Language and Cinema,* the work of the Metzian text analysts, and (briefly) of "The Imaginary Signifier," as "Metz: *Essais I* and Film Theory" asks them of *Essais I.*

This task is not so great as it sounds, not in fact so great as the analysis of *Essais I* alone; because, simply, *Language and Cinema* and the later work are not concerned with film theory at all. They do not provide the missing critique of film theory, they do not open up new relations with film theory or redefine old ones, they do not directly discuss film theory at all. Even the *grande syntagmatique* is discussed only a few times, and briefly. (But these passages are important and "Segmentation" examines them carefully.)

All the explicit relations between film semiotics and film theory are worked out in the first book, *Essais I.* What is settled there is not reopened. Indeed Metz insists repeatedly that the *grande syntagmatique* is a single, unchanging thing. However, as "Segmentation" shows, there are passages in *Language and Cinema* that do alter the definition of the *grande syntagmatique,* or that attempt to do so. Even as he does this, Metz insists that he is merely clarifying what the *grande syntagmatique* means and has always meant.

What are reopened, more than once (in *Language and Cinema* and again in "The Imaginary Signifier"), are fundamental questions of semiotic theory and practice. These imply altered treatment of particular topics, such as the *grande syntagmatique;* though, as we have seen, Metz does not, with a few exceptions, consider the implications of these changes for the *grande syntagmatique* and, when he does, denies that there has been any change. When one considers in addition that Metz has never admitted a role for film theory in his work, neither in *Essais I* nor in later work, it is clear that the question of the relations between film semiotics and film theory in the later work is very difficult to get at. Thus the approach of "Segmentation" is somewhat oblique, but the material itself imposes this.

The immediate point of departure for "Segmentation" is the latter-day usage of the *grande syntagmatique* for general segmentation in Barthes-like textual analyses of film. It asks first how the *grande syntagmatique* came to be used in this way and second whether it is an appropriate tool for general segmentation in such analyses. In *Essais I* the *grande syntagmatique* was promoted in different ways as the chief code of cinema, even as the semiotic mechanism of cinema itself; though other passages call it just one code among many, albeit the one controlling the "large units" of film. *Language and Cinema* resolves this ambivalence unequivocally. It declares that the *grande syntagmatique* is merely a code among others, indeed "a subcode of montage"; it is in no sense a division of the entire film. "Segmentation" shows that using the *grande syntagmatique* as general segmentation principle violates the prescriptions of *Language and Cinema*. It shows also that in doing so the text analysts merely return to the definition of *Essais I*, perhaps carrying a step further tendencies already at work in it. "Segmentation" also elucidates some factors that determine this return: the advent of textual semiotics and the receding of systemic semiotics and the failure of film semiotics to analyze any code other than the *grande syntagmatique*.

As noted, film semiotics does not banish film theory from its realm —except formally. In practice it absorbs the core of film theory and presents it in a new guise. This guise is drawn from the semiotic vocabulary. While this finding tells us that film semiotics does not supplant film theory and sends us back to our film-theoretical investigations, it is itself puzzling and disturbing. It is even more puzzling when we consider that Metz does not just use a semiotic vocabulary to state his findings, he goes through an elaborate semiotic argument, stage by stage, in arriving at them. Our question then is: How does Metz use semiotic methods to arrive at film-theoretical results? The possible answers seem to be: either we mistake the nature of those results, that is, they truly are semiotic; or Metz has not used, or has misused, the semiotic method.

In raising these questions at all, we venture into new terrain. No one has questioned Metz's relation to semiotics and linguistics, neither his followers nor his critics. His fellow semioticians and followers, who are able to question the relation, will not do so for obvious reasons, at least they have not done so. His critics have assumed without question that Metz knows semiotics. What they doubt is that he knows film and its problems; or they massively doubt semiotics as a method; or they say nothing about the method and disagree directly with the results that it produces in Metz's work. Indeed many or most critics of Metz do not know enough semiotics and linguistics to make an evaluation; but the important point is that they have not tried, they cede the point in advance. In nearly all cases they identify Metz's work with semiotics itself, putting themselves in a position where they must make a joint evaluation. One critic wrote a detailed criticism of Metz and called it "Contra Semiology." It is true that critics from several schools do not wish to make finer distinctions than this amalgamation permits. A number of critics argue that film is essentially, in part or whole, a visual medium, therefore that "the linguistic model" cannot apply to it. Such writers wish precisely to reject Metz's work and semiotics in one stroke. If, however, we are interested in understanding Metz's work as fully as possible before we make an evaluation, especially before we declare ourselves finished with that work, then the relations between Metz's work and semiotics must be probed.

In relation to the other essays of Part II, this means probing the relations between film semiotics and film theory once again, this time from the film-semiotic side. "Metz: *Essais* I and Film Theory" considered the interaction of discourses in Metz's first book: semiotics and linguistics, phenomenology, structural analysis of the narrative, and film theory. When it came to evaluation of the overall argument, however, the results of film theory's analysis were laid alongside the results of the film-semiotic analysis, a comparison was made, and conclusions were drawn. "Segmentation" in effect did the same thing apropos the later Metzian work. "Film Semiotics as Semiotics" evaluates the semiotic analysis as such. It begins with the principles of Metz's semiotic method, set forth in Barthes's *Elements of Semiology,* and applies them stage by stage to Metz's argument. It asks whether that argument does, or can, reach its results, notably the analysis of the *grande syntagmatique,* on its own power. It finds that it cannot, that it covertly introduces other concepts, assumptions, propositions, and positions along the way, and that these are the concepts, assumptions, propositions, and positions of film theory. It studies the interactions of the two discourses in great detail. It asks whether, even so, the interaction does not produce something new, and if so, what precisely that is. Is it just the analysis of film theory put into semiotic vocabulary? Or is it an amalgam of some kind?

"Critique of Cine-Structuralism," the final essay of Part II, lies somewhat outside the main lines of inquiry of this book. It deals with theoretical problems of film and its study but not with film theory in the senses in which we have adumbrated it. But it resembles the essays on Metz's work, and casts some light on them, in opposing older and newer modes of analysis in relation to a traditional problem, in this case the place of the author in film production and of the concept of the author in film study. It also relates to and comments on the essays of Part I, notably "The Long Take" and *"Godard on Godard:* Notes for a Reading."

"Critique of Cine-Structuralism" deals with various early uses of "structuralist" discourses in Anglo-American film books and journals. The structuralist sources include the writings of Claude Lévi-Strauss on myth analysis and the *Cahiers du cinéma* textual analysis, "John Ford's *Young Mr. Lincoln."* The Anglo-American texts in question interpret the texts of Lévi-Strauss and of *Cahiers* as compatible with, indeed as supporting, the notion of the film director as author of the film. These include *Signs and Meaning in the Cinema* by Peter Wollen and articles on the *Cahiers* essay by Ben Brewster, Sam Rohdie, and Stephen Heath in *Screen* (14, no. 3 [Autumn 1973]). The immediate occasion for Part I of "Critique of Cine-Structuralism" is a meta-theoretical text by Charles Eckert, "The English Cine-Structuralists," with which "Critique of Cine-Structuralism" is in fundamental agreement on all but a few points. Given these overlaid layers of theory and meta-theory, the argument of our essay is necessarily complex, but its underlying points are simple.

More than the other essays in this book, perhaps because it is more polemical than they, "Critique of Cine-Structuralism" is bound to the historical moment in which it appeared. The conjuncture of discourse and debate in which it intervened has now passed, but the question of the author has not. The debate of which "Critique of Cine-Structuralism" is a part took place at the fringe of a field then, now, and perhaps always dominated by the figure of the author. It is for this reason that we reprint the piece here: a dead horse may be flogged if it bears a living rider. The myth analyses of Lévi-Strauss and the discourses on which *Cahiers* based its study of *Lincoln* are grounded in what Roland Barthes summed up in a brief essay as "The Death of the Author." By this is meant the nineteenth-century notion of the author as creator of works *ex nihilo*. The error of the writers polemicized, Eckert apart, is to join the new discourses to the old author-centered criticism, at once bolstering the latter, extending its life, and taking the edge off of the former, as well as distorting it. Much ingenuity of argument is expended to make this squaring of the circle come right. Our essays attempt to untangle the contorted arguments and sliding senses of terms devoted to this cause.

Chapter 6

Metz: *Essais I* and Film Theory (1975)

Semiotics as we now understand it must always rest on a double support: On the one hand, upon linguistics, and, on the other hand, upon the theory peculiar to the field under consideration.

—C. Metz, *Essais I* (1968)

Two of Christian Metz's three books have appeared for the first time in English this year, *Essais sur la signification au cinéma*, volume I (Paris: Klincksieck, 1968) and *Langage et cinéma* (Paris: Larousse, 1971). The latter is translated straightforwardly as *Language and Cinema* (The Hague: Mouton, 1974). The former becomes *Film Language: A Semiotics of the Cinema,* translated by Michael Taylor (New York: Oxford University Press, 1974). Not yet available in translation is *Essais,* volume II (Paris: Klincksieck, 1972).

Essais I (1968) is already a historical book. It collects essays written between 1964 and 1968 (the English edition omits the bibliographical details of the original). Thus some of its contents have taken ten years to reach these shores. Since 1964, of course, research has advanced and theoretical structures have changed greatly. The book itself has been critiqued and commented on by many writers. Scarcely a line has escaped critical examination.[1]

Metz's own later writings appear to question many of the positions of *Essais I,* though both subsequent books defend the principal theoretical effort of the first, the analysis of the *grande syntagmatique* (GS) of the image track. It is reported that Metz's current lectures are pursuing lines of inquiry quite different from those of all his writings to date, focusing especially on materialist and psychoanalytic approaches to cinema. This is welcome news indeed, though an author's change of mind does not affect the need to read important books. The first attempt to construct a semiotics of the cinema is one of these.

Essais I can be read in two kinds of ways. Since the book contains discussions of many particular questions in semiotics and in film theory, such topics may be discussed apart from the book as a whole and their place in it. When the question of analogy in cinema is discussed, Metz's position is one of those that may be reviewed and criticized. On the other hand, the book as a whole weaves its positions on various questions into a single, overall argument, in this case that leading to presentation of the *grande syntagmatique.* Our interest is in the latter operation, partly because most critiques have tended to deal with Metz's positions one by one. Perhaps the best of these, Michael Cegarra's in *Cinéthique,* is virtually a line-by-line critique. Such analyses are useful though, of course, they are not exhaustive. Attention to this level misses relations, operations, and

---

[1] See, among others, Emilio Garroni, *Semiòtica ed estètica* (Bari: Laterza, 1968); Umberto Eco, *La Structure Absente* (Paris: Mercure de France, 1972), "Articulations of the Cinematic Code," *Cinemantics,* no. 1 (January 1970); Kristeva, Cegarra, *Cinéthique,* Heath pieces in *Screen,* 14, nos. 1–2 (Spring–Summer 1973); Jean-Louis Baudry, "Ideological Effects of the Basic Cinematographic Apparatus," *Film Quarterly,* 28, no. 2 (Winter 1974/75); Brian Henderson, "Critique of Cine-Structuralism, I and II," *Film Quarterly,* 27, nos. 1 and 2 (Fall 1973; Winter 1973/74).

configurations at other levels, particularly the larger patterns of discursive interactions and the relationship of questions posed to questions omitted or suppressed that constitutes the problematic of a
text.

Neither does our attention to the book's overall argument claim
to be exhaustive. We are most interested in the book's claim to inaugurate a semiotics of the cinema and with its claims—explicit and
implicit—that this constitutes a break with previous discourses on
film. Thus we are concerned with examining Metz's deployment of
the discourses of linguistics and semiology. But we are equally interested in the other large discourses that mix with these in the
book, particularly those of phenomenology, film theory, and the
structural analysis of narrative (itself a branch of semiology). We
are interested in differentiating the places of these discourses in the
structure of the argument; in tracing their dynamic interaction, that
is, the mutual pressures they exert; and in charting what may be
called the general economy of the *Essais I* text as it unfolds by virtue
of now one, now another of these discourses, or now a certain conjunction of them, now another.

We begin with certain positions of Metz's that have been much
discussed: the methodological centrality of the narrative film to a
semiology of the cinema, the problem of analogy in cinema, and
whether or not, and if so, in what sense, cinema is a language. We
do not propose to review in detail Metz's positions on these questions,
let alone critiques by others. But minimal review of these positions
is necessary to indicate the overall plan of the argument, specifically
to show how they prepare the presentation of the *grande syntagmatique.*

Several passages of *Essais I* argue the historical supremacy of the
narrative film. It was not unavoidable that film develop along narrative lines, but this is what happened. Going to the movies has
long meant going to see a filmed story. Narrative was the demand
of audiences, but cinema's "inner semiological mechanism" made it
especially well suited to tell stories in any case: "Narrativity and
logomorphism. It is as if a kind of induction current were linking
images among themselves, whatever one did, as if the human mind
(the spectator's as well as the film-maker's) were incapable of not
making a connection between two successive images" (p. 46). Thus
Metz's reinterpretation of Kuleshov. Not scientific montage alone,
any cinematic construction (however random) will be read narratively by viewers.

These historical and mediumistic questions give way to the methodological questions that they mask: what body of films is the semiologist to study and why? Metz grants that the answer depends upon what one wants to study, but he does not leave it at that: "Nevertheless, there is a hierarchy of concerns (or, better yet, a methodological urgency) that favors—in the beginning at least—the study of narrative film" (p. 93). Again Metz mentions the "historical and social fact" of "the merging of the cinema and of narrativity." The feature-length film of novelistic fiction (which is simply called a film) has traced more and more clearly the king's highway of filmic expression. Moreover, non-narrative films are different principally by virtue of their content, not by their language processes: "It is by no means certain that an independent semiotics of the nonnarrative genres is possible other than in the form of a series of discontinuous remarks on the points of difference between these films and 'ordinary' films. To examine fiction films is to proceed more directly and more rapidly to the heart of the problem" (p. 94).

Moreover, historically speaking, it was by virtue of confronting the problems of narration that it came to produce a body of specific signifying procedures. "Thus, it was in a single motion that the cinema became narrative and took over some of the attributes of a language" (p. 96).

Metz seems somewhat embarrassed by these arguments today, and for good reason. They are not only specious, but needless. The narrative film is merely one of many possible objects of film semiotics. If one prefers to study it rather than something else, that choice cannot be justified. Metz's argument serves to enhance his own project and his own choice: "to move to the heart of the problem." This is a delusion that is no longer possible. (Better to say with Barthes: "The text I have chosen . . . is Balzac's *Sarrasine*.") If Metz can provide the groundwork for a semiotics of the narrative film, that is quite enough. To claim (in advance, yet) that this is the semiotics of film itself is ideological in several senses. Cegarra argues that Metz's centralizing the narrative film in his studies is complicit in that cinema's social and economic domination of the world's production and consumption.

We must distinguish Metz's attempt to make narrative film methodologically primary from a very different point. Once one chooses to study the narrative film, a study that has no priority or greater importance than any other kind of film study, then within that study, narrativity is centrally important. Some of Metz's critics lump these two points together, saying that Metz is wrongly concerned with narrativity in film, neglecting other aspects or values. In our view he is wrongly centered on narrative film in relation to a general semiology of film; but, given his study of narrative film, as one among many, he is too little concerned with narrativity itself.

Metz's position on the problem of analogy or iconicity is also fundamental to his overall argument. Each image is unique *because* it reproduces some object or view of the world directly; that is, it does not encode the world, as language does, by translating it into some system other than its own. The diversity of images in cinema is the world's diversity. Metz's subscription to the theory of analogy in cinema and in photographic *duplication* more generally founds his theory of filmic discourse. Speaking of Méliès, Porter, Griffith, the pioneers of "cinematographic language," he says: "Men of denotation rather than of connotation, they wanted above all to tell a story; they were not content unless they could subject the continuous, analogical material of photographic duplication to the *articulations*—however rudimentary—of a narrative discourse" (p. 95).

It is important here to introduce Umberto Eco's critique in "Articulations of the Cinematic Code" of the notion of analogy. Eco concludes:

> Thus we can say that everything which in images appears to us still as analogical, continuous, non-concrete, motivated, natural, and therefore "irrational," is simply something which, in our present state of knowledge and operational capacities, we have not yet succeeded in reducing to the discrete, the digital, the purely differential. As for the mysterious phenomenon of the image which "resembles," it may be enough for the moment to have recognized processes of codification concealed in the mechanisms of perception themselves.[2]

It seems from the footnotes to *Essais I,* written after the original essays, that Metz accepts Eco's critique. This acceptance does not, however, lead to substantial revision of Metz's position. There seem to be two related points or principles that permit Metz to accept this change at one level without corresponding changes at other levels: "Contrary to what I believed four years ago, it does not seem at all impossible to me, today, to assume that analogy is itself coded

---

[2] *Cinematics,* no. 1 (January 1970). Reprinted in *Movies and Methods,* Bill Nichols, ed. (Berkeley, Calif.: University of California Press, 1976), p. 595.

without however ceasing to function authentically as analogy in relation to the codes of the superior level—which are brought into play only on the basis of this first assumption" (pp. 111–112).

The other assumption is that of the first essay in the book, "On the Impression of Reality in the Cinema," in which Metz argues in a phenomenological manner that the correspondence between image and reality in cinema is less important than the fact that viewers perceive or *intend* the images of cinema as reality. Not reality but a certain impression of reality is the basis of Metz's argument.

Thus Metz seeks to "contain" the potentially disruptive effect of Eco's critique. The efficacy of his attempt cannot be considered here. In any case, the structure of Metz's system does not change.

Metz devotes considerably more attention to the problem of whether film is a language. He argues that the early film theorists—Eisenstein, Bazin, and most others—spoke of film as a language, but in fact knew nothing of linguistics. Metz then proceeds to draw upon linguistic science in order to answer the question precisely and authoritatively. He proceeds slowly, carefully, apparently exhaustively through a detailed comparison between the linguistic and the cinematic media, determining point by point what is like and what is unlike between them and what the consequences of these similarities and dissimilarities are. The method is indirect but, he argues,

> To understand what film is not is to gain time, rather than to lose it, in the attempt to grasp what film is. . . . I call one of them the "first stage" because it benefits from the capital of linguistics, which encourages one to begin with it. The "second stage" is properly semiotic and translinguistic; it is less able to depend on previously acquired knowledge, so that, far from being helped, it must, on the contrary, participate—if it is able—in work that is new. Thus it is condemned to suffer the present discomfort of semiotics. (p. 61)

Metz comes immediately to a fundamental dissimilarity: cinema has nothing corresponding to the double articulation of natural language. In the latter, phonemes are distinctive units without proper signification, signifiers without corresponding signifieds. It is only when phonemes are articulated at a second level, by combination into monemes or words, that signification occurs. Only at the second level do phonemes (in combination) acquire signifieds. But in cinema every shot involves signification; every shot has a signified. What is missing is the first articulation. Thus in film, unlike natural language, "it is impossible to break up the signifier without getting isomorphic segments of the signified" (p. 63). A consequence of double articulation is a great distance between content and expression in natural language; in cinema the distance is "too short."

Not only does the cinema have no phonemes—it has no words either. The image or shot corresponds instead to one or more sentences; the sequence is a complex segment of discourse (that is, a paragraph or chapter, a unit composed of several sentences). A shot has nothing incomplete about it; it is "a completed assertive statement." The image is *always actualized*. Even a close-up of a revolver, which would seem equivalent to the word *revolver*, signifies at the very least, "Here is a revolver!" Thus the image is always speech, never a unit of language.

From this Metz moves to a related point. Though the combinatory or syntagmatic possibilities of cinema are very rich, its paradigmatic resources are surprisingly poor. This is another way of saying that every image is unique, therefore, strictly speaking, unsubstitutable. "Every image is a hapax (a unique determination)" (p. 69). Thus images do not (or only very generally) assume their meaning from paradigmatic opposition to other images; whereas words are always more or less embedded in paradigmatic networks of meaning and indeed create meaning by virtue of such systems. But this poverty of the paradigm in film is the counterpart of a wealth distributed elsewhere: the filmmaker can express himself by showing us directly the diversity of the world. Certain camera movements (rear and forward dolly) and techniques of punctuation (dissolve or cut) have the character of low-level paradigms, but their leverage on the total expression is not strong.

Thus, the cinema is not a language system (it is a language of art) because it contradicts three important characteristics of the linguistic fact: a language is a *system* of *signs* used for *intercommunication*. Like all the arts, cinema is a one-way communication. It is only partly a system. Finally, it uses only very few true signs. The image is first and always an image. Therefore the nerve center of the film-semiological process lies elsewhere.

This elsewhere is the large syntagmatic organization of the image track. Here Metz discovers an unusual fact.

> Although each image is a free creation, the arrangement of these images into an intelligible sequence—cutting and montage—brings us to the heart of the semiological dimension of film. It is a rather paradoxical situation: Those proliferating (and not very discrete!)

units—the *images*—when it is a matter of composing a film, suddenly accept with reasonably good grace the constraint of a few large syntagmatic structures. While no image ever entirely resembles another image, the great majority of narrative films resemble each other in their principal syntagmatic figures. (p. 101)

This regularity is due, historically and structurally, to the narrative function of cinema. It was by confronting the problem of narrativity that cinema became a language, historically; and it is by this function that regularity is sustained. The key fact here is that in cinema the denotation itself must be organized.

In still photography this is not so. A photo of a house denotes the house by virtue of its automatic reproduction of its subject. In the cinema, on the other hand, a whole semiotics of denotation is possible and necessary, for a film is composed of *many* photographs (the concept of montage, with its myriad consequences)—photographs that give us mostly only partial views of the diegetic referent. (p. 98)

Metz continues:

Thus a kind of filmic *articulation* appears, which has no equivalent in photography: It is the denotation itself that is being constructed, organized, and to a certain extent codified (codified, not necessarily *encoded*). Lacking absolute laws, filmic intelligibility nevertheless depends on a certain number of dominant habits: A film put together haphazardly would not be understood. (p. 99)

Thus, Metz summarizes, "cinematographic language" is first of all the literalness of a plot. Artistic effects, even when they are substantially inseparable from the semic act by which the film tells us its story, nevertheless constitute another level of signification, which from the methodological point of view must come later.

Thus filmic narrativity gradually shaped itself into forms that are more or less fixed, but not immutable. They are a "synchronic state" (that of the present cinema), which can change only through gradual evolution. With Ferdinand de Saussure one can say that the large syntagmatic category of the narrative film *can change*, but no single person can make it change overnight.

From this point, Metz proceeds to present and analyze the principal types of large filmic syntagma, which organize filmic denotation. Before doing so, he summarizes:

The cinema is certainly not a language system (*langue*). It can, however, be considered as a *language,* to the extent that it orders signifying elements within ordered arrangements different from those of spoken idioms—and to the extent that these elements are not traced on the perceptual configurations of reality itself (which does not tell stories). Filmic manipulation transforms what might have been a mere visual transfer of reality into discourse. Derived from a kind of signification that is purely analogous and continuous—animated photography, cinematography—the cinema gradually shaped, in the course of its diachronic maturation, some elements of a proper semiotics, which remain scattered and fragmentary within the open field of simple visual duplication. (p. 105)

Besides preparing the way for the *grande syntagmatique,* Metz uses his various points to refute once and for all the metaphor of film-as-language. There is no arguing with Metz here. Eisenstein, Bazin, etc., were wrong. Far less certain is how important this point is. Metz seems to think it very important, one of the chief achievements of his work. To establish this, however, one would have to show the precise operational effect that this metaphor had within each theory concerned: show not only that Eisenstein or Bazin used the metaphor but what they used it to think or theorize. Our sense is that the metaphor was in both theories relatively nonoperative. Change the word and you do not fundamentally alter the theoretical position of each or the rhetoric of filmic figures that each adumbrated. If this is the center of Metz's achievement, it is an empty center.

After further preliminaries, Metz's text is prepared to present its own system. ("The time has come for a semiotics of the cinema.") This occurs in chapter 5, section 5, "The Large Syntagmatic Category of the Image Track." [3]

---

[3] Every page (but one) of this fifteen-page passage has at least one footnote, sometimes two, often longer than the page itself. The first four paragraphs, those which inaugurate the system ("The time has come . . .") contain four footnotes, three of which contain important theoretical material, crucial to Metz's project. This does not include the material set off in four sets of parentheses and three sets of dashes, let alone that in the many parentheses and dashes in the footnotes themselves. These graphic/discursive signifiers indicate a text under extreme pressure, in which the smooth surface of discourse is broken again and again by exceptions, doubts, alternative formulations, background information, anticipations of objections, promises of future refinement and development, etc. No other portion of the book exhibits anything like this degree of textual stress. We consider why this is so below.

The first four paragraphs inaugurate the project:

> So far, I have examined only the status of "cinematographic grammar," and I have said nothing about its *content.* I have not given the table of the codified orderings of various kinds used in film.
>
> It is not possible here to give this table in its complete form, with all the explanations required by each one of the indicated orderings, and with the *principles of commutation* between them (and consequently to enumerate them).
>
> Let us content ourselves, then, with the almost unpolished "result"—the table itself in a summarized form—and only that part of it that outlines the large syntagmatic category of the image track (i.e., the codified and signifying orderings on the level of the *large* units of the film, and ignoring the elements of sound and speech). Naturally this problem constitutes only one of the chapters of "cinematographic syntax."
>
> In order to determine the number and the nature of the main syntagmatic *types* used in current films, one must start from common observation (existence of the "scene," the "sequence," "alternate montage," etc.) as well as on certain "presemiotic" analyses by critics, historians, and theoreticians of the cinema ("tables of montage," various classifications, etc.).[4] This preliminary work must account for several points of importance—that is why it in no way precludes the viewing of numerous films—and it must then be organized into a coherent body—that is to say, into a list of all the main types of image-orderings occurring in films under the various headings into which they are naturally classified.
>
> One thus arrives at a first "tabulation" of the syntagmatic components of films—a chart remaining fairly close to the concrete

---

[4] Among the authors who have devised tables of montage, or classifications of various kinds—or who have studied separately a specific type of montage—I am indebted to Eisenstein, Pudovkin, Kuleshov, Timochenko, Béla Balázs, Rudolf Arnheim, André Bazin, Edgar Morin, Gilbert Cohen-Séat, Jean Mitry, Marcel Martin, Henri Agel, François Chevassu, Anne Souriau . . . and one or two others perhaps whom I have unintentionally overlooked.

Because there is not enough room here, I will not (at least in this text) indicate how the various classifications of these authors are distributed in relation to each specific point of my chart. But it must not be forgotten that, among the various "image constructions" identifiable in films, some were defined and analyzed (very ingeniously at times) before the appearance of an actual semiological method. There were also larger attempts at classification, which are extremely instructive even in their failings. Semiotics as we now understand it must always rest on a double support: On the one hand, upon linguistics, and, on the other hand, upon the theory peculiar to the field under consideration (pp. 120–121n).

filmic material, but which, from the point of view of semiological theory, is as yet insufficiently developed. (pp. 119–121)

The balance of section 5 presents Metz's *"la grande syntagmatique,"* the large syntagmatic category of the image track. Presented finally in the form of a chart or general table (pp. 145–146), this is "the table of the codified orderings of various kinds used in film" (p. 119). Metz expounds the *grande syntagmatique* by describing each syntagmatic type in turn, opposing those that might seem similar through example and conceptual distinction. He notes several versions of his table and the crucial difference between the first and the second beyond the addition of two types:

> It appears that the different types and subtypes that composed the first table, where they were presented in the purely enumerative form of a list, can be redistributed into a system of successive dichotomies, according to a procedure commonly used in linguistics. This scheme gives us a better outline of the *deep structure* of the choices that confront the film-maker for each one of the "sequences" of his film. In this way, an empirical and purely inductive classification was later able to be converted into a deductive system; in other words, a factual situation, initially ascertained and clarified, later showed itself to be more logical than one might have predicted (see table). (p. 123)

Reorganized, the table presents a series of seven binary oppositions or rather a system of binary oppositions at six different levels. These are: among autonomous segments, autonomous shots versus syntagmas; among syntagmas, chronological and achronological syntagmas; among achronological syntagmas, parallel and bracket syntagmas; among chronological syntagmas, narrative and descriptive syntagmas; among narrative syntagmas, alternative narrative and linear narrative syntagmas; among linear narrative syntagmas, scene and sequences; among sequences, episodic and ordinary sequences. Metz defines the autonomous segment in general as "a subdivision of the first order in film; it is therefore a part of a film, and not a part of a part of a film" (p. 123). "It is clear nevertheless that the 'autonomy' of the autonomous segments themselves is not an *independence,* since each autonomous segment derives its final meaning in relation to the film as a whole, the latter being the *maximum syntagma* of the cinema" (p. 123). The first and primary division among autonomous segments is that between autonomous shots and syntagmas. The former contain one shot, the latter (including seven subclassifications) all contain several shots. In the unique case of the autonomous plot, a single shot presents an episode of the plot. It is therefore the only instance in which a single shot constitutes a primary, and not a secondary, subdivision of the film. The autonomous shot is by definition not a syntagma, but it *is* a syntagmatic type, since it is one of the types that occur in the global syntagmatic structure of the film. "More generally speaking, syntagmatic analysis is a part of semiotics in which one is *initially* confronted with 'discourses' that are always syntagmas of different magnitudes, but in which the units one *isolates as one proceeds* are not necessarily all syntagmas—for some of them may not be divisible in every case" (p. 124).

Among syntagmas, a second criterion allows the distinction between nonchronological syntagmas and chronological syntagmas. In the first the temporal relationship between the facts presented in the different images is not defined by the film; in the second kind it is. Of nonchronological syntagmas, there is the parallel syntagma, in which montage interweaves two or more alternating motifs, but no precise relationship, whether temporal or spatial, is assigned to them, at least on the level of denotation. This kind of montage has a direct symbolic value. There is also the bracket syntagma, in which a series of very brief scenes represent occurrences that the film gives as typical samples of a same order of reality, without in any way chronologically locating them in relation to each other, in order to emphasize their presumed kinship within a category of facts that the filmmaker wants to describe in visual terms. Each little scene is taken as an element in a system of allusions and therefore it is the series, rather than the individual scene, that the film takes into account. This construction suggests that among the occurrences it groups together there is the same relationship as that between words in a topographic bracket. Frequently the different successive evocations are strung together through optical effects.

In the chronological syntagmas, the temporal relationships between the facts that successive images show us are defined on the level of denotation. But these precise relationships are not necessarily those of consecutiveness; they may also be relations of simultaneity. In the descriptive syntagma, the relationship between *all* the motifs successively presented on the screen is one of simultaneity. It is the only case of consecutiveness on the screen that does not correspond to any diegetic consciousness. Objects in a descriptive syntagma have a relation of spatial coexistence, not any temporal relation.

Chronological syntagmas other than the descriptive are narrative syntagmas, that is, those in which the temporal relationship between the objects seen in the images contains elements of consecutiveness and not only of simultaneity. Among narrative syntagmas, the alternate syntagma interweaves several temporal progressions (the old "parallel montage"). The montage presents alternately two or more series of events in such a way that within each series the temporal relationships are consecutive, but that, between the series taken as wholes, the temporal relationship is one of simultaneity.

The linear narrative syntagma presents a single succession linking together all the acts seen in the images. Succession may be continuous or discontinuous. When succession is continuous, that is, with no diegetic breaks, we have a scene, a spatiotemporal integrity experienced as being without flaws. (This was the only construction known to early filmmakers; it exists as a type among others today.) Here the signifier is fragmentary—a number of shots—but the signifieds are unified and continuous.

Opposed to the scene are the various kinds of linear narrative syntagma in which the temporal order of acts presented is discontinuous: the sequences. These include the ordinary sequence, in which the temporal discontinuity is unorganized (as though scattered). Or the discontinuity may be ordered, and may therefore be the principle of structure and intelligibility in the sequence—the episodic sequence. Little scenes are strung together, usually separated by optical devices, and they succeed each other in chronological order. The scenes must not be taken as separate instances but only in their totality. This construction can be used to condense gradual progressions. In both there is the concept of a single concatenation plus the concept of discontinuity. In the episodic sequence each of the images appears distinctly as the symbolic summary of one stage in the fairly long evolution condensed by the total sequence. In the ordinary sequence each of the units in the narrative simply presents one of the unskipped moments of the action. In the former each image stands for more than itself and is perceived as taken from a group of other possible images representing a single phase of a progression. In the ordinary sequence each image represents only what it shows.

The *grande syntagmatique* concerns the syntagmatic ordering of the denotative meanings of the image track. Though Metz's semiotics of film does not concern the paradigmatic dimensions of filmic communication, he argues also that the system of eight syntagmatic segment-types constitutes itself a paradigm of filmic construction: each segment of a film may be constructed in at least eight ways. Metz's semiotics also excludes connotation. It is concerned with "the literal temporality of the plot, the first message of the film" (p. 117). This is why "filmic orderings that are codified and significant constitute a grammar—because they organize not only filmic connotations, but also, and *primarily,* denotation" (p. 117). Metz defends this exclusion in several ways. First, connotation is more difficult to determine than denotation and always itself builds on denotation as secondary meaning (cf. Roland Barthes, *Mythologies,* trans. Annette Lavers [New York: Hill and Wang, 1972]). Since film semiotics is just beginning and since denotation must be determined first in any case, it is advisable to take on the system of denotation in cinema as a separate topic. Second, in cinema even more than in other semiotic systems, connotation is nothing other than a form of denotation (p. 118): "films are able to connote without generally requiring *special* (i.e., separate) connotors because they have the most essential signifiers of connotation at their permanent disposal: the choice between several ways of structuring denotation" (p. 119).

We note the important consequences of Metz's double choice here. As Cegarra says, citing Barthes, ideology is the signified of connotation. Metz's exclusion of connotation eliminates the study of ideology in cinema from his semiotics. (This is just one of the points on which Metz, apparently following Baudry and other critics, has changed his mind.[5])

---

[5] Note that Barthes too has changed his mind; in S/Z (1970; trans. Richard Miller [New York: Hill and Wang, 1974]) he says that the primacy or centrality of denotation in relation to connotation is itself an ideological illusion, hence the notion of their separability is also. "There is no reason to make this system (denotation) the privileged one, to make it the locus and the norm of a primary, original meaning, the scale for all associated meanings; if we base denotation on truth, on objectivity, on law, it is because we are still in awe of the prestige of linguistics . . . The endeavor of this hierarchy is a serious one: it is to return to the closure of Western discourse (scientific, critical, or philosophical), to its centralized organization, to arrange all the meanings of a text around the hearth of denotation (the hearth: center, guardian, refuge, light of truth)" (p. 7).

"Structurally, the existence of two supposedly different systems—denotation and connotation—enables the text to operate like a game, each system referring to the other according to the requirements of a certain *illusion.* Ideologically, finally, this game has the advantage of affording the classic text a certain *innocence:* of the two systems, denotative and connotative, one turns back on itself and indicates its own existence: the system of denotation; denotation is not the first meaning, but pretends to be so; under this illusion, it is ultimately no more than the *last* of the connotations (the one which seems both to establish and to close the reading), the superior myth by which the text pretends to return to the nature of language, to language as nature . . ." (p. 9).

These are the bare bones of Metz's argument. Let us now examine more carefully the theoretical operations that produce the system of the *grande syntagmatique,* looking especially to the interplay of those discourses that we identified topographically at the outset: linguistics and semiology, phenomenology, film theory, and the structural analysis of narrative.

We begin with a review of film theory and one version of its constituent errors and shortcomings. This will help us to identify the discourse of film theory as it operates in the *Essais I* text, but it will also help to sharpen our principal question: Does the book constitute a semiotics of cinema? Does it break decisively (or at all) with film theory? For classical film theory, its problematic, its concepts, and its structure, constitutes an important part of the background against which the discursive formation of *Essais I* must be traced.

In "Two Types of Film Theory," we characterized the classical film theories of Eisenstein, Bazin, and others as theories of cinematic parts. Both defined the basic filmic unit as the shot and considered different ways of combining these units to form larger units called sequences. Their treatment of this problem mixed descriptive, normative, historical, and philosophic discourses. Neither worked out a theory of cinematic wholes, therefore neither considered problems of part-whole relations in cinema. This was seen as a crippling defect in both theories and in classical film theory generally. Symptomatic of the theoretical problem involved is each theorist's formulation of the concept of the cinematic whole, on the few and incidental occasions on which the problem was treated. Both used genre categories borrowed principally from literary studies. Eisenstein's essay on organic unity and pathos in the composition of *Potemkin* defines the formal organization of the film as a whole as a tragedy in five acts. Bazin wrote of those cinematic genres such as gangster film, horror film, comedy, Western that organize the whole film and hence determine the content of each sequence. Bazin's theory concerns various visual treatments of the sequence; its content and its relation to the film as a whole are taken as "givens" that are not inquired into.

We noted a crucial disjunction in both theories. After detailed, technical analyses of cinematic parts and *their* internal relations, both resort to literary discourse to treat formal organization of the whole film. Why narrative should emerge as the sole category of analysis at the level of the whole, when it has not been a category at all at lower levels, is not explained. Eisenstein and Bazin shift ground at this point. They turn to another problem as though it were the continuation of the first, as though treating a single problem from start to finish. They write as though visual parts added up to a narrative whole.

This is not Metz's critique. He criticizes classical film theory in passages here and there but never questions its foundations, fundamental assumptions, and problematic, a failure that has important consequences for his own theory. Nevertheless, Metz's argument promises at several points to overcome or to bypass the difficulties noted above. First of all, Metz's book seems to derive from those modern theoretical discourses that insist on the multiplicity of levels in any system or text and on the methodological necessity of specifying the level at which a particular analysis is working. Such insistence exposes the error of theories such as the classical film theories, whose one-level epistemological model treats complex objects either by excluding important aspects or by forcing them all within a single plane, as classical film theory did with narrative and visual form. Not only were these forged in a false relation but important aspects of the problem were excluded altogether: those of visual wholes and of narrative parts, among others.

Second, Metz refers several times to that large body of work on the structural analysis of the narrative that appeared in the 1960s (see *Communications,* no. 8 [1966]) and is called by some *narratology.* This work posits and takes for its object the system of narrative in general, regardless of the medium of its realization. It is treacherous to generalize about this work, as Vladimir Propp's analysis of narrative functions differs from Claude Lévi-Strauss's paradigmatic analysis of mythic narratives, A. J. Greimas's narrative grammar seeks to integrate and improve on both, etc. At the least, however, each is concerned with analyzing the relations between narrative parts and wholes within a system that generates both.

On each of these grounds, Metz's text seems to promise a reconstruction of classical film theory.

> There are therefore two distinct enterprises, neither of which can replace the other: On the one hand there is the semiotics of the narrative film, such as the one I am attempting to develop; on the other hand, there is the structural analysis of actual narrativity— that is to say, of the narrative taken *independently from the vehicles carrying it* (the film, the book, etc.). . . . Bremond [studies] . . . that very precise "layer of signification" that a narrative constitutes before the intervention of the narrative "props." I agree with this author as to the autonomy of the narrative layer itself:

> The *narrated event,* which is a signified in the semiotics of narra-
> tive vehicles (and notably of the cinema), becomes a signifier in
> the semiotics of narrativity. (pp. 144–145)

Note that Metz emphasizes here the separation and autonomy of
the levels and of their study. What is implied here is true of the
argument as a whole: Metz does not himself take up the analysis
of the narrative layer of the cinematic complex. He does not analyze
narrative wholes and parts and their relations. His work is to study
another layer of signification, that of cinematic expression. He introduces the structural analysis of narrative not for its own sake, but
to define his project in relation to it. It permits him to define his
object of study more precisely.

Thus Metz does not propose a model of filmic signification in
general, including identification and definition of constituent levels
and a plan of their interaction. Metz instead defines two levels, only
one of which he will address, and says nothing about their interaction. In doing this, he is attempting to define a level without a
model of the overall field. This is a fundamental theoretical failure,
for every designation of "a level" or "a layer" must presuppose some
model of the whole. Where the model is not explicitly and con-
sciously constructed by the text, it is implicit and unconscious. Of
course the latter condition creates confusions and ambiguities because fundamentals of the argument are swallowed and hidden.
More generally, the definition of an object of analysis without a
model defining the field in which this object is constituted commits
the complex of errors called empiricism, in which it is assumed that
the object exists prior to the analysis and therefore can be appre-
hended and analyzed directly. On the other hand, discourses such
as psychoanalysis and historical materialism stipulate that theory
must construct its object and the field that defines it. Exemplary here
is Freud's metapsychology, which organizes the multiple levels of its
object simultaneously from three standpoints, the topographical, the
economic, and the dynamic.

Despite his emphasis on the autonomy and separation of the two
layers, defining the narrative layer in order to specify the level of
expression, other passages in Metz suggest that the units of expression will be defined in relation to the narrative level.

> The reader will perhaps have observed in the course of this article
> (and especially in the definition of the different types of autono-
> mous segment) that it is no easy matter to decide whether the large

syntagmatic category in film involves the *cinema* or the cinematographic *narrative*. For all the units I have isolated are located *in* the film but in *relation* to the plot. This perpetual see-saw between the screen instance (which signifies) and the diegetic instance (which is signified) must be accepted and even erected into a methodological principle, for it, and only it, renders commutation possible, and thus identification of the units (in this case, the autonomous segments).

One will never be able to analyze film by speaking *directly* about the diegesis (as in some of the film societies, *cine clubs,* in France and elsewhere, where the discussion is centered around the plot and the human problems it implies), because that is equivalent to examining the signifieds without taking the signifiers into consideration. On the other hand, isolating the units without considering the diegesis *as a whole* (as in the "montage tables" of some of the theoreticians of the silent cinema) is to study the signifiers without the signifieds—since the nature of narrative film is to narrate.

The autonomous segments of film correspond to as many diegetic *elements,* but not to the "diegesis" itself. The latter is the *distant signified* of the film taken as a whole: Thus a certain film will be described as "the story of an unhappy love affair set against the background of provincial bourgeois French society toward the end of the nineteenth century," etc. The partial elements of the diegesis constitute, on the contrary, the *immediate signifieds* of each filmic segment. The immediate signified is linked to the segment itself by insoluble ties of semiological reciprocity, which form the basis of the principle of commutation. (pp. 143–144)

This zone of discrepancy requires investigation, an assertion of autonomy and separation and an assertion of relation and reciprocity. Also, if Metz defines the visual part in relation to the narrative part, then there might be an advance over classical film theory, which did not do this, even if Metz fails of those other relations: narrative whole/narrative part; visual whole/visual part; narrative whole/visual part; visual whole/narrative part, etc.

The issue arises first in chapter 2, "Notes Toward a Phenomenology of the Narrative." Metz refers to several theorists of narrativity but he does not discuss the differences in their models, let alone choose one as superior to the others or as most appropriate to the needs of his work.

Instead he seems to enlist narratology in general on behalf of his work. As in the passage quoted above, he seems to require only the idea of the narrative plane as autonomous layer in order to found his own study by differentiation. But, as he does not define this other by specifying the differences among narratological systems, his own system has an insecure foundation. To overcome this problem, he seeks more aggressively to reduce the divergent systems of narrative to a usable core. "Although several different methods have been proposed for structurally breaking down the narrated events (which do not initially constitute discrete units), the event is still and always the basic unit of the narrative" (p. 24).

Metz herein collapses the various systems into a single concept, that of the division of the narrative into "events." In fact, each system defines the units of narrative differently and none calls its basic unit the event. Even more important, Metz takes only the concept of unit identification and discards the other elements of the theories involved. Thus, each not only defines units but propounds a syntax (or syntagmatics) governing the combination of narrative units into larger units, as well as an overall model of the operation of the narrative system as a whole. Of course each system determines its own breakdown of units and syntagmas, which means, among other things, that the set of units and the rules governing their combination are strictly correlative. Thus to extract the unit designations of a narrative system without the syntagmatics and the overall model that go with them is meaningless. It indicates a fundamental misunderstanding of the nature of theory construction. As noted, Metz performs not only this extraction but also a reduction and assimilation of the decontexted unit designations into the general category of "the event."

Even Propp, the most empirical and syntagmatic of the group, whom Lévi-Strauss critiqued for ignoring the semantic dimension, is not at all the atomizing theorist that Metz is. Propp defined the basic units of the narrative as functions, each of which is designated by its relation to the "general economy of the tale." It is precisely this overall economic model of the whole that Metz's semiotics of the narrative film lacks. This is true not only of the narrative layer, which he does not take as object of his analysis, but of the expressive layer, which he does take. Metz attempts a syntagmatics of the part, determined empirically, that is, without reference to an overall theoretical model.

Metz provides a justification for his reductive seizure of concepts in chapter 2. This derives from his phenomenological theoretical base. Since the latter influences his argument decisively at several points, its operation here must be examined closely.

It is my intention in the following paragraphs not to advance still another model, but rather, to invite the reader to reflect on what has brought about all the attempts already presented. It seems to me, indeed, that the narrative lends itself to structural analysis because it is primarily, in some way, a real object, which even the naïve listener clearly recognizes and never confuses with what it is not. . . .

It might be said that the main interest of structural analysis is only in being able to find what was already there, of accounting with more precision for what naïve consciousness had "picked up" without analysis. . . .

Let us say, therefore—perhaps a little cavalierly—that structural analysis always assumes, by virtue of an implicit or explicit prior stage, something like a phenomenology of its subject, or, again, that *signification* (which is constructed and discontinuous) renders explicit what had been first experienced only as a perception (which is continuous and spontaneous). It is from this point of view that I would like to explore some answers to the question: How is a narrative recognized, prior to any analysis? (pp. 16–17)

The rest of the essay constructs this "narrative recognized, prior to any analysis." It is his phenomenological method, his appeal to experience, that permits Metz to bracket or to bypass the specifics of the different methods for breaking down narratives into units in favor of a generalized notion of event. The site of this notion, which Metz admits cannot be found in any narratological system, is apparently located in the general experience of viewers. In Metz's epistemology, the experiential, phenomenological order underlies, indeed *founds,* systems of narrative analysis, and all theoretical work. Hence it may be appealed to beyond the particular systems for a more general and more basic, a more originary truth. As he says toward the end of the essay, "My intention is simply to remind the reader that if the narrative can be structurally analyzed into a series of predications it is because phenomenally it is a series of events" (p. 26).

Instances of Metz's phenomenological method are too numerous to collect. Note that chapter 1 of the book, "On the Impression of Reality in the Cinema," is also phenomenological in its orientation. Chapters 1 and 2 form Part I of the book's four parts, called "Phenomenological Approaches to Film." They operate explicitly as one of the book's theoretical and methodological foundations. This fact is obscured, however, for several reasons: first, because most of the book that follows is cast as a search for a method, as a long, slow inquiry into linguistics, semiology, and structuralism, in order to determine principles for film analysis. The book's *own* method is often hidden beneath this overt search for a method. It is nevertheless operative, governing questions posed as well as answers produced. Second, after chapters 1 and 2, it is mostly an invisible text, easily dismissible as holdovers from Metz's early thinking and from the phenomenological period in France. But it is not separable from the book's principal positions. Its phenomenological assumptions operate unseen much of the time but also emerge at certain points into the text's surface. These tend to be textual stress points, at which resort to another level of discourse becomes imperative due to conflicts at the surface level.

Among other emergences is Metz's statement at the end of his long exploration of linguistics and semiology, just before he applies his method to a filmic text: *"The fact that must be understood is that films are understood"* (p. 145). And:

> [M]ovie *spectators* in turn constitute a group of users. That is why the semiotics of the cinema must frequently consider things from the point of view of the spectator rather than of the film-maker. (p. 101)
>
> [The cinema] uses only very few true signs. Some film images, which, through long previous use in speech, have been solidified so that they acquire stable and conventional meanings, become kinds of signs. But really vital films avoid them and are still understood. Therefore the nerve center of the semiological process lies elsewhere.
>
> The image is first and always an image. In its perceptual literalness it reproduces the signified spectacle whose signifier it is; and thus it becomes what it shows, to the extent that it does not have to *signify it* (if we take the word in the sense of *signum facere,* the special making of a sign). (pp. 75–76)

Thus the book does not make a journey from phenomenology to semiology in the course of its argument. The phenomenological text is always there. It founds the semiological inquiry or text by providing the base level of theorization on which that inquiry proceeds as well as determining the method of inquiry and the standard of judgment of its findings. Instead of a replacement, there is a continuity, which is phenomenology's definition of semiology: a set of tools for clarifying what is given in experience, for understanding experience. Semiology builds on and works with ordinary perception.

It permits us to formulate the structures of experience more precisely. It does so, however, only by virtue of that basis and by virtue of its continuity with and true relation to experience. Thus are asserted continuities on the one hand between experience and knowledge in general and between phenomenology and semiology as specific disciplines, that is, at both levels of world and of theory.

On the contrary, psychoanalysis and historical materialism require a break with ordinary experience in order to construct its concept, in order to construct a model of that system which produces ordinary experience either at the psychological or the political level. So, at the level of theory, materialism stipulates an epistemological break with phenomenology as the lattermost stage of empiricism, the large ideological complex of several centuries' duration in philosophy and in theory generally. Even a structuralist like Lévi-Strauss affirmed the necessity of such a break.

> Phenomenology I found unacceptable, in so far as it postulated a continuity between experience and reality. That the latter enveloped and explained the other I was quite willing to agree, but I had learnt from my three mistresses (Freud, Marx, Geology) that there is no continuity in the passage between the two and that to reach reality we must first repudiate experience, even though we may later reintegrate it in an objective synthesis in which sentimentality plays no part. As for the trend of thought which was to find fulfillment in existentialism, it seemed to me to be the exact opposite of true thought, by reason of its indulgent attitude towards the illusions of subjectivity. To promote private preoccupations to the rank of philosophical problems is dangerous, and may end in a kind of shop-girl's philosophy—excusable as an element in teaching procedure, but perilous in the extreme if it leads the philosopher to turn his back on his mission. That mission (he holds it only until science is strong enough to take over from philosophy) is to understand Being in relation to itself, and not in relation to oneself. Phenomenology and existentialism did not abolish metaphysics: they merely introduced new ways of finding alibis for metaphysics. (*Tristes Tropiques,* pp. 61–62)[6]

From the topographical standpoint, the narratological and the phenomenological are equally important systems or discourses in *Essais I.* But their operation in the text is neither equal nor parallel.

---

[6] Trans. John Russell as *A World on the Wane* (New York: Criterion Books, 1961).

Seen from the dynamic standpoint, these discourses exert pressure on each other (and others) throughout; this conflictual interaction produces different resolutions at particular points. In chapter 2, as we have seen, phenomenology rewrites narratology. This transformation seems determinative of the rest of the argument, at least in that an unreduced narratology never asserts itself subsequently. Two later sections on narrative, "A Non-System Language: Film Narrativity" (chap. 3, pp. 44–49) and "Cinema and Narrativity" (chap. 4, pp. 93–96), argue a point already discussed, the primacy of narrativity in film, experientially and historically.

A textual stress point at which all of the large discourses are operative is chapter 5, section 5, summarized in detail above, in which Metz presents the system of the *grande syntagmatique*. It is here that the discourses at work in the text as a whole are arranged and fixed in positions of dominance and subordination, within an overall theoretical conjunction. The first four paragraphs of the section, quoted above, are worth examining in detail, as are the numerous footnotes, parentheses, etc., which indicate a text under stress from within.

Paragraph 4 is particularly interesting. The parallel construction of its first sentence designates the double support of the system about to unfold: phenomenology ("one must start from common observation") and film theory ("as well as on certain 'presemiotic' analyses by critics, historians, and theoreticians of the cinema . . ."). Note the crucial operation of the phenomenological method here.

Common observation is thus to validate theoretical concepts; there is no need to retheorize them or to define them or to justify them theoretically. They are existents. They are real. They are located in the world. (Alain Badiou says that such a conception pretends to find inside of the real, a knowledge of which the real can only be the object. Supposedly, this knowledge is already there, just waiting to be revealed.[7]) Why one must rest on common observation is not stated. It is an imperative that requires/allows no questioning.

The other half of the imperative that launches Metz's system is important also: "as well as on certain 'presemiotic' analyses by critics, historians, and theoreticians of the cinema . . ." It is notable that in this inaugural sentence of the first semiotics of the cinema classical film theory, previously absent except in the form of particular opinions on particular points, makes such a prominent and

---

[7] Alain Badiou, "Le (Re)Commencement du matérialisme dialectique," *Critique*, no. 240 (1967).

surprising appearance. Conspicuously absent at the initiation is the structural analysis of the narrative, whether as a starting point for the semiotic analysis of filmic expression or as *a* reference point for that project or as a parallel inquiry or even as an ingredient to be included in the inquiry at its point of impact. This double marking, the absence of narratology and the sudden emergence of classical film theory—possibly the submerging or replacement of narrative analysis *by* classical film theory—determines the course and the limits of Metz's theoretical enterprise. It inscribes that project as a *combinatoire* of parts within larger parts, but cut off from any connection with the whole. The reliance on classical film theory rather than narrative analysis inscribes the entirety of Metz's own system within the problematic of the former rather than the latter, that is, locks it into a part-oriented, local analysis, cutting it off from that global systemic analysis which is needed.

It is easy to show that Metz's double theoretical foundation of phenomenology (continuity with ordinary experience and terminology) and classical film theory commands the concepts and execution of the *grande syntagmatique* and how they, in conjunction with the elimination of narratological analysis, determine the limitations and inadequacies of the latter. As noted, the *grande syntagmatique* says nothing about narrative parts and wholes and their relation, but it says nothing about the visual or image-track whole either. This level is not theorized as a whole, let alone related to other levels within an overall systematic model. Metz merely defines as untheorized givens, that is, empirical entities, a number of different kinds of segments. The taxonomy that results identifies certain patterns and gives various labels to these, but it says little or nothing about them, neither why these patterns exist nor what is important about them. Metz clearly does not know what to do with the regularities he finds at the segment level. He does not know how to interpret his own findings, so he says merely: these facts are *there*. He has produced some regularities, but he has no theoretical model to fit them into, so as to make use of them, interpret them, declare their importance. And, as there was no theoretical model that launched the inquiry, he cannot account for what led to the collection of these data in the first place. Empirical studies often exhibit this doubly isolated condition.

We asked at the outset whether *Essais I* broke with film theory and established a new semiological discourse.

It is evident that the *grande syntagmatique* does not differ fundamentally from classical film theory itself. Like Eisenstein and Bazin, Metz takes from ordinary experience or from previous discourse a basic unit—the shot—and defines several modes of its combination into the next larger unit, the sequence (which Metz calls the segment). In neither classical film theory nor Metz is there an overall model or economy of sequences within the whole. Like Eisenstein and Bazin also, he does not analyze narrative parts and wholes, nor the system of narrative and image-track relations. The difference is that narrativity theory permits Metz (or anyone now) to analyze the general economy of the narrative layer, including definition of units and part-whole relations. This theoretical work, unavailable to Eisenstein and Bazin, might also permit theorization of the image track, *its* parts and wholes and general economy, but Metz turns away from this possibility. In chapter 2 he eliminates the syntagmatic *and* general systemic dimensions of narrativity theory and also lumps its various and differential definitions of unit into the vague and boundaryless "event."

Given the limitation of Metz's semiotics to the level of the image-track sequence or segment, does it do something new or different here, in relation to classical film theory? Possibly there are two things it does differently. First, classical film theory only discussed ways of combining shots into sequences, that is, quasi-syntactic or rhetorical plans, strategies. It did not discuss or *name* or define the resulting or emergent units themselves. Thus we could say in "Two Types of Film Theory" that, strictly speaking, neither produced a theory of the sequence. Perhaps, with his taxonomy and conceptual distinctions among sequence types, Metz *does* achieve a theory of the sequence, even if an inadequate, falsely based one because empirical, lacking a model of the whole, etc. Second, and harder to determine precisely, Metz's *grande syntagmatique* has at least a narratological flavor, because it seems to deal, however inadequately, with the time-and-space relations signified by various shot groupings. This Eisenstein and Bazin did not do, attempting a purely formal definition of shot relations. This difference may be the theoretical basis for Metz's ability to produce a theory of the sequence and a plan of sequence types.

But even this operation is rather vague and somewhat suspect for several reasons. First of all, time-and-space relations are only one aspect of narrativity study. Other aspects, correlative with and determinative of time-and-space relations, such as actantiality, Metz excises. Also, again, it is doubtful that time-and-space organization can be theorized or studied adequately at the level of the segment alone. The narrative as a whole, both particular narrative texts and the system of narrativity that commands such texts, disposes of time-and-space relations in the narrative text as a whole. The time-and-space relations between and among sequences or segments themselves (not just within sequences among shots) Metz says nothing about; his model cannot deal with this level, which determines time-and-space orderings within each segment, even if in standardized ways along the lines that Metz's taxonomy suggests.

Second, the imprecision of Metz's one narratological concept of "event" merges with the imprecision of his phenomenological method to prevent any theoretical or systemic rigor, even in the *grande syntagmatique*. Thus, in section 11, quoted above, Metz speaks of the ambivalent locus of the GS categories in the film or in its narrative and of the "perpetual see-saw" between the screen instance that signifies and the diegetic instance that is signified. He says this must be accepted and even erected into a methodological principle (for it makes commutation possible). Given the initial vagueness of the narrative side of this seesaw, "the event," it is clear that nothing nearly as precise as linguistic commutation is achieved here. This vagueness and the seesaw instead permit Metz to define cinematic units as he pleases, often making up ad hoc principles of a narratological sort to differentiate units.

This is evident especially in chapters 6 and 7 where Metz applies his system to a film text, *Adieu Philippine* (1962) by Jacques Rozier. In addition to, and probably because of, its theoretical failings, Metz's *grande syntagmatique* proves to be quite troublesome in application. Any sort of experimentation in film, even narrative experimentation, creates an immediate gap, but there are also substantial problems even with conventional narrative. Critics in France have noted many discrepancies or misapplications in the *Adieu Philippine* reading. Indeed, Metz's own text raises a large number of doubtful cases, regarding which GS category applies to a segment, or even more fundamentally, *how* the borders of "a segment" are to be determined in a particular case—since Metz's phenomenological base assumes that segments are given, that is, that they come already identified in viewer experience of the film. As noted, he resolves these difficulties by appeals to various, utterly heterogeneous principles and criteria. Gödel's second theorem states that every system generates contradictions at its higher levels. Metz's system generates a number of conflicts even at its first level.

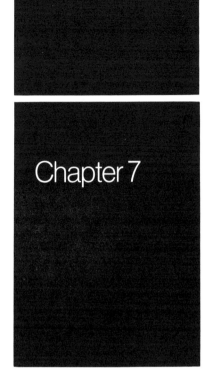

Chapter 7 Segmentation (1977)

The earth it selfe being round, every step wee make upon it, must necessarily bee a segment, an arch of a circle.

—*John Donne,* Sermon *lxvii*

In film studies as in other disciplines, old problems tend to reappear under new names. What are the basic units of film? How are they, or how should they be, combined in the filmic composition? These are perhaps the oldest, most frequently asked questions in film theory. Film semiotics has its own history within the larger history of film theory, though it has always presented itself as bypassing or supplanting earlier efforts. Since it first appeared in the early 1960s, film semiotics has undergone a complex evolution—in relation to the old problems of film theory as well as to the new ones it defined. In the present, at the (temporary) end of this history, we find textual semiotics. This is a new system and in it we find a new problem, one that faces every analyst of a filmic text: the problem of *segmentation*. It asks: How shall I divide up the filmic text in order to talk about it?

This essay concerns the problem of segmentation and its theoretical context. Its principal focus is the development and treatment of this concept within the texts of film semiotics. The relation of segmentation and the theories that support it to film theory is a large topic that will have to be pursued elsewhere. But concern with such relations is implicit in the inquiries undertaken here.

Any discussion of segmentation must include Roland Barthes, particularly his S/Z.[1] This study has had enormous impact on textual semiotics in many domains, including notably that of film. Thus the first questions to be raised are predictable. Can a segmentation scheme and set of prescriptions for the textual analysis of literature be used for film texts? Have those using the scheme and prescriptions made a theoretical bridge from the textual semiotics of literature to that of film? If so, what are its components and is it adequate? These questions catch others—some perhaps more interesting —in their nets. In any case, they serve to open up an area that has been virtually unexamined.

S/Z deals with many subjects besides segmentation, but this is our interest at the moment. Barthes seems to say that when it comes to segmentation, total permissiveness is the rule. The working convenience of the analyst governs. The analyst may divide up the text in any way conducive to the analysis. In any case, in the new textual semiotics, it no longer seems possible to prescribe or proscribe theoretically, that is, in advance of the *praxis* of reading, any system of segmentation. Barthes says:

> If we want to remain attentive to the plural of a text . . . we must renounce structuring this text in large masses, as was done by classical rhetoric and by secondary-school explication: no *construction* of the text: everything signifies ceaselessly and several times, but without being delegated to a great final ensemble, to an

[1] Roland Barthes, S/Z (1970), trans. Richard Miller (New York: Hill and Wang, 1974).

ultimate structure. Whence the idea, and so to speak the necessity, of a gradual analysis of a single text.

It is . . . to substitute for the simple representative model another model, whose very gradualness would guarantee what may be productive in the classic text; for the *step-by-step* method, through its very slowness and dispersion, avoids penetrating, reversing the tutor text, giving an internal image of it: it is never anything but the *decomposition* (in the cinematographic sense) of the work of reading: a *slow motion,* so to speak, neither wholly image nor wholly analysis.

We shall therefore star the text, separating, in the manner of a minor earthquake, the blocks of signification of which reading grasps only the smooth surface, imperceptibly soldered by the movement of sentences, the flowing discourse of narration, the "naturalness" of ordinary language. The tutor signifier will be cut up into a series of brief, contiguous fragments, which we shall call *lexias,* since they are units of reading. This cutting up, admittedly, will be arbitrary in the extreme; it will imply no methodological responsibility, since it will bear on the signifier, whereas the proposed analysis bears solely on the signified. The lexia will include sometimes a few words, sometimes several sentences; it will be a matter of convenience: it will suffice that the lexia be the best possible space in which we can observe meanings . . . (pp. 11–13)

What do Barthes's specifications mean for the textual analysis of film? What have they meant so far? What has happened in film textual analysis to date? When we move to film, the first fact we encounter is the overwhelming predominance of the Metzian *grande syntagmatique* (GS) in nearly all semiotic textual analyses thus far. Typically, the problem of segmenting the text is posed—usually by that name—at the beginning of the analysis. Almost without exception, the method of segmentation chosen and applied is that of the GS. One may say generally that any textual analysis in *Screen, Communications, Ca-Cinema,* or even occasional American journal issues on film such as *Sub-Stance* and *Film Reader,* will use the GS in whole or part, or explain why it is not used. (Certain of the latter passages read like apologies.) Since these are precisely the journals where textual analyses (in the post-structuralist, Barthesian sense) are most likely to appear, one soon discovers that the problem of segmentation in film analysis has in effect been settled, apparently by common agreement.

This de facto unanimity is odd, however. It has followed no theoretical debate on the matter—no editorials, manifestoes, or theoretical statements, setting forth, defending, deriving, or justifying the general line of GS segmentation. Hence it is a practice, or set of practices, without a theory. No one has shown that the GS can or should serve as a universal scheme of segmentation for film textual analysis. Nor can the demonstration be found in the writings of Metz, who has not considered the question. The question has not been raised by anyone. Most interesting of all, however, is that practice proceeds as though the question had been raised and definitively resolved, so that it need never be raised or even referred to again.

There is a logical paradox here that we should explore, as it might clarify our inquiry if we do and ensnare it if we do not. We may say that we have defined so far the posing of a question and the suggestion of an answer to that question. The question is What mode(s) of segmentation of films would be homologous to Barthes's segmentation mode in S/Z? (This question is posed against the background of a more general one: What would be a textual semiotics of film, homologous to Barthes's textual semiotics of literature in S/Z?) The answer: The GS, as presented by Christian Metz in *Essais sur la signification au cinéma* (*Essais I*), (1968),[2] and discussed in later works also. As noted, this answer is a practical one. It consists of the unanimous resort to the GS by textual analysts, a *fait accompli*. It seems to be regarded as such by its practitioners also, since its use has no need of theoretical elaboration or defense.

The armature of the paradox is that the GS premise is both an answer to a question and a question in itself. It is an answer to the question What segmentation mode? But this answering leads to the posing of a question at another logical level. What is the large syntagmatic arrangement of film in general or of a particular film? The fact that it is also a question allows it to lose its answer status, hence its dependency on another question or other logical level. When it loses its status as answer, the question that initially defined it disappears also. Attention is focused on the second question, as question, entirely. Thus the second question substitutes itself for the first and supplants it, even as it answers it. It eclipses the first, blocks it, and thereby prevents its being asked, raised, or even seen again.

Practically speaking, this has happened. Text analysts consider no other segmentation modes; nor do they ever relate the problem of segmentation to S/Z directly. They do not derive the method they use from Barthes's theory of textual analysis, or justify their opera-

---

[2] Trans. Michael Taylor as *Film Language: A Semiotics of the Cinema* (New York: Oxford University Press, 1974).

tion in its terms. The GS, as answer to the question, cuts off access to it. Under these conditions the answer ceases to be an answer to anything; it is self-standing. It proceeds on its own authority both as specific question and as unspoken set of assumptions that eliminates other questions and authorizes this one. Not only is the first question obliterated, so is the connection of the answer to it.

Arguably, this substitution effect is more important than the question of the merits/demerits of the GS as a mode of analysis; because it cuts off inquiry, experimentation, and research in an entire domain of intellectual work. This is a frequent phenomenon in scientific investigation, philosophy, and theoretical endeavor of various sorts. A wrong answer, an incomplete one, sometimes even a right one may effectively stop further investigation of a problem for a few years or centuries. Of course the situation is far worse where there is no reasoned defense of the solution, where it is buried in the solution itself. It is also worth noting that the imposition of one method of analysis—*any* method—opposes Barthesian pluralism.

What is the position of our analysis in relation to the problem of the two questions that might also be called the problem of the collapsed questions, as there is but one visible question in place of two? Our task is to liberate the first question, currently eclipsed and submerged. To liberate it means to expose it beneath the structure that obscures it, to permit it to be asked and answered. Once this is done, the question may be addressed and work may be done on it. We do not propose to address the first question in the present essay— enough to discern and expose it.

How to proceed? We shall promote liberation of the first question by analyzing and clarifying the second and its operation of substituting for the first. This will entail considering as many aspects of this question as possible. Besides examining the general facts that (1) the GS as general segmentation is unfounded, even unexplained; (2) that universal resort to the GS blocks consideration of other modes; and (3) the theoretical question, why *this* mode?; we are also concerned with the *operation* of the GS as general segmentation principle in textual analysis. The operational question is in two parts: (*a*) the theoretical specifications of the GS and how these have developed, and (*b*) the actual studies using the GS themselves. In the present essay, we shall consider the former, at some other time the latter. Both parts bear upon the second question, but work toward clarification of the relations between the second and the first, and thereby toward liberating the first.

There has been no discourse on the GS as general segmentation of texts, but there is a considerable literature on the GS. We shall examine the Metzian texts carefully, asking by what process of development the GS came to serve as general segmentation principle, a question both historical and theoretical. We shall look particularly at those concept structures that qualify it/disqualify it as general segmentation principle.

We shall proceed by returning to the original GS and noting subsequent changes and transformations in relation to it. The GS was proposed in *Essais I*. This is by far the fullest treatment of the GS, but we shall not dwell on it long since this book and the place of the GS in it have been the subject of much discussion. (See, among others,[3] "Metz: *Essais I* and Film Theory," *Film Quarterly* [Spring 1975].) In *Essais I*, Metz put the basic concepts of linguistics to work in analyzing cinema. His method derived closely from Roland Barthes's *Elements of Semiology* (1964),[4] though he no doubt went back often to his linguistics sources also. His initial and recurring method is to ask what is semiotic in cinema, that is, to search for a site on which semiotic analysis might begin, a precise object which it might address. (Possibly a paradox—Metz uses the semiotic tools of *Elements* to determine that site and then uses the same tools to investigate it.)

After discussions of many topics, he determines this site to be the syntagmatic type. The analogic diversity of film, the uniqueness of each image, cannot be the basis for a semiotics of cinema. Rather it is the manner in which these diverse images are combined in what Metz calls syntagmatic types, which constitutes the object for such a discipline. Thus the *grande syntagmatique,* a rather grand name for the eight syntagmatic types that Metz develops, is translated as "the large syntagmatic category of the image track." Metz sometimes suggests that the GS comprises what there is of language or system in cinema. At other times he suggests that it is just a code among others. Thus a crucial ambivalence about the GS begins in its first enunciation. Though later ambivalences are not necessarily reducible to this, they very often relate to it in some way.

It was perhaps the placing of the GS exposition at such a theoretic crossroads that promoted the sense of its primacy, even more than explicit indications of this in the text. Placed at the end of the

---

[3] See chapter 6, "Metz: *Essais I* and Film Theory."
[4] Trans. Annette Lavers and Colin Smith (New York: Hill and Wang, 1964, 1967).

first sustained inquiry into film semiotics, it is inevitably read as its result/consequence/justification. Such placement makes difficult effective argument that the GS is only one code among many. (Moreover, the exact nature of the primacy of the GS in *Essais I* and later is itself unclear and shifts depending upon the discussion involved. Is it the primary code, a base code, a/the central code or, as the overall cast of the argument suggests, "the semiotic mechanism" of cinema itself? Still other passages suggest it is one code among others.)

Language and Cinema (LC) (1971) [5] addresses the vacillation of *Essais I* on the status of the GS. LC acknowledges this vacillation (though it also vacillates on the vacillation, not to mention the acknowledgment).

> In our *Essais sur la signification au cinéma* (pp. 212–234), we studied a certain sub-code of montage, the large syntagmatic category . . . of the picture-track in the classical film narrative. It was said in various places (notably pp. 122 and 138) that this is only one cinematic code among others; however, in certain passages (p. 138+ *passim*), the importance of this code in relation to the ensemble of the cinematic material is clearly overestimated, and the idea that one could really be dealing, if not with the single code of the cinema, at least with a privileged and particularly central code, was not sufficiently avoided. This vacillation explains, and justifies in part, some of the criticism which has been levelled against us, and which nevertheless remains unfounded. One has especially reproached the study of the large syntagmatic category for not having mentioned certain cinematic elements whose importance is unquestioned . . . [These signifying configurations (such as sound, dialogues, visual point of view, etc.)] stem from other codes, the study of which, from the beginning, was excluded by the very definition which we gave the large syntagmatic category (p. 122). However, the expose did intrinsically lay itself open to these criticisms, to the extent that it failed to establish explicitly enough the pluricodical nature of the cinema, such that the only code (or rather sub-code) which, in the passage in question, was studied in detail tended to appear, from a somewhat hurried reading, as the only code of the cinema. (p. 189)

LC makes crystal clear that the GS is not a primary or privileged code, or a basic or fundamental one in any sense. It is merely one code among many, indeed a "subcode" of the code of montage. The

---

[5] Trans. Donna Jean Umiker-Sebeok (The Hague: Mouton, 1974).

vacillation concerns whether Metz contradicted this point earlier, failed to make it clearly enough, or what. This point need not concern us here. In itself it is rather unimportant, except that Metz's refusal to admit error or even change is symptomatic of his discourse throughout, and sometimes affects its structure.

LC defines the status of the GS unequivocally—it is one subcode among others, no more, no less. This settles the question as much as unmistakable prescription can. By this we mean that the question of the status and definition of the GS must now be pursued at a deeper level than that of explicit definition and proclamation. (Here we will reconnect with the problem of segmentation also.)

LC declares the GS to be merely one code among many, but the matter is not so simple as this. To see why, we must return to *Essais I* and *LC* and the relations between them. The GS was an attempt to divide up the filmic chain into successive "autonomous segments"—the GS of the picture track. An Italian semiotician, Emilio Garroni, criticized the GS on just this point in *Semiòtica ed estètica* (1968). Garroni's principal point concerns "the codical heterogeneity of the aesthetic object." Applied to cinema, this becomes "the codical heterogeneity of the cinematic language." On this basis, Garroni criticizes the very project of the GS—its division of the filmic chain into autonomous segments. For Garroni, the overall filmic message is a pluricodical text. If one splits this overall filmic message into smaller material branches (parts), one has not really analyzed it; for one obtains in the end segments that are just as completely heterogeneous but simply smaller in size.

Metz responds to this criticism of the GS with characteristic denial.

> This criticism would be valid only if our theory of the types of sequences (= autonomous segments) were presented as a tool for the *total* analysis of the filmic message: but, in our opinion, it constitutes only an attempt to elucidate *one* of the codes of the film, the one which organizes the most common spatio-temporal logic within the sequence. This logical combinatorics is only one of the systems which make up the "grammar" of the cinema (and thus *a fortiori* which instructs the total message of the film). Concerning the deliberately fragmentary nature of this attempt, the reader is referred to our discussions in . . . (*LC*, p. 189)

Immediately following this passage, Metz absorbs the substance of Garroni's critique into his own position, in this case the definition of the status of the GS.

Thus it is quite true that each of the autonomous segments recognized in a film remains a heterogeneous conglomerate *in other respects,* and constitutes an authentic unity only within a certain perspective, i.e., in the perspective of one of the formal models which may be—as we have said—constructed by abstraction from the concrete text: the autonomous segment is not a unit "of the film," but a unit of one of the systems of the film. Our attempt thus leads in the same direction as do Emilio Garroni's thoughts on the codical heterogeneity of the cinematic language. It would, moreover, be an unusual coincidence if the different systems of the film all gave rise to units, within the filmic chain, whose boundaries coincided exactly with their syntagmatic positioning: it is thus normal that the units of this particular code (= the autonomous segments) are not units for other filmic codes; but we have not said that they were. (p. 190)

Thus pluricodicity becomes one of the principal themes of *LC* generally. On this point, Metz cites Louis Hjelmslev (Danish linguist, 1899–1965) as well as Garroni. There are in fact more references to Hjelmslev in the book than to anyone else. Pluricodicity was a concept much discussed in the late 1960s and Hjelmslev was in vogue in semiotic circles (especially Parisian) then.

Metz goes on to denounce *all* attempts to devise or determine systems of basic units of the cinema. "[I]t is astonishing that, in so few years of research, so many minimal units have been proposed . . . each author thinking of a particular code or a particular group of codes, which he more or less clearly identified with the cinematic fact in its entirety" (p. 188).

All these propositions would be more interesting—and their coexistence would provoke less confusion—if, instead of being supposed to apply globally to the "cinema," they clearly focused on some particular, explicitly designated cinematic code (or group of cinematic codes). (*Ibid.*)

Though acknowledgment of previous ambiguity is uncertain, the standing of present theory is clear in *LC,* settled by unequivocal prescriptions. From the perspective of the present, these prescriptions of *LC* seem utterly incompatible with the GS as general segmentation principle. They implicitly prohibit any such usage (perhaps explicitly), but we know that the GS *is* used for general segmentation and that when it is, it does precisely divide up the entire filmic chain. We asked originally: How did it come about that the GS is used as segmentation principle in textual analyses? At this point we ask it again, with greater force, more urgency, and a sense of paradox, for there seems no reasonable path across these polar oppositions, neither in logic nor in experience.

We note two important factors, operative between 1971 and 1975 and after, working to undermine *LC*'s clarity about the place of the GS in the codic domain. Interestingly, each may be seen already at work in the text of *LC*, though the importance of each in film semiotics has grown with each passing year. One factor is the failure of film semiotics to produce any codic analyses besides that of the GS, and the implications of this. The other is the advent of textual semiotics until it not only predominated over the older, systems-oriented ones, but had virtually effaced them.

We recall that the GS is the only code analyzed in *Essais I*. Far more important: it is the only code analyzed in *all* of Metz's texts. This fact plus its placement in the discourse of the first book virtually insure a continuing reading that the GS is a or the primary code of cinema, if not itself equal to what is semiotic in cinema, despite explicit pronouncements to the contrary.

Metz's later books could not alter the initial placement of the GS discussion, though their own placements of GS discussions were quite different. But it *was* to be expected that they would alter its status as the only code of cinema analyzed by Metz. Not so. Metz's subsequent two books and many essays do not analyze any additional codes. A partial exception that proves the rule is a beginning analysis of filmic punctuation in *Essais II*,[6] which turns out to be a kind of footnote to the GS, concerning the ways in which the large syntagms are connected to each other in the filmic text.

This absence of new analyses tends strongly to hold the GS in the central place where most readers, despite occasional warnings, have always placed it. It is also in itself somewhat scandalous. Let us examine the point briefly, taking as focus the explanation of this absence in *LC*, the only place where it is mentioned.

Why have there been no other Metzian analyses of codes or subcodes? *Essais I* barely had space to do the GS, but what of *LC*? Called by Metz "a notional book," it is concerned with defining the fundamental notions and concepts of film semiotics. He says in the Conclusion, "The study of the cinema thus involves two great tasks: the analysis of the cinematic language system and the analysis of

---

[6] Christian Metz, *Essais sur la signification au cinéma,* vol. II (Paris: Klincksieck, 1972).

filmic writing" (p. 286). The analysis of the cinematic language system involves the study of cinematic codes and subcodes. Indeed the codes and subcodes that are cinematic constitute, as a block, the cinematic language system. The relations of these and other fundamental notions are elucidated in a passage in chapter 7, section 6 titled "The Systemic and the Textual."

> the semiotics of the filmic fact ought constantly to make use of three concepts which it can always use with ease. Having defined them, let us repeat them. They are:
> (1) filmic texts, which may present different degrees of material scope, the privileged one being the single and entire film (the notion of "film" in its distributive sense);
> (2) textual filmic systems, i.e., filmic systems which correspond to these different texts; and
> (3) non-textual filmic systems (codes), which themselves present different degrees of generality (the distinction between code and sub-codes), and which, according to the individual case, may be cinematic or extra-cinematic; those which are cinematic constitute, as a block, the "cinematic language system."
> We could thus summarize the task of the semiotics of the filmic fact as follows: to analyze film texts in order to discover either textual systems, cinematic codes, or sub-codes. (pp. 149–150)

LC certainly does seem to address "the analysis of the cinematic language system," but it does *not* enumerate, analyze, or even identify particular codes and subcodes, neither cinematic nor noncinematic, neither "as a block," nor individually. And yet the passage above defines the cinematic language system *as* the aggregate of cinematic codes and subcodes. As a consequence, either *LC* does not after all study the cinematic language system (CLS), hence does not pursue the task of the semiotic study of cinema or there are other ways to study the cinema than analyzing the CLS or other ways to study the CLS than by the study of cinematic codes and subcodes. Metz recognizes the problem, at least in part. This is his answer, also located in the four-page Conclusion:

> In regard to the first task itself, the reader will perhaps be surprised at not having found here an explicit enumeration of specific codes. This omission was intentional. First, because to study the *status* of a phenomenon (to define it intensionally) and to deploy its entire content (to define it extensionally) are two distinct steps and that, when the "phenomenon" is rather a constructed notion (as is the case for the cinematic language system),

> the detailed exposition of distinctiveness is what should take pride
> of place. Next, because cinematic studies are not yet developed
> enough, one is not able to seriously advance an explicit list of all
> the codes and sub-codes. It is, of course, possible, even desirable,
> to proceed already to a preliminary listing, to propose a beginning
> of an enumeration, even if incomplete and still approximate. But
> even this is a task which, in order to be useful, demands specifica-
> tions which would require a separate book. (p. 286)

Its status as the only code analyzed by film semiotics insures the
GS a continuing primacy and centrality. Given the battles waged
over it, and the unremitting defense of the GS by the Metzians,
there perhaps was pressure to use it in some way, to show that it
was useful, beyond the analysis for demonstration purposes done
by Metz on *Adieu Philippine* in *Essais I*. Both factors probably con-
tributed to the ascendancy of the GS as principle of general segmentation.

But there is another factor that made it theoretically possible for
the GS to rise to and occupy this ascendancy. This is the rise of
textual semiotics, to which we turn. (More specifically it is the rise
of textual semiotics in *relation* to the GS that we explore. The
theory of the text is "external" to the GS and its early history; but
when they interact, it plays upon and brings to the fore concepts and
doctrines "internal" to the GS. [On the latter, see "Metz: *Essais I*
and Film Theory."] Of course "internal" and "external" are constructs of the analysis, not of the texts under consideration, and
even at that level soon become indistinguishable.)

The older semiotics—of *Elements,* of Todorov's *Grammaire du
Decameron,* of Metz's *Essais I*—made system primary, in logic and
method, and text secondary. The text was the message or instance,
which was implicit or potential in the system and hence logically
subsumed by it. This congeries of methods (sometimes called
"structuralist") came to seem reductive in the late 1960s, as in
Barthes's remark that narratologists seeking the single model of narrative were like monks attempting to see the world in a bean.

One avenue of break from the model derived from a refinement
of it—the notion of a multiplicity of systems and codes at work in
a particular message or text. As these could not all operate in a
frictionless way, interaction involved the possibility of transformation. Once even this much was admitted, a shift of focus from system to text had begun. It came to be seen that it was this transformation process itself which was truly interesting and the most truly

semiotic. The textual process—destroying, creating, transforming—was itself the center, if there was any; systems and codes were secondary, peripheral, abstract—the mere materials on which textual process worked. The latter alone was concrete. Kristeva, Derrida, and others formulated theoretical models of textual process.

LC is perhaps the highpoint of Metz's classical semiotics work—sharply distinguishing code/message, system/language, etc. Nevertheless, several elements, theories, terms, formulations, *parti pris* of the new textual semiotics begin to operate importantly in *LC*. This does not make for "consistency"—the book threatens to come apart, both at the level of chapters and within particular chapters. Thus the book's conclusion is called "Cinematic Language System and Filmic Writing." Its four pages suggest retrospectively what the goals of the book have been, but also signal the book's systems versus text semiotics tension.

> The study of the cinema thus involves two great tasks: the analysis of the cinematic language system and the analysis of filmic writing. This book, as its title indicates, dealt essentially with the first of these. If the second was discussed, it was in order to try to define its connections (and its differences in distinctiveness) with the first, in order to *situate* them in relation to one another. (p. 286)

Chapter 5, "From Code to System; Message to Text," chapter 6, "Textual Systems," and chapter 7, "Textuality and 'Singularity,'" are devoted to filmic writing and indeed seem different from the other chapters, devoted to the cinematic language system, as though written later. There is no attempt to address the differences between the two groups of chapters, or to bridge the differences between them.

The well-known (re)definition of film semiotics of pages 149–150 (quoted above) attempts to strike a balance between the demands of systemic and textual semiotics. It is still mainly systemic, attempting to acknowledge the text but projecting it as the non-transformative combination of clear and knowable codes.

Later work by Metz will shift this balance decisively in favor of text, and transform the model of their comparison. *Essais II* has little concern with the question of text, principally perhaps because nearly all of it was written before *LC*, though it appeared the year later (1972). But there is reference to text, indeed it is the only reference to his previous work, in "The Imaginary Signifier" (1975). Metz here rejects his former concept of *a* textual system in favor of multiple textual systems; or, as he puts it alternately, "the indefinite textual system as I now see it . . . this perpetual possibility of a finer, or else less apparent structuration . . . of the registration of a new *significatory pressure* which does not annul the preceding ones (as in the unconscious where everything is accumulated) . . ."[7]

The increasing emphasis on the filmic text has entailed as one important consequence the loosening of the firm outlines of codes and of their differentiation from each other, established by LC. In the latter we have codes "interacting" with each other. Later, including other parts of LC, we have codes transforming each other in the textual process; and still later, talk of "significatory pressures" (based, it seems, on the Freudian theory of drives and their representations). Perhaps at this point, the notion of code itself recedes or disappears.

It is against this background that the GS becomes less and less a code among other codes, for codes themselves tend to recede and the borders between codes to disappear. But its original function as division of the filmic chain remains and, like a long-repressed chamber of the unconscious, rises to the surface when there is no longer any force to oppose it.

The theoretical operator that triggers this final ascendancy is a fundamental principle of the new semiotic constellation—the freedom of the analyst in choosing an analytic procedure, including a segmentation mode. The mantles of various prescriptions were off; one could do what one wanted. So why not use the GS—familiar to all from early days, even a kind of habit. And, while we're at it, why not the earlier GS, understood to divide the entire text-message—choosing one's reading of a method was part of the new freedom also. Under "analyst's free choice," the old constraints on the GS division of the message no longer applied. The GS had come full circle, or rather moved in a spiral, for it had arrived not where it had been but at a new place, in some ways parallel to it.

A question we have not examined carefully is whether use of the GS as general segmentation of the filmic text necessarily implies a division of the message in Garroni's sense? Can it be read as a division for purposes of the analysis only, which implies no judgment concerning the filmic message as a whole? It merely divides up the text in an arbitrary way in order to be able to talk about it.

The substance of our argument has been that the GS is *not* an arbitrary system of division, that it is heavily determined by a number of assumptions about the filmic message as such, despite dis-

---

[7] *Screen* (Summer 1975), p. 35.

claimers and occasional declarations to the contrary. Also, the notion of segmentation or the practice of segmentation, or both, implies a virtual segmentation of the message, even if theoretically nonbinding on later work. At the least it works *as though* it segmented the message, both in its own operation and for those stages of the analysis that follow segmentation.

Proof: the GS cannot be itself a codic analysis, because it is the division on which the codic analyses will operate. This is why segmentation is always and must be the *first* step of a textual analysis. It proposes that division of the material upon which the analysis proper will operate. On the contrary, Barthes's segmentation cuts out a piece *as it goes,* in order to watch the codes pass and intertwine through, around, in relation to it. Barthes's segmentation is a dividing of the text, but this dividing has no standing other than convenience. Another reading, another reader, another historical epoch, another social formation—each will involve a different segmenting. GS segmentation, on the other hand, is always the same for a given message; this is how the GS was originally defined and there has been no redefinition, in theory or practice. No one has considered or proposed that the GS might be something different from before in its general segmentation phase. At least the GS originally aspired to such repeatability, objectivity, universality and is still defined so. How could the GS segmentation of one film hold good for all subsequent analyses of it unless it operated on the message itself rather than as an extension of this text analysis only?

This is inevitable where an a priori scheme is involved; it is the meaning of a priori. The level of generality at which general segmentation must operate and the uniformity and nonadaptability of the GS concept itself—when combined with the installation of the GS as general segmentation principle—perhaps make it what it never was before, even in *Essais I,* an a priori scheme for the division of the filmic message in the abstract and therefore of all particular filmic messages.

This question and various others we have pursued lead us to consideration of the GS-based textual analyses themselves. Many further questions of interest can be dealt with only on that ground. But this takes us beyond the present piece. For now, we shall make a few summary points concerning what we have done here.

The advent of textual semiotics has been the principal factor in enthroning the GS as a scheme of general segmentation. Needless to say, this occurred in the special situation of film semiotics, film theory, the GS, their particular concept structures, etc. It is not inherent in, or a general result of, textual semiotics itself. It is useful to trace the interactions between this advent and the GS stage by stage in very close detail—a study we have only sketched.

The use of the GS as general segmentation is not authorized by any Metz text. Yet the users of the GS write as though its use in this way was clearly authorized and well understood. In fact, as general segmentation, it is a method without a theory. Resting in principle on the preference of the analyst, each of the latter defers to it as to authority. Conclusion: the text analysts use a tool they do not understand for reasons they know not why. In a partial sense at least, they do not know what they are doing.

The use of the GS reflects its complex history including those theoretical disputes carried on in its name. Textual analysis cannot claim to be free of these conflicts but must deal with them.

The use of the GS as general segmentation is not the segmentation discussed by Barthes. Even in his strictures of permissiveness, there are restraints and specifications. Resort to a priori codical analysis such as the GS is not what Barthes's discussion indicates. The analyst has freedom, but also responsibility for the method(s) used, their appropriateness to the task, etc.

It might be argued that the analyst's choice is real, but by habit and familiarity, the analyst chooses the GS. It is, in any case, the only scheme around. But habit and convenience are matters of history and culture, not of nature. Habit must be questioned, interrogated, justified. Also, resort to "habit" may result in a logical shifting of levels, hence in the transformation of apparently constant objects. This occurs when an old habit is put to work on a new problem. Such a case is that of a scheme of codical analysis, familiar also from theoretical dispute, resorted to by habit for the division of the whole film.

Chapter 8

Film Semiotics as Semiotics

"Metz: *Essais I* and Film Theory" finds that film semiotics does not dismiss film theory, as it claims to do; it absorbs its core and presents it in new guise. Precisely what is the nature of this guise and precisely how it is arrived at are the questions of "Film Semiotics as Semiotics."

"Metz: *Essais I* and Film Theory" tells us that film semiotics does not supplant film theory and hence sends us back to our film-theoretical investigations. But these findings are themselves puzzling and disturbing, the more so when we consider that Metz does not just use a semiotic vocabulary to state his findings—he goes through an elaborate semiotic argument, stage by stage, in arriving at them. Our question then is *how* does Metz use semiotic methods to arrive at film-theoretical results? The only possible answers seem to be either that we have mistaken the nature of those results, that is, they are truly semiotic; or that Metz has not used, or has misused, the semiotic method.

Answering our question means probing once again the relations between film semiotics and film theory, this time from the semiotic side. "Film Semiotics as Semiotics" evaluates Metz's semiotic analysis *as* semiotics. It begins with the principles of the method Metz uses, set forth in Barthes's *Elements of Semiology,* and uses them to evaluate Metz's argument stage by stage. It asks whether that argument reaches its results, notably the analysis of the *grande syntagmatique,* as it claims to do, on the power of the semiotic method. It finds that it does not, that it covertly introduces other concepts, assumptions, propositions, and positions along the way, and that these are the concepts, assumptions, propositions, and positions of film theory. It then studies the interactions of the two discourses in great detail. It asks whether those interactions may not, after all, produce something new and, if so, precisely what that is. Is it simply the analysis of film theory put into semiotic vocabulary? How can that be simple? Is it rather an amalgam of some kind, a mutation of film theory by the transformer of semiotic method?

Barthes's *Elements of Semiology* [1] is the guidebook for all of Metz's books, but most particularly, and most literally, the first. It is the closest thing to the codebook for *Essais I.* This means that we may use it not only to understand the book but to evaluate its argument: to critique it.

The sole aim of *Elements* is to extract from linguistics analytical concepts that Barthes thinks a priori to be sufficiently general to start semiological research on its way. He does not expect that these will remain intact during the course of research or that semiology will always be forced to follow the linguistic model closely. *Elements* seeks only to furnish a principle of classification of the questions. "These elements of semiology will therefore be grouped under four main headings borrowed from structural linguistics:

I.   Language and Speech
II. Signified and Signifier

---

[1] Roland Barthes, *Elements of Semiology,* trans. Annette Lavers and Colin Smith (New York: Hill and Wang, 1964, 1967).

III. Syntagm and System
IV. Denotation and Connotation"

Essais I and *Langage et cinéma* are explicitly organized in relation to these concepts, often by chapter title. They are almost equally pervasive in *Essais II,* though somewhat less so in "The Imaginary Signifier."

Barthes notes that there could not possibly be a linguistics of speech, since any speech, as soon as it is grasped as a process of communication, is *already* part of the language: the latter only can be the object of a science. Thus speech must always be studied before language (the opposite is impossible); on the other hand, one *can* study speech immediately only inasmuch is it reflects the language. "It is just as useless to wonder *at the outset* how to separate the language from speech: this is no preliminary operation, but on the contrary the very essence of linguistic and later semiological investigation: to separate the language from speech means *ipso facto* constituting the problematics of the meaning" (pp. 16–17). Of course the relation between the language and speech will be different in different semiotic systems. Indeed the semiological extension of the language/speech notion itself brings with it some problems, which coincide with the points where the linguistic model can no longer be followed and must be altered.

The semiological sign, and therefore the relation between signifier and signified, differs from the linguistic sign in (at least) two fundamental respects. First, only language is doubly articulated. Among linguistic signs, there are significant units, each endowed with one meaning and which form the first articulation (= words or monemes); and there are *distinctive units,* which are part of the form but do not have a direct meaning, and which constitute the second articulation (= the sounds or phonemes). The second point concerns the relation between signifier and signified, specifically the signifier's (material) mediation of the signified. This relation may be *arbitrary,* as in language, or *motivated,* as in some semiotic systems. A sign is motivated when the relation between its signified and signifier is *analogical.* (Of course the problem of analogy in cinema is a fundamental one in film-theoretical texts, including all of Metz's. See below.)

The relationships between linguistic or semiotic terms can develop on two planes, each of which generates its own particular values. The first is that of the *syntagms:* the syntagm is a combination of signs, which has space as a support. This space is linear and irreversible, each term here derives its value from its opposition to what precedes and what follows. The second plane is that of the *paradigms.* Besides the discourse (syntagmatic plane), the units which have something in common are associated in memory and thus form groups within which various relationships can be found. Each group forms a potential mnemonic series, the terms of each are united in absentia. The two planes are united by a close relation: each linguistic or semiotic unit in a discourse may be located along both. The syntagm cannot progress except by calling successively on new units taken from the paradigmatic plane. The paradigmatic plane has a very close connection with the language as a system, while the syntagm is nearer to speech. What is true at the level of basic units is also true at the level of discourse: there will be discourses of the metaphorical (paradigmatic) and of the metonymic (syntagmatic) types. Neither type implies the exclusive use of one of the two models—*both* syntagm and paradigm are necessary to all discourse—but only implies the dominance of one of them. In the metaphoric order, associations by substitution predominate, in the metonymic order, syntagmatic associations predominate.

The main part of semiological analysis consists in distributing the facts that have been listed on each of these axes. It is logical to begin the work with the syntagmatic division, as this is the operation that supplies the units that must be classified in paradigms; however, when confronted with an unknown system, it may be more convenient to start from a few paradigmatic elements empirically obtained and to study the system before the syntagm. The logical order, however, goes from the syntagm to the system.

The syntagm presents itself in the form of a chain, it is continuous, yet it cannot be the vehicle of a meaning unless it is articulated (meaning can arise only from an articulation, that is, a simultaneous division of the signifying layer and the signified mass). Thus the problem that arises again with every system of signs: How shall we divide the syntagm? Iconic syntagms, founded on a more or less analogical representation of a real scene, are infinitely more difficult to divide. In spite of these difficulties, the division of the syntagm is a fundamental operation, as it must yield the paradigmatic units of the system. It is in the very definition of the syntagm to be made of a substance that must be carved up. How can one spot in this text without end the significant units, that is, the limits of the signs that constitute it?

In linguistics this is done by the commutation test. This consists of artificially introducing a change in the plane of expression (signifiers) and in observing whether this change brings about a corresponding modification on the plane of content (signifieds). This is to create an artificial homology, that is, a double paradigm, at one point of the text, in order to check whether the reciprocal substitution of two signifiers has as consequence the reciprocal substitution of two signifieds. If the commutation of two signifiers produces a commutation of the signifieds, one is sure of having got hold (in the fragment of syntagm submitted to the test) of a syntagmatic unit. This operation can be conducted reciprocally by starting from the signifieds; but the commutation is usually applied first to the plane of the signifiers, as it is the syntagm that has to be divided. One can resort to the signifieds, but this remains purely formal; the signified is not called upon for its own sake, by virtue of its substance, but merely as an index of the signifier: it *places* the signifier, that is all. In the ordinary commutation test, one calls into use the form of the signified (its oppositional value in relation to other signifieds), not its substance.

The commutation test supplies significant units, that is, fragments of syntagms endowed with a necessary sense. These also must be already systematic units (even though they are not yet classified), because each one of them is part of a potential paradigm. (In linguistics only, by virtue of double articulation, a second commutation test is then performed, yielding the distinctive units [phonemes]. These units have no meaning in themselves, but play their part in the production of meaning, because the commutation of one of them changes the moneme it is part of.) In semiology, it is impossible to guess in advance the syntagmatic units that analysis will discover for each system.

Barthes deals with connotation (in *Elements*) as a staggered system, following his earlier analysis in *Mythologies:* [2] where a system of signification (plane of expression, plane of content, and a relation between the two planes) becomes the plane of expression or signifier of the second system, the first system is the plane of denotation and the second system the plane of connotation. A connoted system is a system whose plane of expression is itself constituted by a signifying system. Barthes notes that the units of the connoted system do not necessarily have the same size as those of the de-

---

[2] Roland Barthes, *Mythologies* (1957), trans. Annette Lavers (New York: Hill and Wang, 1972).

noted system: large fragments of the denoted discourse can constitute a single unit of the connoted system.

Thus, in very broad summary, the tasks and procedures of a
semiotic analysis are these: The goal is to separate language from
speech. The first operation is the analysis of the sign or discourse
into signifier and signified elements (or planes). This makes possible the commutation test, which alone can determine units and
hence permit division of the syntagm. Once the syntagm is divided
and the units are determined, the resulting units are classified into
paradigms. They can then be distributed along two axes. This in
turn makes possible a definition of language and speech: the paradigms and their interrelation correspond to language, so also does
the syntagmatic form of utterances, the combinative constraints. But
the latter two also define the speech function as the combinatory
act, governed by constraints as well as by freedoms, that results in
syntagms.

Metz's position on the problem of analogy is fundamental to his
overall argument. In "Metz: *Essais I* and Film Theory" we specified
Metz's position that cinema and the cinematic sign are basically and
inherently analogic in nature. Each image is unique *because* it
reproduces some object or view of the world directly. That is, it does
not encode the world, as language does, by translating it into some
system other than its own: The diversity of images in cinema is the
world's diversity. Metz's subscription to the theory of analogy in
cinema and in photographic *duplication* more generally founds his
theory of filmic discourse. Speaking of Méliès, Porter, Griffith, the
pioneers of "cinematographic language," he says: "Men of denotation rather than of connotation, they wanted above all to tell a story;
they were not content unless they could subject the continuous,
analogical material of photographic duplication to the *articulations*
—however rudimentary—of a narrative discourse." [3]

Metz's position on analogy is clear, simple, unequivocal, and
indeed well known. It remains the same for all of *Essais I* and indeed for all the rest of Metz's work. It is virtually the same as C. S.
Peirce's definition of iconic signs. (Analogic signs and iconic signs
are virtually identical notions.) Peirce defines the icon as a sign
that "may represent its object mainly by its similarity," or as "a sign
which refers to the object it denotes merely by virtue of characters

---

[3] Christian Metz, *Film Language: A Semiotics of the Cinema*, trans. Michael
Taylor (New York: Oxford University Press, 1974), p. 95.

of its own." [4] Charles Morris's definition of the iconic sign in *Signs, Language and Behaviour* is essentially the same. "An iconic sign . . . is any sign which is similar in some respects to what it denotes." [5] Iconicity is thus a matter of degree.

We must however distinguish Metz's position on analogy, a particular doctrine that may be summed up statically, from his use of that doctrine in his overall argument. The former is static, it may be defined statically and exhaustively. The latter is a dynamic process, it can only be defined dynamically—"in action." Metz's position on analogy is not difficult to state. It is far more difficult to determine how the doctrine of analogy functions in Metz's argument as a whole, and how it functions differently at different stages and at different levels of that argument.

We note first that the question of analogy is closely bound up in Metz's work with the question of the possibility of a semiotic analysis of cinema, and the questions how, where, and precisely on what is that analysis to operate. Applied literally, across the boards, the doctrine of cinema as analogy precludes the possibility of a semiotics of cinema.[6] It is chapter 3, "The Cinema: Language or Language System?," that most fully considers the implications of cinematic analogy for semiotic analysis. Surprisingly, most of chapter 3 is quite pessimistic about the possibility of a semiotic analysis of cinema. A late passage sums up the main theme of chapter 3: "It is true that, for an actual semiotics of cinema, analogy serves as a kind of stopping block: Whenever analogy takes over filmic signification (that is, notably the meaning of each visual element taken separately), there is a lack of specifically cinematographic codification" (*Film Language,* pp. 110–111).

---

[4] *Collected Papers of Charles Sanders Peirce,* ed. Charles Hartshorne and Paul Weiss, 6 vols. (Cambridge: Harvard University Press, 1931–1958), bk. 2, pp. 276, 247.

[5] In *Writings on the General Theory of Signs* (The Hague, Mouton, 1971), p. 273. For an opposing view see Umberto Eco, "Introduction to a Semiotics of Iconic Signs," *VS,* 2 (January–April 1972), pp. 1–15.

[6] Of course to say that the cinematic sign is an analogic sign is itself a semiotic analysis. But it is an analysis of the taxonomic sort—it consists in making a classification according to a scheme, applying the right generic name to the object in question. It is a one-stage analysis. It is not an analysis of the *Elements* sort, an analytic procedure of several stages addressing "the problematics of meaning" in a given system. Though analogy is itself a semiotic notion and the analysis that pronounces it is necessarily a semiotic analysis, it is a terminal operation, which does not constitute the problematics of the meaning of, or otherwise address, the semiotic *system* involved.

Chapter 3 considers whether the categories of linguistics, which are also the categories of semiotics, may be applied to cinema; or, more precisely, which may be applied and which not and in exactly which ways. In section after section of chapter 3 Metz uses the concept of cinematic analogy to defeat in advance every stage of an *Elements* analysis. Because of cinematic analogy, it is impossible to distinguish firmly between signifier and signified, denotation and connotation, paradigm and syntagm, and more generally, between signification and expression, and communication system and art.

Metz's argument is as follows: In the cinema every signifier has its analogic signified (and vice versa). Thus one cannot break up the signifier without getting isomorphic segments of the signified; in effect this means that there can be no distinction between signified and signifier, no division of the syntagm to determine basic units, no distribution of units along syntagmatic and paradigmatic axes, hence no constitution of the problematics of meaning. This line of reasoning explicitly rules out the possibility of an *Elements* analysis of cinema. Metz nevertheless proceeds with his general comparison between language and cinema. He finds that the image corresponds to one or more sentences (spoken not written), the sequence to a complex segment of discourse. At the same time, the image is "always actualized," that is, it has no paradigmatic dimension, it exists only *in praesentia*. Put another way, every image is a *hapax*. The poverty of the paradigmatic resources of cinema is contrasted by Metz to the richness of its possible syntagmatic arrangements, however. Whereas literature is an art of heterogeneous connotation (expressive connotation added to nonexpressive denotation), the cinema is an art of homogeneous connotation (expressive connotation added to expressive denotation). Thus cinema can never be purely aesthetic—it is always also representational; and it can never be purely denotative—it is always also connotative.

This generalized comparison between language and cinema does not overcome cinema's analogism or the consequences of the latter for semiotic analysis. Rather it develops certain aspects of that analogism.

Thus it is not surprising that in the last two sections of chapter 3 (pp. 84–91) Metz seems to be at the end of his semiotic rope. Using the tools of Barthes's *Elements* (and the Saussurean linguistics behind it), he has painted himself into a corner. In the last pages of the chapter Metz resorts to desperate measures by considering several alternatives to the Saussure-Barthes tradition. Having come this far with Saussure-Barthes and getting nowhere, he seems now to consider abandoning that line of analysis entirely to try other modes of analysis. In these few pages Metz proposes several other models for the analysis of cinema—the linguistics of the sentence (p. 89), the linguistics of speech (p. 84), the "linguistics" of discourse (p. 89), and the analysis of types of speech (p. 90). None of these methods is pursued, in this chapter or later. They are invoked as though to keep the "filmolinguistic" venture alive at the moment of its imminent doom.

Just before the end of the chapter Metz considers giving up the project.

> One can of course conclude that the cinema is not a language, or that it is so only in a sense that is altogether too figurative, and, consequently, it should not be dealt with through semiotics. (p. 89)

This is only two pages from the end of the chapter, and its concluding line: "The time has come for a semiotics of the cinema" (p. 91). How does Metz effect this dramatic reversal? The intervening two pages adduce *no* new points or arguments, *no* inversions or reinterpretations of points and arguments already made. Metz turns the tide by sheer will, by a burst of Emersonian resolve when adversity is the strongest and prospects for success the dimmest.

> But this is a very negative point of view, particularly in the case of a social fact as important as the cinema. The result of this attitude would be that one would study traffic signals because they have a very obvious paradigmatic structure, while paying no attention to a means of expression that after all carries a little more human weight than roadside signs! (p. 89)

Two more pages discuss film theory and filmology as important components of any semiotics of the cinema, but do nothing to lift the pall of impossibility with which the previous discussion has shrouded that project. The last paragraph of the essay is a final burst of resolve, an act of faith beyond reason.

> De Saussure did not live long enough to remark on the importance the cinema has assumed in our world. No one disputes this importance. The time has come for a semiotics of the cinema. (p. 91)

Of course this is rhetoric not argument. The remark about Saussure is either a truism or a suggestion that a break with Saussurean method is necessary to deal with cinema. In an earlier passage Metz does suggest such heresy but he follows it with statements so contradictory that the passage makes no clear point at all.

> Naturally, anything that even approximately resembles a *linguistics of speech* is a departure, it would seem, from the thought of the Genevan scholar. The objection had to be pointed out. It is, however, not insurmountable, and it would be to respect the great linguist very narrowly indeed if one were to block all innovative research under the pretext that one could not risk even grazing a study of speech. And I say: *grazing*. For it often happens in the study of nonverbal means of communication that the actual nature of the material under consideration causes one to resort to a "linguistics" that is neither that of language nor that of speech, but rather is one of *discourse* in Émile Benveniste's sense. . . . Between words—pure "sign events" as they are called in American semiotics, events that never occur twice and cannot give rise to a scientific study—and language (human language, or the more systematic and formalized language of machines), which is an organized, coherent instance, there is room for the study of "sign designs," sentence patterns, transphrastic organizations, "writings" in the Barthesian sense, etc.—in short, *types of speech.* (pp. 89–90)

Precisely what these suggestions mean and why Metz places them here are unclear. In any case they remain suggestions only—for Metz does not develop any of these possibilities in later discussions. This in effect nullifies them, for they are at most threads to be developed in detail later if they are to have impact on the overall argument. If they are not this, they are nothing.

Since chapter 3 virtually admits that an *Elements* analysis of cinema is impossible, chapter 4 must confront the problem and deal with it successfully if the inquiry is to continue. The challenge faced by chapter 4 is to restore, or rather to establish for the first time, the applicability of Barthesian semiotics to cinema; or, on the other hand, to develop another analytic method, semiotic or other, for dealing with it. From the hints dropped in the last few pages of chapter 3, the reader expects that another method will be developed, derived from other sources and proceeding in other directions than the Saussurean-Barthesian principles of *Elements*.

In fact chapter 4 does not mention chapter 3, neither does it address the overall finding of chapter 3 that cinema is analogic and therefore that Barthesian semiotics does not apply. Astonishingly, chapter 4 starts in *all over again* to consider the relations between cinema and language—as though the problem had not already been treated at length by chapter 3. This new treatment is quite different from the earlier one—in conclusion, mode of procedure, and tone. Notably missing in chapter 4 are (1) the pessimism about the possibility of a semiotics of cinema and (2) the hinted apostasy from the Saussurean-Barthesian semiotics of chapter 3. Among other things, chapter 4 is a sustained, uncritical reaffirmation of orthodox semiotic method. Indeed, as it does not mention the doubts of chapter 3, it is simply an *affirmation* of classical semiotics, for no shadow, counter-argument, or possible deficiency of application to cinema is ever admitted, hence none needs to be overcome.

If chapter 4 does respond to the issues underlying chapter 3, it is obliquely and indirectly, by proceeding in different ways and in a different direction. Chapter 3 poses a choice: show that cinema is *not* analogic in nature *or,* if it is analogic, resort to non-Saussurean linguistics and non-Barthesian semiotics in analyzing it. Chapter 4 takes neither option—in effect it rejects the choice itself and the analysis that poses it. It never denies cinema's pervasive, dominant analogism; it argues that there are linguistic dimensions, operations, and aspects at other levels than the analogic. These comprise an object or site that Saussurean-Barthesian semiotics may analyze.

Chapter 4 is called "Some Points in the Semiotics of the Cinema." Its purpose is

> to examine some of the problems and difficulties confronting the person who wants to begin undertaking, in the field of "cinematographic language," de Saussure's project of a general semiotics: to study the orderings and functionings of the main signifying units used in the filmic message. (p. 92)

The entire chapter is structured around the term "cinematographic language," specifically whether use of the term is justified. This is the central question of chapter 3, though posed and treated differently, for if the term "cinematographic language" is justified, then Saussurean-Barthesian semiotics applies; if not, then not. The introductory section of chapter 4 concludes with a passage that makes this explicit.

> The very term "cinematographic *language*" already poses the whole problem of the semiotics of film. It would require a long justification, and strictly speaking it should be used only after the in-depth study of the semiological mechanisms at work in the filmic message had been fairly well advanced. Convenience, however, makes us retain, right from the start, that frozen syntagma—

"language"—which has gradually assumed a place in the special vocabulary of film theoreticians and aestheticians. Even from a strictly semiological point of view, one can perhaps at this time give a preliminary justification for the expression "cinematographic language" (not to be confused with "cinematographic *langue*" (language system), which does not seem to me acceptable)—a justification that, in the present state of semiological investigations, can only be very general. I hope to outline it in this essay and especially on the next-to-last page. (pp. 92–93)

Exactly what do these words mean? Chapter 4 proposes to give "a preliminary justification" for the expression "cinematographic language," a justification that in the present state of semiological investigations can only be "very general." More correctly, chapter 4 proposes "to outline" this preliminary justification. Metz notes that the term cinematographic language "already poses the whole problem of the semiotics of film." Put together this means that chapter 4 proposes to give us the *outline* of a *preliminary justification, very general,* of *the whole problem of a semiotics of film.* As noted, this means a justification of the "filmolinguistic" project itself: if the term "cinematographic language" is justified, then Saussurean-Barthesian semiotics may be applied to it.

How does Metz make this justification, or rather, its outline? What he does in each section of chapter 4, though differently in each and not linked logically from section to section, is to isolate, establish, and explore linguistic features of cinema or, to be precise, features of cinematographic language. Of course these are precisely the features that differentiate cinema from pure analogy and hence that justify the application of *Elements.* Not only do they justify the use of *Elements* in the analysis of cinema, they comprise the materials on which an *Elements* analysis will work and the site at which it will operate. To find linguistic features in cinema (that is, semiotic features) is at once to justify in advance the project of a semiotic analysis and already to locate the site and to isolate the materials of such an analysis. Moreover, just as calling cinema analogic is already a semiotic analysis, so here finding that cinema has semiotic features and stating what they are can only be the *results* of a semiotic analysis already performed.

Thus Metz uses the results of a semiotic analysis in making the argument that the project of a semiotic analysis of cinema is justified. This is the logical fallacy of *petitio principii*—assuming as a premise that which is to be proved by the argument itself. One might also

say that what Metz does under the cover of a preliminary justification of the semiotic project is to conduct that analysis itself! This
permits him later to declare the semiotic analysis (or parts of it)
already accomplished when, formally speaking, it has not yet begun.
Both of these factors operate in Metz's text. Their operation in it is
possible because of the odd way that Metz has set up his overall
argument. Why did he not proceed directly to the *Elements* analysis
of cinema? It is in making the analysis itself that one can see what
difficulties arise, what further analyses are needed, what methodological alterations are required. Metz proceeds by asking in advance
whether there can be a semiotics of the cinema and by raising in
advance a number of questions, doubts, and difficulties concerning
that application. There is, however, no way to determine the question in advance; the only way to determine it is to attempt to do it.
Besides, there is no method for determining the question in advance
except the semiotic method itself—in any case Metz provides none.

We must ask ourselves *why* Metz has proceeded as he has, why
he has cast his argument as a series of preliminaries, repeated again
and again, even through chapter 5, to the brink of the semiotic
analysis that he finally makes (or seems to). What would a straightforward *Elements* analysis, presented step-by-step, do to his argument? What would it reveal about his analysis of cinema?

As noted, each section of chapter 4 attempts in a different way
to isolate and define linguistic features of cinema, that is, features
of cinematographic language that may be analyzed by Saussurean-
Barthesian semiotics. Metz does not propose to conduct that analysis
in chapter 4, or even strictly speaking to begin it, but only to justify
it. Especially in light of chapter 3, but also in light of points made
in chapter 4, justifying semiotic analysis means clearing away or
breaking through or working around the absolute barrier to semiotic
analysis constituted by cinematic analogy. This is done by defining
linguistic features of cinematic signification—those that are irreduc-
ible to analogy, in addition to it, or simply different from it.

The first section, "Cinema and Narrativity," begins by asking
what body of films shall the film semiologist study. "Is the corpus
to be made up of feature films . . . or, on the contrary, of short
films, documentaries, technological, pedagogical, or advertising films,
etc.?" (p. 93). He decides that there is "a hierarchy of concerns,"
indeed "a methodological urgency" that favors, in the beginning at
least, the study of narrative film. "To examine fiction films is to
proceed more directly and more rapidly to the heart of the problem"
(p. 94). "Metz: *Essais I* and Film Theory" criticizes the substance

of this argument (see pp. 120–122). Our question here concerns the *placement* of this discussion. In the course of an essay offering the outline of a preliminary justification for the project of a semiotics of the cinema, Metz is discussing what body of films the semiologist should analyze.

Nor does "Cinema and Narrativity" isolate and define any film-linguistic features. Instead it makes the general point that such features may be grasped more easily by studying narrative films. After noting that the earliest films were simple duplications of visual spectacles, that is, they were simply analogic, Metz argues

> Now, *it was precisely to the extent that the cinema confronted the problems of narration* that, in the course of successive gropings, it came to produce a body of specific signifying procedures. . . . Thus, it was in a single motion that the cinema became narrative and took over some of the attributes of a language. (pp. 95–96)

This is a general historical point about the development of cinematic language: it does not isolate or define any features of such a language. It is moreover a first principle of Saussurean studies that "language" of any kind must be studied and understood synchronically—in its operation as a system. After this is established, a diachronic study of the formation, change, and development of the language as a system becomes possible. Metz violates this canon by making a diachronic argument stand in for a necessary systemic one.

Thus "Cinema and Narrativity" does nothing to realize the project of chapter 4, the definition of linguistic features in cinema. The question it does deal with—What body of films shall the semiologist study?—belongs to a later phase of the argument, itself dependent upon chapter 4's making out its case. It seems that Metz is going ahead with his semiotic analysis in the course of an essay devoted to a preliminary justification of such an analysis.

Compounding this flash-forward method considerably is an argument that Metz makes in the course of defending the semiotic primacy of narrative films.

> Nonnarrative films for the most part are distinguished from "real" films by their social purpose and by their content much more than by their "language processes." The basic figures of the semiotics of the cinema—montage, camera movements, scale of the shots, relationships between the image and speech, sequences, and other large syntagmatic units—are on the whole the same in "small" films and in "big" films. (p. 94)

How and when have "the basic figures of the semiotics of the cinema" been determined? This passage occurs in the first section of a preliminary justification of the semiotic project itself. Nothing like *any* stage of an *Elements* analysis has yet been done. In this section Metz introduces the "basic figures" point as the established premise in an argument concerning the body of films to be used in semiotic analysis, itself dependent on conclusions that the essay in which these arguments occur is devoted to establishing. Thus the goal of the analysis as a whole is used as a premise to reach a conclusion belonging to the middle of the argument, in the course of an argument devoted to preliminaries. This is a compound, impacted instance of the *petitio principii* fallacy.

Section 2 is "Studies of Denotation and Studies of Connotation in the Semiotics of the Cinema." Metz assumes that cinematic denotation and connotation can be sharply distinguished for analytical purposes and, indeed, analyzed in separate stages (see pp. 130–131). He proposes that film semiotics address denotation first and connotation later. Connotation is in any case "superimposed over the denoted meaning" (p. 96). Paraphrasing Barthes's *Mythologies,* Metz argues that connotation takes over both the signifier and signified of denotation, making them the signifier of a new signified of connotation. *Elements* discusses this under the heading "Staggered Systems" (see p. 131n for Barthes's criticism of his own earlier position).

After making this point, Metz concludes abruptly: "The study of the cinema as an art—the study of cinematographic expressiveness—can therefore be conducted according to methods derived from linguistics" (97). What is entailed in this "therefore" is explained after the conclusion is stated. He assumes, also in advance of establishing it, that semiotics *can* study filmic denotation. The Barthesian "overlay" theory makes filmic connotation a function of filmic denotation and thereby brings it within the orbit of film semiotics.

Of course this argument works only if it is shown that film semiotics *can* study filmic denotation. The argument that should come first in this line of reasoning, Metz places last. Metz asserts: "[It is] also, and even first of all, through its procedures of *denotation,* [that] the cinema is a specific language" (p. 97). Metz introduces the concept of diegesis, "the film's represented instance," "the sum of a film's denotation,"

the narration itself, but also the fictional space and time dimensions implied in and by the narrative, and consequently the characters, the landscapes, the events, and other narrative elements, in so far as they are considered in their denoted aspect. How does the cinema indicate successivity, precession, temporal breaks, causality, adversative relationships, consequence, spatial proximity, or distance, etc.? These are central questions to the semiotics of the cinema. (p. 98)

Once again Metz makes a statement about film semiotics that can only be the result of a complete *Elements* analysis. Once again he introduces it as a premise in the argument of a preliminary point, well prior to the premise in logical sequence and indeed itself necessary to establish the premise.

Of course Metz has not established the denotation point, he has merely asserted it. He argues that cinematic denotation, unlike photographic denotation, must itself be

> constructed, organized, and to a certain extent codified (*codified*, not necessarily *encoded*). Lacking absolute laws, filmic intelligibility nevertheless depends on a certain number of dominant habits: A film put together haphazardly would not be understood. (p. 99)

Note the nonspecific formulations of Metz's conclusion: codified "to a certain extent," "a certain number of dominant habits" not equal to absolute laws. These terms and the propositions that assert them are too vague to sustain the argument that film semiotics should address denotation first, let alone the argument that semiotics can analyze filmic denotation, let alone to define the semiotic operations of cinematic denotation itself. Neither does the section succeed in isolating or defining features of cinematographic language. To say that a film put together haphazardly would not be understood is not to say anything concrete about filmic language.

Section 3, "Paradigmatic and Syntagmatic Categories," addresses a topic already discussed in chapter 3. Metz concludes as before that "more than paradigmatic studies, it is the syntagmatic considerations that are at the center of the problems of filmic denotation" (p. 101).

The next section, "An Example: The Alternating Syntagm," concerns one of "the principal types of *large* filmic *syntagma*" (p. 102) or, rather, "some of the characteristics" of that type. This discussion and the syntagmatic type it treats are later abandoned by Metz in a long footnote that accompanies the reprinting of this section in

Film Language. It is supplanted entirely as a syntagmatic type by the analysis and table of the *grande syntagmatique* in chapter 5, section 5, in which it does not appear.

Though there is a "Conclusion" section, it is the next-to-last section, "Other Problems," that provides an extensive summary of chapter 4. It concerns the "important differences between the semiotics of the cinema and linguistics itself" (p. 105). Metz here repeats a number of the main points of chapter 3: film has no second articulation, all of its units are directly significant and they occur only in the actualized state. "The commutations and other manipulations by which the semiotics of the cinema proceeds therefore affect the large significatory units" (p. 105).

In this passage "therefore" is unjustified—the absence of semiotic units at one level does not prove that they exist at another level. (This is the logical fallacy "affirming the consequent.") Metz repeats chapter 3's finding that the cinema is not a language system (*langue*), but that it "can be considered as a *language,* to the extent that it orders signifying elements within ordered arrangements different from those of spoken idioms and . . . not traced on the perceptual configurations of reality itself" (p. 105). Derived from purely analogous, continuous signification,

> the cinema gradually shaped, in the course of its diachronic maturation, some elements of a proper semiotics, which remain scattered and fragmentary within the open field of simple visual duplication. (p. 105)

Again a diachronic argument is used to stand in for a needed synchronic one, the Saussurean-Barthesian semiotic analysis of cinema as a system that Metz still has not begun. Moreover, what are these "some elements"? Where is the semiotic analysis that derives and/or justifies them?

In the "Conclusion" Metz finds:

> The concepts of linguistics can be applied to the semiotics of the cinema only with the greatest caution. On the other hand, the methods of linguistics—commutation, analytical breakdown, strict distinction between the signified and the signifier, between substance and form, between the relevant and the irrelevant, etc.— provide the semiotics of the cinema with a constant and precious aid in establishing units that, though they are still very approximate, are liable over time (and, one hopes, through the work of many scholars) to become progressively refined. (p. 107)

Thus, though the problems of chapter 3 are not dealt with, chapter 4 affirms the applicability of Saussurean-Barthesian semiotics to cinema. Chapter 4 does not even begin the Barthesian analysis of cinema. Rather it affirms the possibility and necessity of such analysis—without, however, dealing with the objections of chapter 3 or itself laying the theoretical groundwork for such an analysis to come.

This stasis beneath apparent motion characterizes the "Conclusion" also. The *concepts* of linguistics do not apply to cinema— phoneme, morpheme, moneme, syntax, and grammar in the strict sense. But no one has supposed that they did, not even the strictest Saussurean. Barthes makes this point many times in *Elements*. But the *methods* of linguistics do apply to the semiotic analysis of cinema: commutation, strict distinction between signifier and signified, etc. This too is not new; it is simply the program of *Elements*.

In any case, the "Conclusion" makes clear that chapter 4 is an unqualified return to the Saussurean-Barthesian position, overriding the doubts of chapter 3 and the flirtations with other models at the end of that chapter. One expected chapter 4 to take up one of these hints and to develop it into a method for analyzing cinema semiotically; or to return to the problems raised by chapter 3 and, by careful analysis, to dismiss them and to reinstate the applicability of the *Elements* method to cinema analysis. Instead Metz asserts the latter without having dealt with any of the problems raised by the former.

In one sense chapter 3 and chapter 4 cancel each other. At the end of chapter 4 the argument stands exactly where it stood at the start of chapter 3—with *Elements* in hand, about to begin the semiotic analysis of cinema. As we have seen, the body of chapter 3 moves as far from this point as possible, short of abandoning the semiotic project altogether; then chapter 4 moves back toward an affirmation of Saussurean-Barthesian method as the proper tool for the analysis of cinema. (Beyond the level of literal argument as such, this pair of chapters accomplishes more than a simple, useless venture out and back. What this more is we consider below.) This means that chapter 5 must conduct the *Elements* analysis itself. That promised analysis was first postponed from chapter 3 to chapter 4, then from chapter 4 to chapter 5. How does chapter 5 handle it?

Chapter 5 is called "Problems of Denotation in the Fiction Film." A prefatory paragraph asks where the language of cinematography (the phrase is used now without qualification, as though fully earned) differs most from language itself, for here film semiology encounters its greatest obstacles. There are two points of maximum difference: the problem of the motivation of signs (the question of the arbitrariness of signs) and the problem of the continuity of meanings (the question of discrete units). Sections 1 and 2 deal with the first problem. Sections 3 and 4 deal with the second problem. Thus sections 1 through 4 of chapter 5 consider yet one more time issues treated, though not resolved, by chapters 3 and 4. In several senses, these sections protract the ambivalence and irresolution of the earlier discussions. In one or two respects, however, a determinative direction is taken.

Section 1, "Cinematographic Signification Is Always More or Less Motivated, Never Arbitrary," argues that in cinema connotation overlays denotation but also exceeds it. Metz makes a few other remarks on connotation but "will not insist upon the problems of cinematographic connotation here, for this is a study of denotation" (p. 109).

Section 2 is titled "Range and Limits of the Concept of Analogy." This title (at last) poses directly the problem that chapter 3 and chapter 4 have dealt with obliquely and contradictorily. The concept of analogy *must* be limited if there is to be a semiotic analysis of cinema. If it cannot be limited, there can be no semiotics of cinema. Hence the question of the limits of the concept of analogy, that is, whether it can be limited, is fundamental to the semiotic project. Section 2 acknowledges for the first time in Metz's argument the fundamental importance of overcoming this problem if there is to be a semiotics of cinema at all. He says, "Wherever analogy takes over filmic signification (that is, notably the meaning of each visual element taken separately), there is a lack of specifically cinematographic codification" (p. 111).

Declaring analogy "a stopping block" to semiotics, Metz considers alternate avenues/sites for construction of a semiotic analysis, as he *must* do if his analysis is not to come to a halt at this "stopping block." Just following the passage above, Metz pivots to other sites for semiotic analysis.

That is why I believe filmic codes must be sought on other levels: the codes peculiar to connotation (including partially "motivated" codes, for the pure "arbitrary" does not exhaust the codifiable field) or the codes of denotation-connotation related to the discursive organization of image groups (see also, for example, the "large syntagmatic category in the image track," pages 119–34). (p. 111)

The first topic under this new rubric is those "extracinemato-graphic" codes that "intervene on the screen under cover of analogy" (p. 111). Through its duplication function, visual and aural, cinema activates a very large number and variety of codes of the culture generally. These are of interest to a "general semiotics," though not to a semiotics of cinema. To make this clear, Metz distinguishes between *cultural* codes and *specialized* codes. Cultural codes define the culture of each social group. They are so ubiquitous and well assimilated that viewers consider them to be "natural." The handling of these codes requires no specialized training. Specialized codes concern more specific and restricted social features; their use requires special training. The "purely cinematographic signifying figures" studied by the semiotics of cinema are specialized codes.

This distinction, and exclusion from his project, brings Metz back to his seeking of filmic codes on "other levels." Sections 3 and 4 concern "the problem of the continuity of meanings," that is, the question of discrete units. Section 3, "The Cinema as Such Has Nothing Corresponding to the Double Articulation of Verbal Languages," considers the basic unit—the shot. Section 4, "The 'Grammar' of Cinema: A Rhetoric or a Grammar?," concerns the grouping and arrangement of shots in larger units.

Section 3 repeats several of the formulas of chapter 3 and chapter 4. The cinema has no distinctive units.

> Even with respect to the signifying units, the cinema is initially deprived of discrete elements. It proceeds by whole "blocks of reality," which are actualized with their total meaning in the discourse. These blocks are the "shots." The discrete units identifiable in the filmic discourse on another level—for, as we shall see, there is another level—are not equivalent to the first articulation of spoken languages. (p. 115)

Metz then argues that montage is in a sense an analysis, a sort of articulation of the reality shown on the screen. But this is not a true articulation in the linguistic sense—even the most partial "shot" still presents a complete segment of reality.

On the other hand, "the film *sequence* is a real unit—that is to say, a sort of coherent *syntagma* within which the 'shots' react (semantically) to each other" (p. 115). This recalls, up to a certain point, the manner in which words react to each other within a sentence, but the old film theoreticians' equations of the shot with the word and the sequence with the sentence were "highly erroneous identifications." Metz then discusses "five radical differences between the filmic 'shot' and the linguistic word" (p. 115), which largely recapitulate earlier discussions.

In section 4 Metz considers whether the "grammar" of cinema is not "a rhetoric rather than a true grammar, since the *minimum unit* (the shot) is not determined, and consequently codification can affect only the *large units*" (p. 117). Enlarging this question, Metz refers to "the *dispositio* (or large syntagmatic category), which is one of the principal parts of classical rhetorics, consist[ing] in prescribing determined orderings of undetermined elements" (p. 117).

Metz complicates his question by noting that, in the case of cinema, *"this rhetoric I have just mentioned is also, in other aspects, a grammar"* (p. 117). They constitute a grammar in that they organize not only filmic connotation, but also, and *primarily,* denotation. "The thing that characterizes the *functioning* of filmic orderings is that it is primarily thanks to them that the spectator understands the literal sense of the film" (p. 118). Here Metz again brings in his historical myth: at first stories were told on film with iconic analogy; in order to enhance their connotations, filmmakers resorted to devices like moving the camera and editing that altered cinema's denotation. In cinema connotation is nothing more than a form of denotation. "Films are able to connote without generally requiring *special* (i.e., separate) connotors because they have the most essential signifiers of connotation at their permanent disposal: the choice between several ways of structuring denotation" (p. 119).

Sections 1 through 4 of chapter 5 do not accomplish a semiotic analysis of cinema, or even the first stage of such an analysis. Their failure to do so postpones the promised analysis yet one more time, this time to chapter 5, section 5, in which the *grande syntagmatique* is presented. But sections 1 through 4 do accomplish something beyond what chapters 3 and 4 do. We must determine precisely what that is in order to understand what comes later in the argument.

Sections 1 through 4 may be reduced to these propositions:

1. Analogy is a stopping block to semiosis.

2. But semiotic analysis *is* possible at another level than the analogic, that of the syntagmatic ordering of images or shots.

3. Under analogy many cultural codes intervene in cinema (and in the filmic text). Metz is interested only in the *specifically cinematic* codes.

4. Cinema has no discrete units at the first or analogic level. There it proceeds by "whole blocks of reality." But there *are* discrete units identifiable in the filmic discourse at another level.

5. Montage constitutes *analysis* but not true *articulation* in the linguistic sense—even the most partial shot presents a complete segment of reality.

6. On the other hand, the film *sequence* is a real unit, that is, a sort of coherent syntagma within which the shots react simultaneously to each other.

7. This recalls, but is unlike, how the word operates in the sentence—Metz lists five major differences.

8. The cinema, at the *sequence* level, is both a rhetoric and, in a very limited sense, a grammar.

9. The rhetorical *dispositio* is a precedent for the semiotic operation of cinema, specifically the cinema, as Metz has defined it: the determined ordering of undetermined units; that is, units themselves undetermined in size and nature. Cinematic sequences do the same by their syntagmatic ordering of undetermined analogy pieces—the shots.

10. But the semiotic process of cinema is also, in other respects, a grammar, in that it orders denotation.

Let us direct our attention to those points bearing directly on the main problems and the overall themes of Metz's argument as a whole, its attempts to achieve a semiotics of cinema à la *Elements*. We are then left with 1, 2, 6, 9: Analogy does stop the semiotic analysis of cinema, but there is another level of cinema—the syntagmatic, at which shots react to each other semantically—at which semiotic analysis is possible. This amounts to saying that there can be a semiotic ordering of units that are not themselves semiotic, that is, a determined ordering of indeterminate elements. There is a precedent for this in rhetoric, the *dispositio,* though cinema goes beyond the rhetorical and takes on elements of the grammatical.

What sections 1 through 4 of chapter 5 entail is that Metz explicitly abandons his former program for the semiotic analysis of cinema, his entire approach to the question thus far. He has not made out this new analysis itself; he has only announced a program to do it. But it is a new program and at last he has announced it, after one hundred pages of asserting the impossibility of the semiotics of cinema. The semiotic analysis itself is again postponed, but we now have a program to test that analysis against. What Metz has not done is to relate his new program to his methodological sources, specifically to *Elements;* he has not delineated, even generally, a method of analysis that can realize his program by *Elements* means. In other terms, Metz has so far only asserted that there can be a semiotic analysis of cinema at the syntagmatic level, he has not done it or demonstrated its possibility. In short, he has not related the syntagmatic analysis of cinema to the canons and stages of analysis specified by *Elements.*

Chapter 5, section 5, at last presents Metz's semiotic analysis of cinema. As such it is oddly couched and shrouded in qualifications and reservations. The first four paragraphs of the section are quoted and comments made on them above (pp. 127–128). This section presents the *content* of cinematographic grammar, the codified orderings of various kinds used in film. (Previous sections have been concerned with establishing the *status* of this grammar.) But it is not possible to give the table in its complete form, with all the explanations required for each ordering, with the principles of commutation between them given. We must content ourselves with "the almost unpolished 'result' "—the table itself in summarized form— and only that part that outlines the large syntagmatic category of the image track—the codified and signifying orderings on the level of the *large* units of the film, and ignoring the elements of sound and speech. This problem in any case constitutes only one of the chapters of "cinematographic syntax."

> In order to determine the number and the nature of the main syntagmatic *types* used in current films, one must start from common observation (existence of the "scene," the "sequence," "alternate montage," etc.) as well as on certain "presemiotic" analyses by critics, historians, and theoreticians of the cinema ("tables of montage," various classifications, etc.). This preliminary work must account for several points of importance—that is why it in no way precludes the viewing of numerous films—and it must then be organized into a coherent body—that is to say, into a list of all the main types of image-orderings occurring in films under the various headings into which they are naturally classified.
>
> One thus arrives at a first "tabulation" of the syntagmatic components of films—a chart remaining fairly close to the concrete filmic material, but which, from the point of view of semiological theory, is as yet insufficiently developed. (pp. 120–121)

After some remarks on the development of his analyses through several earlier stages, Metz says:

At present, then, I distinguish eight main types of autonomous segments, that is, "sequences" (but henceforth I will reserve the term sequence for only two of these eight types, numbers 7 and 8).

The autonomous segment is a subdivision of the first order in film; it is therefore a part of a film, and not a part of a part of a film. (If an autonomous section is composed of five successive shots, each one of these shots is a part of a part of the whole film—that is to say, a nonautonomous segment). It is clear nevertheless that the "autonomy" of the autonomous segments themselves is not an *independence*, since each autonomous segment derives its final meaning in relation to the film as a whole, the latter being the *maximum syntagma* of the cinema.

In distinguishing between the "shot" and the "sequence," everyday language clearly indicates that there are two things in the cinema (without prejudice to eventual intermediate levels): On the one hand there is the minimum segment, which is the shot (see above, pages 106–7), and on the other hand the autonomous segment. This, as we will see shortly, does not prevent a minimum segment from being occasionally autonomous. (pp. 123–124)

At this point, Metz plunges into a ten-page presentation of the eight syntagmatic types. This material is summarized on pages 128–130 above.

The *grande syntagmatique* and the analytical scheme that supports it comprise Metz's semiotic analysis of film—long promised, long postponed. At least it is all of such an analysis that Metz provides. Of course we wish to examine it carefully.

Metz's analysis (of the *grande syntagmatique*) rests on a two-level model: level one is the shot, level two is the sequence or segment, the syntagmatic ordering of shots in one of eight possible ways. We recognize at once that these operations correspond to two fundamental operations of an *Elements* analysis. One is the determination of the basic unit of a system of communication; the second is determination of "the syntagmatic form of utterances," which Barthes calls "combinative constraints" and places on the side of language rather than of speech.

Metz's two-level analysis—the result of his overall argument—has the *form* of the result of an *Elements* analysis, but it has not been arrived at by the procedures specified by *Elements*. At least we cannot recall such an analysis when we finish reading chapter 5. The analyses and arguments necessary to an *Elements* analysis have not been performed. But, as this question is of central importance, we must reexamine Metz's presentation carefully to be sure that it is not of the *Elements* type. It is at least hypothetically possible that in the labyrinthine coils of Metz's arguments, obscured by their repetitions as well as their gaps, he manages to make out one or another of the stages of an *Elements* analysis, or even all of them.

We begin with the first level: the designation of cinema's basic unit as the shot. How did this occur? Where did it occur? By what analytic means was it established?

Of course the shot is designated as the basic unit of cinema in chapter 5, section 5, itself, in which it is adopted by reference to "common observation" and to "certain 'presemiotic' analyses" and to "everyday language":

> In distinguishing between the "shot" and the "sequence," every-day language clearly indicates that there are two things in the cinema . . . : On the one hand there is the minimum segment, which is the shot . . . , and on the other hand the autonomous segment. (pp. 123–124)

But the designation occurs before this, in sections 1 through 4 of chapter 5, specifically in section 3.

> Even with respect to the signifying units, the cinema is initially deprived of discrete elements. It proceeds by whole "blocks of reality," which are actualized with their total meaning in the discourse. These blocks are the "shots." (p. 115)

It is this section that enacts the movement of Metz's argument from the shot to the syntagm level once and for all (more or less), though of course the syntagm is precisely a syntagm of shots.

> It is true that the film *sequence* is a real unit—that is to say, a sort of coherent *syntagma* within which the "shots" react (semantically) to each other. (p. 115)

(He then lists "five radical differences between the filmic 'shot' and the linguistic word.")

But, well before these passages, we find the shot identified as the basic unit of cinema in the conclusion to chapter 4.

> The "shot"—an already complex unit, which must be studied—remains an indispensable reference for the time being, in some-what the same way that the "word" was during a period of lin-guistic research. . . . [I]t constitutes the largest *minimum seg-*

ment . . . since at least one shot is required to make a film, or part of a film—in the same way, a linguistic statement must be made up of at least one phoneme. To isolate several shots from a sequence is still, perhaps, to analyze the sequence; to remove several frames from a shot is to destroy the shot. If the shot is not the smallest unit of filmic *signification* (for a single shot may convey several informational elements), it is at least the smallest unit of the filmic chain. (p. 106)

We also find references to the shot as cinema's basic unit in earlier sections of chapter 4. In the fourth section, "An Example: The Alternating Syntagm," Metz provides his first discussion of a cinematic narrative syntagm, albeit one he retracts and rejects when he gives the *grande syntagmatique* table of syntagm types in chapter 5. A syntagm is necessarily a syntagm of something. Here Metz's terminology alternates between "images" and "shots." What an alternating syntagm or *any* ordering of "images" might be *other* than an ordering of shots is not clear. Metz specifies or suggests no other sense. In any case, he uses the terms interchangeably here and in other sections.

Even earlier than the fourth section, we find mentions of the shot in the third section, "Paradigmatic and Syntagmatic Categories," in both text and footnotes. Here the shot is not identified explicitly as the basic unit of cinema—it is treated as a site of codification in a section devoted to different kinds of codification in cinema. Of course it is significant that the *only* unit discussed is the shot. To be the site of codification is, of course, one definition of a basic unit (though Metz attributes codifications to other units, such as the syntagm, also).

The second section of chapter 4, "Studies of Denotation and Studies of Connotation in the Semiotics of the Cinema," also does not primarily concern the problem of the basic unit. But when it argues that in cinema denotation is constructed out of parts, unlike still photography, Metz establishes the point by showing that a number of (interrelated) shots is necessary to construct it.

The first section of chapter 4, "Cinema and Narrativity," does mention the word shot in passing but does not say much about it.

If we go all the way back to chapter 3, we find the shot already mentioned as basic unit—rather, assumed as basic unit, for we find no derivation or justification of the shot there either. On page 67, "The shot is the smallest unit of the filmic chain . . ." From this statement Metz immediately proceeds to a discussion of the richness and exuberance of the syntagmatic arrangements possible in film.

Of course these are syntagmatic arrangements of shots. Also from chapter 3:

> But at a certain point in the division into units, the shot, a "completed assertive statement," as Benveniste would call it, is equivalent to an oral sentence.
>
> Nevertheless the shot, a "sentence" and not a word (like the proverb), is indeed the smallest "poetic" entity. (p. 66)

Mentions of the shot and assertions of the shot as the basic unit of cinema go all the way back in Metz's argument to its earliest beginnings. Where, when, and how is this justified? Where is the unit of shot derived semiotically or at least defined or redefined by semiotics? If it is simply borrowed from other disciplines (film theory), how is that borrowing justified as comprising a fundamental stage of a semiotic argument? The answer is that it never is. When one looks for the semiotic argument deriving or justifying the shot as basic unit, one does not find it, late or early in Metz's work. When one traces the shot back to its first mentions in Metz's discourse, one has the sense of pursuing an infinite regress. In fact, the shot is never introduced in Metz's writings. It is *always already* there as the basic unit of cinema.

Instead Metz assumes the shot as the basic unit for film semiotics, as for other discourses on film, and proceeds to the syntagmatic level. Of course the analysis of the syntagmatic level rests on, depends upon, the unit of the shot, because the segment of that level is a higher unit than the shot and because what is syntagmicized or combined at the (higher) syntagmatic level are, precisely, shots.

Of course *Elements* specifies the semiotic determination of a system's basic units as a fundamental stage of any semiotic analysis and as necessary to any further step. There is no way to get around or avoid this step and still perform a semiotic analysis. Its absence in Metz's argument means simply that Metz has not performed a semiotic analysis of cinema.

But we must look at the syntagmatic level also for completeness sake. In any case, given the absence of a semiotic derivation and/or justification for the shot unit, it is interesting to see just what Metz is doing at the syntagmatic level—which he says is the true semiotic operation in cinema—and just how he does it.

To provide the content of cinematographic grammar can only be the result of a semiotic analysis; but Metz presents just the table itself. The first four paragraphs of chapter 5, section 5, short-circuit the process of semiotic analysis: "Let us content ourselves, then, with the almost unpolished 'result'—the table itself in a summarized form" (p. 119). Just as in Part I Metz began with the basic unit of cinema instead of arriving at it through an *Elements* analysis, so his section on the syntagmatics of cinema begins with the table of autonomous segments, and only then presents their definitions, commutations between them, etc.

One could argue that the second case involves merely a reversal of presentation. But the most fundamental material is not presented— the *Elements* analysis that justifies and derives the table of syntagmatic types. Presenting results first and analysis later masks this omission. It permits whatever omissions the analyst desires, because the analysis is not made responsible for the table: It has instead the character of supplementary information, of which the reader may be given more or less depending upon space and authorial inclination. Correspondingly, the reader accepts the commentary as the author's gift, rather than as an obligation. When the analysis precedes the presentation of results, the latter must be derived point by point, stage by stage, from the analysis. Metz's rhetoric effectively covers these omissions. (One way he does this is to defend the *grande syntagmatique* table by putting principles of *Elements* together with others from earlier chapters that effectively nullify them. This permits the principles of *Elements* to "lead to" or "conclude" what Metz wants them to conclude.)

By presenting the *grande syntagmatique* table first and defending it later, Metz's after-the-fact explanation of the table is able both to stand in for a reasoned defense and to presuppose that such a defense has *already* taken place and may be referred to and even quoted selectively. "It is not possible here to give this table in its complete form, with all the explanations required by each one of the indicated orderings, and with the *principles of commutation* between them (and consequently to enumerate them)" (p. 119). What Metz says following the presentation of the table has the *form* of a *commentary* on it: a commentary may be long or short, may skip topics, etc. But it is evidently to *function* as a closely reasoned defense also, it is in any case the only one we are given. Overlaying this form and this function permits Metz to appear to give a reasoned defense, yet to leave out what he wishes to skip. It also provides scope for the manipulation of stated and unstated premises in order to produce a desired result.

Is it possible to conduct a semiotic analysis at one particular level, within an overall analysis that is not semiotic? Where specifically the units of one's analysis at that level have been borrowed and are used without an analysis or (re)thinking? It seems unlikely. But we shall proceed as though it were possible to do this, in order to explore and elucidate and perhaps critique at a new level Metz's semiotics of cinema. We shall accept Metz's basic film units as given, or even suppose them to be the result of a semiotic analysis. Then the question becomes: even with the minimal units "supplied" without benefit of semiotic analysis, what do we have in the *grande syntagmatique?* Our review of the *grande syntagmatique* analysis/ presentation as semiosis is made possible by temporarily disregarding the results of our critiques of analyses at other levels of Metz's overall semiotic analysis. This is difficult because these levels impinge on the *grande syntagmatique* level logically and the *grande syntagmatique* level logically depends on them.

In examining the *grande syntagmatique* presentation as semiosis, it is useful to return to the statement of the essentials of the *Elements* method presented above. The goal is to separate language from speech in any system. The first operation is the analysis of the sign or discourse into signifier and signified elements (or planes). This makes possible the commutation test, which alone can determine units and hence permit division of the syntagm. Once the syntagm is divided, and the units are determined, the resulting units are classified into paradigms. They can then be distributed along two axes. This in turn makes possible a definition of language and speech: the paradigms and their interrelation correspond to language, so does the syntagmatic form of utterances—the combinative constraints. The latter two define the speech function as a combinatory act, governed by constraints as well as by freedoms, that results in syntagms.

Metz contrasts the autonomous shot as a syntagm type with all seven other kinds of autonomous segments. The reason is that the autonomous shot has only one shot, all the others have multiple shots. (Thus the latter are all *syntagmas,* whereas the autonomous shot is a syntagmatic type.) Metz contrasts this difference with all the differences *among* the other seven syntagmas. "Finally, it can be said that the first dichotomy—which separates the autonomous shot from the seven other types, i.e., from all the syntagmas—is based on a characteristic of the *signifier* (i.e., 'a single shot, or several shots?'), whereas the distinctions between the syntagmas are derived from the signified (despite various identifiable traits in the corresponding signifiers)" (p. 133n).

The "commutations" of the syntagmas 2 through 8 discussions do indeed contrast signifieds only, they do not mention signifiers at all. At no point, except partially in the discussion of 1 (the autonomous shot), is there even an analysis of the autonomous segment, the cinematic sign that Metz analyzes, into signifier and signified. There is no discussion of the signifier whatever in these cases. Regarding the autonomous shot, there is discussion of only one signifier feature, that is, singleness of shot; one signified aspect is mentioned, a corresponding unity of action. The only signifier aspect of 2 through 8 discussed is that they have more than one shot, but this is not sufficient to differentiate *any* one segment from *any* other, let alone from *all* the rest. All seven segments have more than one shot, by definition.

Without analysis of the sign into signifier and signified, there can be no commutation test properly speaking. Without a commutation test, there can be no determination of the units of the system. Hence there can be no division of the syntagm according to its units. (We shall not reiterate that Metz does not semiotically derive his base units: shot, sequence, segment.) What "commutation" comes down to *at* the *grande syntagmatique* presentation level is that Metz, having presented his table, must then justify it through commutation of the designated units at that level. This he cannot do simply because of his failure to derive units semiotically at lower levels. What concerns us now, however, is the failure at the *grande syntagmatique* level itself—to demonstrate it and to explore its implications. (These implications are not identical to those of the failures at other levels, therefore they might teach something about film semiotics and film theory.)

Not only can 2 through 8 not be commuted any one with another, 1 cannot be commuted with the others (except 6), beyond the obvious point that it has one shot and is a segment, they have more than one and are segments. Here there is no common ground on which to compare signifieds, as each (2 through 8) signifies something different—some are narrative, some are not, etc. The seven syntagm types have seven different kinds of signifieds.

There is one genuine commutation in the group, that between 1 (autonomous shot) and 6 (scene). Alone among syntagms, the scene signifies continuous diegetic time; it has this fundamental element in common only with the autonomous shot. The difference is in the signifiers: one shot in the case of 1, more than one in the case of 6. We notice immediately that this "commutation" is one of the fundamental analyses of classical film theory: the long take versus montage option in the construction of the sequence. Metz's formulation is perhaps more precise in specifying "montage" as many narrative functions. Only one, by far the most common one, used far more often than the others combined, is commutable with the long take.

In any case, Metz has now "divided the syntagm," that is, *declared* it divided, without analysis of signifier-signified relations at the level of the basic unit, a step necessary to divide the syntagm, but also necessary for later operations. This absence is naturalized by the structure of Metz's argument in conjunction with his "semiotic method." *Once one has the basic units, one assumes that there has been an analysis, a mutual segmentation of signifier and signified, etc.* Not so here—in the extraordinary case in which the basic unit is defined a priori.

Having skipped the essential requirement at the basic stage, Metz now proposes to use commutation to define the eight syntagmatic types and then to differentiate them from each other. Though Metz has not used commutation to *determine* the unit of the autonomous segment, he is going to use it at this later stage to differentiate the types of that unit from each other. We have determined to evaluate this stage on its own, so far as possible. But a more serious problem arises here. To construct a paradigm of eight syntagmatic types (or of any unit), the analyst must differentiate the units according to distinctive features. Under usual conditions, signifier and signified would already have been analyzed and determined at the autonomous segment level (for them to be considered a unit at all!). As noted, Metz never defines the autonomous segment in signifier terms, only in narrative (here the signified) terms. What is most surprising is that Metz does not make up this gap when he constructs his paradigm of the eight types. For the latter are specified, each in itself and in relation to the other seven, solely by narrative designations. There are eight kinds of time ordering in narrative cinema, eight ways to order the temporal signified. Each segment type is defined as a certain ordering of events of the narrative. It is the *whole* segment alone that comprises the time ordering, not any subdivision. Hence it is only the entire segment that signifies as a whole. (As Metz says, one must read the entire syntagm to know its meaning.) Otherwise there would not be a *unit* at all.

But Metz is not interested in analyzing "the cinematic narrative" as such. As he notes, this is the province of a semiotics of narrative, specifying film as only one narrative vehicle among many. "On the one hand, there is the semiotics of the narrative film, such as the one I am attempting to develop; on the other hand, there is the structural analysis of actual narrativity." "The narrated event . . . is the signified in the semiotics of narrative vehicles (and notably of the cinema)" (pp. 144–145).

Metz is not interested in providing a typology or paradigm of narrative constructions in cinema but that is what he has done in the *grande syntagmatique*. Given his project, his analytical attention must be devoted to the *signifier*. Why then has Metz resorted to the signified of narrative construction first (and indeed, last and only)? This is as unusual a procedure in constructing a paradigm as in performing an initial commutation to divide the syntagm. Indeed, it is semiotically improper. As Barthes says, commutation always begins with the signifier first, then moves to the signified, because it is the signifier that must be classified.

> We must take note of the fact that the commutation is usually applied first to the plane of signifiers, since it is the syntagm which has to be divided; one can resort to the signifieds, but this remains purely formal: the signified is not called upon for its own sake, by virtue of its "substance," but merely as an index of the signifier: it *places* the signifier, that is all. In other words, in the ordinary commutation test, one calls into use the form of the signified (its oppositional value in relation to other signifieds), not its substance: "The difference between the significations are of use, the significations themselves being without importance" (Belewitch). (*Elements*, p. 66)

Metz uses the substance of the signified not just to place but to *define* the signifier. It could be argued that Metz *is* using the signifieds of the eight figures oppositionally: these eight narrative figures are opposed to each other by Metz, these oppositions constitute his paradigm. What he does not do, however, what he *never* does, is to arrive at the signifier. His paradigm is really a classification of signifieds and as such it is an operation that belongs to a semiotics of narrativity and *not* a semiotics of "narrative vehicles (and notably of the cinema)."

Metz returns to the *grande syntagmatique* at several places in his later texts, though never as extensively as in *Essais I*. Chapter 7, "Segmentation," discusses a number of the most important of these, notably those of *Language and Cinema*, "The Imaginary Signifier" —which has only indirect references to the *grande syntagmatique*— and the work of the Metzian text analysts. "Segmentation" concerns itself primarily with the changing place and definition of the *grande syntagmatique* within the developing semiotic context of these books and essays.

But the topic is discussed importantly in at least two other places —in a long interview with Raymond Bellour in volume II of *Essais sur la signification au cinéma* (1972) and again— indirectly, without explicit reference—in chapter 8, section 4, "Circularity of Paradigmatics and Syntagmatics," of *Language and Cinema*. We examine these at some length below in order to make our analysis of the *grande syntagmatique* and of Metz's semiotic analysis of cinema generally, more complete.

Essais sur la signification au cinéma, volume II, was published in 1972, the year following the publication of *Language and Cinema;* but all but three of its collected essays had appeared before *Language and Cinema.*[7] We are interested here only in Part IV of the book, "Semiologie du semiologue," which consists of a 1970 conversation between Raymond Bellour and Christian Metz on the semiology of cinema. The interview is a transition between *Essais I* and *Language and Cinema.* Since we have already considered *Language and Cinema,* much of the interview material is repetitious. Thus pluricodicity; the distinctions between study of the cinematographic language system and that of textual systems; progress, strategies, and limits of semiological research, these are covered more fully in the later treatise. There is also considerable overlapping of *Essais I:* the differences between semiotics and linguistics, presentation-summary of the *grande syntagmatique,* etc.

We are interested in approximately eight pages of the book (pp. 200–207) in which a single idea is discussed: the possibility of a doubled chart of the large syntagmatic category of the image track (*grande syntagmatique*). Although the discussion is inconclusive, and indeed no later Metz text takes it up, it is important for several reasons. First, it is the only text in the Metzian corpus after *Essais I* that explicitly reopens the question of the *grande syntagmatique* and that explicitly considers a retheorization. *Language and Cinema* in effect changes aspects of the theory of the *grande syntagmatique,* but does so, as it were, by altering its semiotic context, without inquiring into the *grande syntagmatique* itself. As a result, as we've seen, the consequences of these changes, most often not acknowledged as

---

[7] *Essais sur la signification au cinéma,* vol. II (Paris: Klincksieck, 1972), unpublished translation by Diane Abramo for the 1972 Oberlin Student Conference on Film Study; *Language and Cinema,* trans. Donna Jean Umiker-Sebeok (The Hague: Mouton, 1974).

changes, are uncertain. It is as though, in that book, Metz is trying to manipulate the *grande syntagmatique* theoretically without taking responsibility for a complete reconsideration. Thus his theorizations of or relating to the *grande syntagmatique* have the quality of assertions or ascriptions—this *is* the theory of the *grande syntagmatique*. He does not however show that, or how, it is so by working it through the mechanics of the *grande syntagmatique,* neither does he consider how the newly theorized element will affect other elements within the overall *grande syntagmatique* theoretical model. Difficult as the situation is in itself, Metz's presentation frequently makes it more so by making these assertions and ascriptions retrospective: the theory of the *grande syntagmatique* has always been this way.

In the interview, which is often quite interesting, the atmosphere is lighter. On the question of pluricodicity and the *grande syntagmatique,* for instance, Metz's remarks are freer and more candid than the tight denial-admission of *Language and Cinema.*

> I chose to closely study one cinematographic code, which I called the code of the large syntagmatic category. This is one cinematographic code among many others. Today, I realize this very well, but at the time that I was conducting my research, the whole thing was much less clear in my mind. I was studying *one* code in the cinema, but without ridding myself of the vague impression that this was perhaps *the* code in the cinema (the wavering is apparent in my book). (p. 200)

Bellour raises the question of the double table, referring to a footnote to the presentation of the table in *Essais I* in which Metz mentions this possibility. Metz responds:

> It is possible, in particular, that the autonomous shot (type 1 of my table) is a class rather than a single, terminal type, for it includes fairly numerous and varied image structures; it is the only one of my types having so many subtypes—and this sort of "bulge" may indicate insufficient formalization of the corresponding point. Also, as we shall see in Part 6 below, the autonomous shot is somehow apt to "contain" all the other varieties of shot. Finally, it can be said that the first dichotomy—which separates the autonomous shot from the seven other types, i.e., from all the syntagmas—is based on a characteristic of the *signifier* (i.e., "a single shot, or several shots?"), whereas the distinctions between the syntagmas are derived from the signified (despite various identifiable traits in the corresponding signifiers). These three reasons might eventually compel us to revise the status of the autonomous shot which would

entail bringing some changes to the general disposition of the chart. Perhaps there are even *two* tables of the syntagmatic category in the image track (ultimately very similar to each other, or at least *homologous* on many points); a table of the syntagmas and one of the combinations internal to the autonomous shot ("free" and "determined" syntagmatic categories, as with morphemes in American linguistics)? The situation would then resemble—in methodology if not in substance—that of many languages, whose phonological systems are more easily understood if one conceives of them as comprising two subsystems, one of "vowels" and one of "consonants."

Bellour says:

> It seems that the constitution of the large syntagmatic category runs into an obstacle that you emphasize in a long note, an obstacle that results from the very high degree of complexity of the first type of the table, the autonomous shot. You go as far as expressing the idea that it could perhaps be necessary to create *two* syntagmatic tables of the picture track. What do you mean by that?

Metz responds:

> There is indeed a complication due to the autonomous shot, and in particular to the "sequence-shot," which is one of its sub-types (I am leaving aside the other sub-types, that is, the inserts).
>
> The sequence-shot, an especially long and complex type of autonomous shot, gives rise to a whole interior construction—"interior montage," as is sometimes said—which plays upon the length of the continuous shooting (. . .), upon the axial superimposition of the visual elements (the problem of depth of field . . .), upon their lateral spacing (width of field . . .), upon the entrances into and exits from the field, etc.: in short, a whole ensemble, a whole arrangement of spatio-temporal relations, that the filmic discourse brings about without resorting to splicing, and within a single shot.
>
> What also strikes me is that in the sequence-shot one can find (at least up to a certain point) various spatio-temporal schemes that also appear in the types I numbered 2 through 8. This or that logical connection which, in the latter, is effected by montage in the narrow sense of the word, can be accomplished in a sequence-shot as well by means of camera movement. We find here an idea that Jean Mitry put forward clearly: montage in the broad sense

(the general activity of syntagmatic arrangement) goes much further than "collage." A *description* for example can be accomplished in several shots (. . .): it is then a "descriptive syntagm" (type No. 4); but it can also be treated in a single shot, the succession of the visual elements being achieved by a pan shot. Now, the logical scheme is the same in both cases. Consecutiveness of the signifying elements equals simultaneity of the corresponding signifieds (this is the actual definition of "description").

In this direction, the methodological task would consist in identifying which of my "syntagmas" (types 2 through 8) are capable of having equivalencies within the shot-sequence, because all of them are not; it is evident, for example, that the bracket syntagma or the episodic sequence could not be achieved in a single shot.

We would thus arrive at a second table of the large syntagmatic category which would be concerned with "interior" montage itself; it would be in a relation of partial and lacunary homology to the table of syntagmas. As for the large syntagmatic category itself, it would be somewhat bifurcated: the present type No. 1 would no longer be placed on the same classificatory axis as the other seven.

However, I left it as it is for the time being. The fact is that the sequence-shot (as the name indicates, moreover) is commutable with a true sequence (*une séquence véritable*) and represents, in relation to the whole film, a subdivision of the same rank.—Some linguists believe that in order to get to the bottom of the phonological system of this or that language, it is more economical to set up distinct sub-systems, that of the vowels and that of the consonants; however in languages like French, a consonant can be commuted with a vowel, and this substitution can suffice to distinguish between two morphemes whose phonological tenor is otherwise identical. As you can see, these problems have only a methodological resemblance to mine; but that counts too, and it helped me to catch a glimpse—and only a glimpse at this stage—of the possibility of dividing my typology of "classical" sequences into two parts. (pp. 203–205)

Just below this passage, Bellour asks:

I would like to know, in this connection, if the eight types that you have defined seem to you to respond with equal fidelity to the material fact of film, or if some of them could—without bringing about a schism in the table, as with the sequence-shot—compel you to complicate the table on its very axis.

[Christian Metz]—[Y]our . . . hypothesis . . . corresponds to the attitude I have towards my own work. In the book we are talking about, the numerous and copious footnotes take into account my dissatisfactions and the problems that remain unresolved (the concepts of "alternating syntagma," "frequentative variant of a syntagma," etc.). I think there remains much to be done.

Moreover, I criticize my classification in its present state for putting types that I would call hard and others I would call *soft* on the same plane. Thus the bracket syntagma and the non-diegetic insert are presented as very clear-cut and particular configurations that can be "recognized" for certain without any possible error: at the other pole, the ordinary sequence and the scene have rather fuzzy outlines, and it is sometimes difficult to pull them out of the formless and isolate them from the general filmic flow.

I feel that we must not hide the fact that the semiotics of the cinema is a completely stuttering discipline. . . . (p. 206)

These passages are extremely interesting for our inquiry—because it is the one reopening of the *grande syntagmatique* in all the Metzian literature and because an important alternative to the *grande syntagmatique* form is considered. But also because it is highly revealing to see how the Metzian discourse defines its weaknesses or errors and how it goes about correcting them. This doubling of the Metzian text back on itself is rare and is far more revealing than its usual proceeding ahead to consider new topics. The relations between the text's operation in doubling back on itself and the signified of the text, the doubled *grande syntagmatique* table, invite a more sophisticated text analysis than we can do here.

What is the difficulty or the embarrassment of the *grande syntagmatique* table that Metz and Bellour respond to here? They seem to be close to criticisms of the *grande syntagmatique* that we developed above: only two terms of the original table rest on an opposition of signifiers, the others rest on oppositions of signifieds. As long as this condition remains, the semiotic analysis of cinema is not just incomplete but aborted. Also, as Metz says, the autonomous segment *swells* with so many subcategories that it presses out toward a new formalization. But this alone would not be sufficient to launch a parallel table, for one could just as easily open up a bracket or otherwise list all the subcategories as subheadings. It is not clear that a separate table overcomes the problem any better (more economically or elegantly). Do both tables now order the signifier? Both the signified? One the signifier and the other the signified? The answer is unclear. And, as Metz says, there is still a commutation between the autonomous shot and the scene. In the scheme of the double table, this is stretched (or stranded) somewhere between the two blocks. (This is given by Metz as a reason why he holds back from the double table.) If this commutation does not imply a single table, it tends strongly in that direction.

In brief, there are imperative factors leading to a double table and equally imperative factors leading back to a single table. Doubling the *grande syntagmatique* scheme is both necessary and impossible. How are we to read this Metzian dilemma, which of course the Metz texts do not merely confront, but in the first instance, and more importantly, generate? What splits the table and leads to the problems Metz identifies as lying deeper than his analysis goes?

For now we can go no further than to pose these questions. The dilemmas discussed by Metz in his conversation with Bellour seem insoluble. In any case, Metz never returned to them.

Chapter 8 of *Language and Cinema,* "Paradigmatic and Syntagmatic," inscribes important revisions both in semiological theory and in the application of theory to the *grande syntagmatique.* Syntagm-paradigm is as important a semiological site as that of the distinctive unit, and the two are related. This chapter, in the guise of a "return" and a "correction," in effect rethinks aspects of the *grande syntagmatique* and provides a new theoretical setting, but does not change the *grande syntagmatique* itself.

Given our own analyses above, it is interesting to note that Metz titles section 8.4 "Circularity of Paradigmatics and Syntagmatics." After noting that syntagmatics and paradigmatics constantly refer back and forth to each other and that a code is both a paradigmatic and a syntagmatic mechanism, Metz launches into an extended discussion of the notion of sequence. We quote this in full, because the passage is redolent of many of the issues we have noted and discussed above.

8.4   CIRCULARITY OF PARADIGMATICS AND SYNTAGMATICS

Let us return to syntagmatics. We have already said that it belongs to the code as much as does paradigmatics. It is necessary to add at this point that, in this code, syntagmatics and paradigmatics constantly refer back and forth to one another and are, properly speaking, inseparable. (If one sometimes forgets this, it is because the syntagm and the paradigm may be examined separately for a certain time, as we have done here.) But as soon as one begins to examine the mechanisms of operation, the structure of syntagms and that of paradigms appear as closely corrrelated one with the other. This is one reason—the second—for not giving way to the simplistic idea that a code is a paradigmatic mechanism, an idea which this chapter is trying to criticize. A code is both a paradigmatic and a syntagmatic mechanism.

Thus, in the cinematic domain, it is impossible to define the notion of *sequence* other than by its differences with other forms of syntagmatic ordering, i.e., with different sorts of non-sequences, for example, the filmic segments which place end-to-end images which are separate and which do not "go together" (for certain films, or certain parts of films, do not contain sequences, and this fact is essential in order to understand what is a sequence in films where they are present). Thus, when one wishes to define, beyond the sequence-tokens, the sequence as an element of the code— as a distinctive unit of syntagmatics—one is immediately led to introduce paradigmatic considerations (sequence/non-sequence commutation). Similarly, the only way to enumerate the diverse sub-types of sequences is to rely on their mutual differences: sequence of parallel montage, sequence of cross-cutting montage, strictly "chronological" sequence, etc. However, each sort of sequence is a syntagmatic unit (a series of several shots), and remains so; but it was possible to delineate it only by means of a paradigmatic comparison. One thus arrives, as we have begun to do in another work, at the enumeration of the principal models of *sequential* organization between which the film has a *choice:* the catalogue which results, no matter what its details, will be a paradigm of syntagms.

The reverse process may also be found. Let us suppose that one defines the "sequence of cross-cutting montage" as that which follows the distributional scheme A-B-A-B-A-B-A-B-A-B-, etc., in contrast to other principles of ordering such as A-A-A-B-B-B-, etc., or A-A-A-B-A-A-A-, etc. One has a definition which is, in principle, of a syntagmatic type, since it consists in stating an *order.* But what is the exact nature of the "elements" which come to be arranged in the order indicated? What does each "A" and each "B" represent? It is here that paradigmatic considerations necessarily reappear, and this time in another fashion. For these "elements" are not exactly elements but rather classes of elements: in order to be able to identify a cross-cutting montage as such it is necessary to *reduce* alternate images to "A" and "B"; in the cross-cutting montage, as may be directly seen in films, one never finds two images, but numerous images which may be classified into two categories (or, in other cases, into three categories, into four, etc.). Without this classification, one would be unable to distinguish cross-cutting montages with two series from those which have three or more series. In addition, one would be unable to speak of "series," for each series is precisely one of the classes of images which alternate. However, outside of the act of categorization, there would not even be any *cross-cutting*. If one adopted as a unit the image rather than the class of images, one would discover only a *succession,* since each image is different and unique. There would remain no difference between a sequence of cross-cutting montage and a non-cross-cutting sequence, so that it is the very notion of cross-cutting montage which would disappear. The latter is thus completely linked to the taking into account of classes of images (distinctive units). However, the only criterion which makes it possible to classify several different images into "A" is that they are not "B" (and vice versa). Thus—and to take a particularly banal example of a cross-cutting montage with two terms—one would put into "A" all the images which show the chasers, and into "B" all those which show those being chased in a chase scene. Finally, the simple enunciation of the syntagmatic scheme ("A-B-A-B-A-B-, etc.") would itself only be possible thanks to the play of a logical opposition ("A/B"), i.e., of a paradigmatic scheme. (Certainly, what is *also* characteristic of A and B is that they alternate: a syntagmatic notion; but, once again, one can only know that they alternate if one has already established categories.) Thus, the terms of the syntagm (A-B) are at the same time members of the paradigm (A/B): one properly calls the "paradigm" an opposition between two classes, and not between two tokens. A moment ago we defined the "catalogues" which enumerate different syntagmatic types ("catalogues of montage," for example) as *paradigms of syntagms.* We find at present that each syntagmatic type is in itself a *syntagm of paradigms,* or more exactly a syntagm of members of paradigms: a class of sequences of classes of elements, as American distributional linguistics would say (e.g., Zellig S. Harris). (pp. 170–172)

This passage is most interesting. There is not time to examine it in detail. For our purposes, there are two essential points. Point one is that without saying it, or even implying it, Metz manages to acknowledge a fundamental aspect of the criticisms we have been developing: that there is no specification of signifier features in the *grande syntagmatique* analysis. Point two concerns what Metz does about this problem. We note first the placement of this discussion in a chapter on paradigm and syntagm. The placement of the discussion as an "example" of the theoretic problem of paradigm and syntagm is surely a ruse, conscious or unconscious, for reintroducing this topic without admitting a prior lack, irresolution, or faulty argument. In principle, for that purpose, it could be brought in as an "example" anywhere. Metz reintroduces the *grande syntagmatique* question in chapter 8, section 4, for a specific reason; he uses the "circularity of paradigm and syntagm" point to explain away what appeared as a lack in the earlier argument, and thereby to overcome it. What seemed to be a fault in the analysis is now seen to be an ineluctable property of the problem itself. It seems that Metz is grasping at the straw of a later theoretical refinement of one point of *Elements* semiotic method as a way of justifying an analytical lack in his own work. This perhaps explains the highly indirect way in which the point is introduced and developed. Just as Metz did not state openly the problems his analysis encountered, so here his reconsideration is not conducted openly. On the second time around, the entanglements required to keep the problem underground become even more complicated and involuted. Now even the *name* of the topic is suppressed.

Chapter 9

Critique of Cine-Structuralism

I (1973)

Several recent texts put the question of structuralist study of cinema back on the agenda: Charles W. Eckert's *Film Comment* article, "The English Cine-Structuralists"; the new edition of Peter Wollen's *Signs and Meaning in the Cinema*, which reconsiders aspects of the 1969 original; and the *Screen* translation of the *Cahiers du Cinéma* collective text on *"Young Mr. Lincoln."* [2] The last is ex-

---

[1] This text originally appeared in two parts in *Film Quarterly*.

[2] *Film Comment,* 9, no. 3 (May/June 1973), pp. 46–51; *Signs and Meaning in the Cinema* (Bloomington, Ind.: Indiana University Press, 1972); *Screen,* 13, no. 3 (Autumn 1972), pp. 5–47.

plicitly a critique of structuralism and itself a post-structuralist work. It appears in English with an afterword by Peter Wollen, which provides the occasion for a specific confrontation. These critical texts are more readily comparable in that they all deal, directly or indirectly, with a common object, the films of John Ford. According to *Tel Quel*, "the exact value of a text lies in its integration and destruction of other texts."[3] The texts we are concerned with have value by this test. Wollen's book destroyed and/or integrated in whole or part many previous film-critical texts. Eckert partially destroys the auteur-structuralist texts, even as he seeks to valorize them. The *Young Mr. Lincoln* text lays waste four entire areas of film study. The present text seeks to integrate and destroy these texts in turn; more precisely, it inaugurates this task. This is its only praise, for most film-critical texts are not worth destroying and are certainly not to be integrated.

Eckert's article concerns those English critics who refurbished the *politique des auteurs* with the critical apparatus of structuralism in the late 1960s: Geoffrey Nowell-Smith, Peter Wollen, Jim Kitses, Alan Lovell, and Ben Brewster. He distinguishes three forms of structural criticism of special interest to film critics: (1) the study of linguistic structures in narrative (Tzvetan Todorov and Roland Barthes); (2) the semiological study of the language of cinema (Christian Metz, Pier Paolo Pasolini, Umberto Eco), which attempts to determine how cinema signifies and whether it can be analyzed like a language; and (3) Claude Lévi-Strauss's study of the underlying structures of thought and of the codes employed in the dialectical systems that operate in mythic thought. The last form of structural study most closely approximates that used by the auteur-structuralists and is the one Eckert concentrates on. (He finds the other two studies "unpromising" and "limited in scope and in the applicability of the insights they achieve."[4]) Eckert

---

[3] *Théorie d'ensemble* (Paris: Seuil, 1968), p. 75.

[4] This text very nearly reverses Eckert's findings, concluding that (3) is not promising, at least as pursued so far. For reasons not fully developed here, we find (1)—perhaps more along the lines of Jean-Pierre Oudart than of Christian Metz—and (2) of considerable promise. See Alan Williams, *Film Quarterly*, 26, no. 5 (Fall 1973), for a study of narrative mechanisms in *La Ronde*. Such study does not reduce the text to "underlying structures." It works on the traces of the film, it does not bypass the inscription in favor of systems that allegedly underlie it. It not only works on the signifiers, whereas auteur-structuralism bypasses the signifiers to get to the signifieds; it studies the *production* of signifiers, specifically those mechanisms that generate narrative. If this is not comprehensive study of inscription, as in the *Cahiers* "Young Mr. Lincoln," it is necessary preparation for such study.

proposes to assess the work of these critics by comparing their methods with those formulated by Lévi-Strauss and then to define the achievements and the promise of auteur-structuralism and of structuralism in general.

The first influential work in English cine-structuralism was Nowell-Smith's *Luchino Visconti* (1967; New York: Doubleday & Company, 1968). The purpose of criticism, according to it, is to uncover behind the superficial contrasts of subject and treatment in a director's work a structural hard core of basic and often recondite motifs. The drawbacks to this approach, noted by Nowell-Smith, were the possibility of variable structures due to changes in an author's work over time and the temptation to neglect the myriad aspects of a film's production and aesthetic effect that a study of motifs does not impinge upon. Indeed in his own study, Nowell-Smith does not find a simple and comprehensive Visconti structure because the latter developed over the years and adopted many styles of filmmaking. His book also studies many aspects of production, history, and stylistic influence that have no bearing upon structure. Nevertheless, Eckert's dominant impression of the book is that structural themes are indeed at the core of Visconti's enterprise and of Nowell-Smith's critical interest.

Wollen's *Signs and Meaning* quotes Nowell-Smith's theory of criticism then takes up the films of Howard Hawks as a test case for the structural approach. He dichotomizes Hawks's films into two categories, the adventure drama and the crazy comedy. These types express inverse views of the world, the positive and negative poles of the Hawksian vision. Wollen cautions that an awareness of differences and oppositions must be cultivated along with the awareness of resemblances and repetitions usually found in thematic or motif-seeking criticism. He then cites the main sets of antinomies in Hawks's work and notes how they break down into lesser sets, any of which may overlap or be foregrounded in different movies. But Wollen's "most intensive criticism" is saved for John Ford, in whose work he finds the master antinomy of wilderness and garden (terms derived from Henry Nash Smith). His analysis of Ford reaches its principal conclusion in this statement: "Ford's work is much richer than that of Hawks and . . . this is revealed by a structural analysis; it is the richness of the shifting relations between antinomies in Ford's work that makes him a great artist, beyond being simply an undoubted auteur." For Eckert, this statement captures the essence of Wollen's species of structuralism, just as the search for a hard core of basic and recondite motifs defines Nowell-Smith's.

Both definitions were harmonious with the intentions of Jim Kitses's *Horizons West* (1969; Bloomington, Ind.: Indiana University Press, 1970). To him, the auteur theory meant the idea of personal authorship in cinema and the concomitant critical responsibility to examine systematically all of a director's work, in order to trace characteristic themes, structures, and formal qualities. Kitses also takes from Henry Nash Smith the insight that the image of the West has a dialectical form. Central to the form of the Western is a philosophical dialectic, an ambiguous cluster of meanings and attitudes that provide the traditional thematic structure of the genre. Kitses lists the principal antinomies involved and notes that polar terms may be transposed in the course of an auteur's development. (These three books led to articles by other English critics, some favorable to structuralism [Alan Lovell and Ben Brewster], some unfavorable [Robin Wood].)

Following his review of these texts, Eckert does not proceed immediately to the promised evaluation of the auteur-structuralists. Instead he returns to Lévi-Strauss, nominally to derive the principles with which to conduct this assessment. "I will take up the most provocative of Lévi-Strauss's insights in the general order of their importance and breadth of application." The oddity of this long section is that Eckert uses only two of the many points it develops in his subsequent return to the auteur-structuralists. These are: that every myth is only a limited application of the pattern that emerges as the analysis of a body of myths proceeds, hence many myths must be analyzed before a valid structure can be discerned; and that figures in myths have meanings only in relation to other figures in that myth, they cannot be assigned set meanings.

Nowell-Smith makes a careful analysis of relationships in individual films and is especially attentive to the shifting nature of these relationships and to dialectical progressions, but his initial premise is that Visconti developed too much as an artist to make a comparative study of his films possible. Hence he considers each film singly, attempting to bring out its relationship, hidden or overt, to the rest of Visconti's work. The absence of a thoroughly comparative method not only qualifies Nowell-Smith's structuralism, it raises the issue whether or not the body of films produced by a director can qualify as a set of myths. Kitses does analyze a director's work as a single body of myth, but his individual figures are defined in archetypal and iconic terms; their meanings are traditional rather than dependent upon relationships within each film. Only his emphasis on the dynamic interaction of the figures and their tendency to form antinomic pairs resembles Lévi-Strauss's analysis. (Lovell's method is very close to Kitses's, employing a mixture of archetypal and structural insights.) Peter Wollen shows the closest familiarity with Lévi-Strauss's writings. His analysis of Hawks and Ford, though only intended to be exploratory and suggestive, (1) is less attuned to archetypes and is thoroughly directed at bundles of relations, and (2) is founded on the premise that it is only the analysis of the whole corpus that permits the moment of synthesis when the critic returns to the individual film.

Eckert enlarges upon the two principles before concluding. Lévi-Strauss's "The Structural Study of Myth" settled that meaning in mythology cannot be found in the isolated elements that enter into the composition of the myth, but only in the way those elements are combined.[5] So much (Eckert adds) for father figures, traditional icons, and wilderness and garden. Accepting such set meanings may blind us to important shifts of relationship and commit us to the surface meaning of the myth. Traditional meanings may well emerge from the process of analysis, but the point is that they will be discovered rather than established a priori. The question of the degree of unity in an auteur's work is less easily resolved. The main premise implicit in the auteur theory is that a director's body of work possesses unity. The alternative notion, that an artist evolves through stages of thought and technique, is a nineteenth-century conception, attuned to purposive evolution. The modern study of myth has attacked evolutionary schemes in favor of synchronic studies of motifs, types, and forms. We must use judgment in deciding to what degree a director conforms to unity and invites a mythic analysis; and we must anticipate that an apparent evolution in style and theme may only mask what is recurrent in a body of work. Eckert concludes overall that the structural method will probably be productive in proportion to the discretion and intelligence with which it is applied. Its promise, however, is undeniable. "There remains much to be done beyond what current auteur-structuralism has suggested."

Why does Eckert return to basic Lévi-Strauss between his review and his evaluation of auteur-structuralism, when so much of what he develops seems nonoperative in relation to that project? Why,

---

[5] Claude Lévi-Strauss, *Structural Anthropology*, trans. Claire Jacobson and Brooke Grundfest Schoepf (Garden City, N.Y.: Doubleday Anchor Books, 1967), p. 202.

in defending auteur-structuralism, does Eckert begin again from zero by asking whether "film can be equated with myths" and questioning "the suitability of a structural study of a director's body of work —or of films in general"? Either the auteur-structuralists have covered this ground before or they haven't. If they have, then Eckert's reconsideration is either repetitious or it is a critique of their foundational work, apparently a covert critique as this section makes no reference to their texts. If they have not covered this ground, then Eckert's defense of the auteur-structuralists uncovers an absence vastly more important than the virtues he finds in their work—their failure to found their criticism theoretically, the absence of an auteur-structuralist epistemology. In activating these texts, Eckert has activated the scandal of their lack of foundation. Attempting to integrate them, they have come apart in his hands. The middle section of his article is then a kind of glue or *bricolage* that attempts to put them back together.

Eckert's text provides a cue, in the form of a speech against itself, which turns us back to the original texts. Neither Kitses nor Nowell-Smith discusses Lévi-Strauss. Wollen does, to be sure, but in ways that avoid rather than confront the problem of founding the method he proposes. This avoidance is inscribed in the rhetoric of Wollen's second chapter of *Signs and Meaning*, "The Auteur Theory." The latter begins with the historical origins of the auteur theory, then quotes Nowell-Smith and applies the structural method to Hawks. It is only then that it discusses foundations—in two paragraphs squeezed between Hawks and Ford, a foundational discourse in the form of a transition between main headings and delivered on the run.

> Something further needs to be said about the theoretical basis of the kind of schematic exposition of Hawks's work which I have outlined. The "structural approach" which underlies it, the definition of a core of repeated motifs, has evident affinities with methods which have been developed for the study of folklore and mythology.
>
> There is a danger, as Lévi-Strauss has pointed out, that by simply noting and mapping resemblances, all the texts which are studied (whether Russian fairy-tales or American movies) will be reduced to one, abstract and impoverished.
>
> This means of course that the test of a structural analysis lies not in the orthodox canon of a director's work, where resemblances are clustered, but in films which at first sight may seem eccentricities.
>
> The protagonists of fairy-tales or myths, as Lévi-Strauss has

pointed out, can be dissolved into bundles of differential elements, pairs of opposites . . . We can proceed with the same kind of operation in the study of films, though, as we shall see, we shall find them more complex than fairy-tales. It is instructive, for example, to consider three films of John Ford and compare their heroes . . . (pp. 93–94)

In the four passages quoted, Wollen's text proceeds from a notation of similarities to a tenuous equation to an achieved integration to a wholesale importation which moreover cautions itself to proceed carefully. Needless to say, each of these stages is unearned, including the first, a notation of affinities at the phenomenal level that asserts its own evidence. The apparent progress of the passage is a feat of rhetoric. The fundamental questions—whether films are like myths, whether modes of myth study are applicable to film study, and whether the auteur theory is compatible with Lévi-Straussian structuralism—are avoided by Wollen, elided by a skillful rhetoric that seems to answer them.

There are some theoretical passages following the discussion of Ford but they do not return to the problem of foundations. Here Wollen discusses the "noise" of camera style and acting, arguing that films, like myths, exist independently of style. Hence, despite noise, "the film can usually be discerned," "film" here meaning auteur-structure. Pivoting on the sentence: "It is as though a film is a musical composition rather than a musical performance . . . ," Wollen then launches into a dazzling essay on the distinction between composition and performance in music, painting, and theatre as they developed over several centuries. Following this, he concludes that the director is not simply in command of a performance of a preexisting text, but himself a composer also. The incidents and episodes of the original screenplay or novel are

> the agents which are introduced into the mind (conscious or unconscious) of the auteur and react there with the motifs and themes characteristic of his work. The director does not subordinate himself to another author; his source is only a pretext, which provides catalysts, scenes which fuse with his own preoccupations to produce a radically new work. Thus the manifest process of performance, the treatment of a subject, conceals the latent production of a quite new text, the production of the director as an auteur. (p. 113)

The chapter concludes with a reminder that the task begun by the original auteur critics is still far from completed.

Founding auteur-structuralism would mean beginning with structuralism and its foundations and moving from it to film study, specifically to the study of auteurs, deriving the principles of the latter study from structuralism. As has been seen, Wollen does not do this. Instead he begins with auteurism, establishes it as an on-going activity, then turns to structuralism as another ongoing activity, and then discovers affinities and similarities between the two.

Let us look more closely at these "affinities" and at the text's "discovery" of them. We note first that at least four different senses of "the auteur theory" may be distinguished in Wollen: the French original, Nowell-Smith's transformation, Wollen's transformation (1969), Wollen's transformation (1972). Yet Wollen refuses to differentiate these senses, speaking at all times of "the auteur theory," as though it were one thing now and had always been one thing. Besides blurring the first two senses, Wollen himself redefines the auteur theory, even as he affirms its singularity of meaning. Most readers may be aware that Wollen is transforming the auteur theory, not merely expositing it; but they may not be aware of how this device affects his argument, precisely because the rhetoric that this collapse of multiple meanings permits is so persuasive. So we ask: Why does Wollen's text deny that it is altering the auteur theory as originally developed? Why does it pass off its transformation as a "discovery" of what already exists? That is, *why does it deny its own work?* The collapse of multiple meanings takes place in several stages. First, by presenting Nowell-Smith's definition of the auteur theory as a "summary" of it "as it is normally presented today,"[6] Wollen denies the latter's transformation of the auteur theory even as he imports it into his own discourse. Not long after this Wollen discovers affinities between the auteur theory and structuralism. Since it is obvious that Nowell-Smith's 1967 book was already influenced by Lévi-Strauss and his followers, this "discovery" is less than fortuitous. Wollen has already imported a basic structuralism on the "auteur theory" side of his exposition. As the essay proceeds, he brings this structuralism more specifically into line with the Lévi-Strauss original, though still under cover of expositing a singular and constant auteur theory. What Wollen's assertion of constancy entails, at this point, is not only that auteurism and structural-

---

[6] Note the crucial repetition of the word *indispensable,* before and after the Nowell-Smith quote, on p. 80. Two things equal to the same thing are equal to each other.

ism are literally the same thing, but that *they have always been the same*. It is only this impossible contention that relieves Wollen from having to provide foundations for auteur-structuralism. If he admitted that he was transforming the auteur theory, specifically that he was seeking to merge the auteur theory with structuralism, then he would have had to found or justify his action theoretically.

Wollen says at one point:

> There are other kinds of code which could be proposed [besides that of auteur-structure], and whether they are of any value or not will have to be settled by reference to the text, to the films in question.[7]

Several other passages put the emphasis on results. There is a way of reading chapter 2 that says: all questions of logic and foundation aside, auteur-structuralism is justified because it works—that is, because it produces (excellent, true) results when applied to films. This reading of Wollen's text is supported by its rhetorical organization. Auteurism is established by the Hawks discussion before Lévi-Strauss and structuralism are introduced; then, after two paragraphs, it turns to an even longer discussion of Ford. (Auteur-structuralism is happier in the field than in the theoretical laboratory.) The organization of the chapter makes these critical discussions carry the principal weight of its argument. To a considerable degree, they *are* its argument. Leaving aside the merits of Wollen's results, let

---

[7] *Signs and Meaning*, p. 168. Wollen's ambiguous use of the word *code* confuses his text at several points. Many of these confusions are carried over into Eckert's text where they generate new ones. One can argue that codes function at the level of meaning analyzed by Lévi-Strauss, but these must be differentiated from the other codes referred to by Wollen. Lévi-Strauss isolates what Hjelmslev would call the form of content. It is perhaps preferable to refer to *structure* at this level and to reserve *code* for the levels of expression. Thus structuralism, concerned with form of content, indeed—positing many layers of content—with a deep structure within the form of content, may be distinguished from semiology, which is concerned with moving from the level of expression to the level of content via codes. But, as noted in the text, structuralism is often used globally to refer to all work influenced by Lévi-Strauss and structural linguistics.

Wollen consistently confuses codes of expression with form of content, according them an equal status, perhaps in an attempt to make his "structures" seem more legitimate. Asking whether particular codes are of value or not compounds the confusion. It is evident that all codes have value in the production of meaning in film. The question can only embody a preference for certain types of meaning and methods of analysis over others. The answer depends on the principle of pertinence chosen and the results desired by the analyst.

us look at this argument itself. What can be said against the argument of good results? Marxist theory, philosophy, and semiology have operated singly and conjointly to dismantle the ideological, conceptual, and linguistic foundations of empiricism. Any system of interpretation *generates* its own results. Every system of interpretation will produce "results" that are in full accordance with its methods. Hence justification by results is circular. As Roland Barthes says in *On Racine,*

> One seeks, and naturally one finds . . . We must not complain about this—the demonstration of a coherence is always a fine critical spectacle—but is it not evident that, though the episodic content of the proof may be objective, the postulate that justifies looking for it is utterly systematic? [8]

Even more importantly, any system that simply produces results as a kind of spectacle, that is, without dismantling and questioning its own foundations, assumptions, problematic, and operations (the means by which it produces results), is necessarily and entirely ideological.

The explanation of Eckert's middle section, too long and wandering for the project proposed in the first section and concluded in the third section, is that it attempts to provide for auteur-structuralism those foundations that the latter does not provide for itself. In doing so, it answers a question that it does not ask, that it cannot ask without calling attention to the scandal of its absence in the work of the auteur-structuralists, thereby undermining their work and possibly itself also. What of Eckert's foundational attempt? In fact it is no more than a sketch, far from the systematic and thorough study that would have been needed to carry its project. Still, it is interesting in several respects. It is genuinely foundational in that it grounds itself in Lévi-Strauss and attempts to move forward toward auteurism. It proceeds in this task only by constructing a highly fragile latticework of premises, inferences, evidences, and connections, many of which are questionable yet each one of which is necessary to make the link that Eckert seeks.

> Whether these codes [of physical objects and of qualities in films] are part of a careful, logical system can only be established through

---

[8] (1960; New York: Hill and Wang, 1964), p. 170.

research. My own preliminary attempts at analysis suggest that they are—[9]

The most interesting aspect of the section is that it moves in a direction nearly opposite to that of auteur-structuralism, toward a criticism of the *many* codes of cinema (most of which Wollen dismisses as "noise," "inaccessible to criticism"[10]) rather than the single code of auteur-structure, and toward an understanding of cinema as myth very different from that of auteur-structuralism:

> The dioscuric union of film-makers and their audience produces a strange Janus of art—myths made by mythmakers that are only certified as true or untrue after they have been created. Perhaps the best index to authentically mythic films, then, is the yearly box-office ratings. (p. 50)

This is very nearly the antithesis of auteur-structuralism. Having reached this point, how does Eckert rearrive at auteur-structuralism, as promised in the first section? He does so only by an authorial *coup de force*—through an abrupt discontinuation of the foundational discourse, which amounts to its abandonment if not its repeal, and an arbitrary jump back to the original discourse. All of which constitutes an extreme and uncharacteristic scriptural violence and the second major way in which Eckert's text criticizes itself, effectively demonstrating the impossibility of arriving at auteurism through a Lévi-Straussian discourse. Immediately following the "box-office" statement Eckert says, "Two more of Lévi-Strauss's stipulations deserve brief consideration," whereupon he adduces the two principles discussed above, which have no connection with his foundational discourse or with the point at which he arrived in considering the box office, but which provide the occasion for a none-too-smooth return to the auteur-structuralists.

---

[9] "The English Cine-Structuralists," p. 49. Again, a confusion regarding codes. To the extent that a film produces meaning at all, one must assume the operation of codes at the level of expression. Codes are by definition logical in that they are constructed by a logical system of analysis.

[10] *Signs and Meaning*, pp. 104–105. *Noise* for Wollen has quite a different meaning than for most semiologists. He seems to consider as noise anything deriving from the level of expression. If camera style and acting were the noise that Wollen suggests, that is, if they resisted codification, then no form of content could emerge from film at all. Hjelmslev would argue that one must posit a total parallel (not identity) between expression and form for the process of signification in cinema to be conceivable at all. Wollen revises his theory of noise in the 1972 edition, but, as argued in the text, with considerable ambiguity regarding the question of codes.

> The issue of how figures are to be interpreted takes us to the heart of the whole enterprise I have characterized as auteur-structuralism. (p. 50)[11]

We have let the auteur-structuralist texts speak for themselves and in speaking, through their gaps, omissions, rhetorical strategies, and contradictions, destroy themselves. We have seen not only that the auteur-structuralist texts have no theoretical foundations, but also that what is present in these texts, their specific traces, can only be understood in relation to this absence. That is, these texts as they exist constitute themselves as an ersatz built over and in relation to this absence, which nevertheless warps them from the inside. We have not asserted positively that auteurism and structuralism are incompatible, that they *cannot* be combined. Nor do we intend to do so, for that would involve first constructing such a foundation as we have demanded and then destroying it, a useless operation. Nor do we suppose that we would do a better job at this than the auteur-structuralists. On the contrary. In relation to the practical problem of directing film-critical energies, however, we shall consider briefly the problems faced by anyone attempting to do this. This will also help explain the failure of the auteur-structuralists, for they are clearly not unintelligent. The difficulty lies in the contradictory project of auteur-structuralism itself, which exists in its purest form in Wollen: the attempt to merge auteurism with structuralism *without altering either in the process*. But, as Eckert's middle section indirectly reminds us, for Lévi-Strauss myths have no origins, no centers, no subjects, and no authors. Bodies of films organized by auteur signature are obviously defined by their origin, which is a subject and an author as well as a definitive center.

---

11 Eckert's text criticizes itself only covertly and unconsciously. At this point we are reminded of Nowell-Smith's book, which (as Eckert himself presents it) contains an explicit critique of structuralism even as it seeks to apply the method. Nowell-Smith's text is demoted by Eckert for its failed structuralism; but when we move outside of the Wollen and Eckert problematic (based on commitment to auteur-structuralism and, in Eckert's case, on the question of which auteur-structuralism most closely resembles Lévi-Strauss's method) and raise our own questions, we are not bound by Eckert's evaluation (which is consistent with his premises). Then we are free to reconsider Nowell-Smith's text and perhaps find it the most interesting of the three, in part for its explicit critique of structuralism, both theoretical and practical. To another problematic it is considerably less disappointing that Nowell-Smith found himself unable to exclude "many aspects of production, history, and stylistic influence that have no bearing upon structure" in considering Visconti's films.

Wollen attempts to deny this or at least he considers it important when he says, in the 1972 edition of *Signs and Meaning*, that the auteur is not a conscious creator but an unconscious catalyst and even (revising his theory of "noise") that the auteur-structure is only one code among many that are discernible.

> What the auteur theory argues is that any film, certainly a Hollywood film, is a network of different statements, crossing and contradicting each other, elaborated into a final "coherent" version. Like a dream, the film the spectator sees is, so to speak, the "film facade," the end-product of "secondary revision," which hides and masks the process which remains latent in the film "unconscious." Sometimes this "facade" is so worked over, so smoothed out, or else so clotted with disparate elements, that it is impossible to see beyond it, or rather to see anything in it except the characters, the dialogue, the plot, and so on. But in other cases, by a process of comparison with other films, it is possible to decipher, not a coherent message or world-view, but a structure which underlies the film and shapes it, gives it a certain pattern of energy cathexis. It is this structure which auteur analysis disengages from the film. ("The English Cine-Structuralists," p. 47)
>
> The structure is associated with a single director, an individual, not because he has played the role of artist, expressing himself or his vision in the film, but because it is through the force of his preoccupations that an unconscious, unintended meaning can be decoded in the film, usually to the surprise of the individual involved. The film is not a communication, but an artifact which is unconsciously structured in a certain way. Auteur analysis does not consist of re-tracing a film to its origins, to its creative source. It consists of tracing a structure (not a message) within the work, which can then post factum be assigned to an individual, the director, on empirical grounds. (*Signs and Meaning*, pp. 167–168)

Wollen twists and turns and makes vocabularic concessions to recent theoretical work, but he does not escape the criticisms he is aware of because he retains the subject as producer of unique or distinctive meaning. In the passage above, Wollen confuses a methodological point with a foundational one. Since auteur-structuralism works empirically (from the works to the director, rather than a priori, from the director to the works) and since it is not interested in the person of the director (his condition as actual subject—biography, psychoanalysis, personal ideology) but only with the structures that are labeled with his name, Wollen supposes that he has solved the foundational problems of auteur-structuralism out-lined above. But he has not. To do so, he would have to explain how it can be that individual subjects produce unique or distinctive meanings (structures), which moreover have the integrity and con-stancy of mythic meanings and can be studied in the same way. In short, he would have to provide that theory of the subject that Lévi-Strauss deliberately and systematically omits, because his work is founded upon the interchangeability of subjects in the production of meaning. The contention that (some) individual directors can and do stamp their films with a distinctive or unique meaning (structure) cannot be grounded in Lévi-Strauss. Nor is the problem overcome if it is stipulated that the auteur-structure is only one meaning among many, for the problem of accounting for the production of this meaning remains.

Wollen is, in any case, ambiguous about his opening out to other codes and the implications of this opening for his method. The greatest source of ambiguity is that the 1972 edition of *Signs and Meaning* reprints chapters 1 through 3 *without change* but adds a new conclusion that seems to reconsider several issues, yet explicitly retracts nothing bearing on auteur-structuralism, neither critical dis-cussions nor theoretical formulations. Wollen continues to speak of "the auteur theory," even though he makes a few changes of em-phasis. Now the director's structuring activity is unconscious whereas before it was "conscious or unconscious." Before it was the script or novel that acted as catalyst to the director, now it is the director who acts as catalyst to his materials. As noted, however, Wollen retains auteur-structure, nominally as one code among many, but really in a privileged position as he continues to identify structure with auteur-meaning and therefore meaning with auteur-structure. Above all, there is nothing in the 1972 edition that recants or re-vises the fundamentals of auteur-structuralism or overcomes the latter's foundational lack—its disconnection with Lévi-Strauss. The latter's name is not mentioned in the new chapter. Wollen wishes to retain his critical achievements and his critical method, though he is willing to change his vocabulary to facilitate this. Hence the long reaffirmation of the auteur theory (pp. 167–173), which is not at all retracted in his remark that chapters 1 and 3 (not 2) are "the most valuable sections" and his remark that "I do not believe that development of auteur analyses of Hollywood films is any longer a first priority." This does not mean abandonment of his previous auteur studies, indeed it freezes them in the eternity of a completed auteurism. As he says in the next sentence, "This does not mean that the real advances of auteur criticism should not be defended and safeguarded."

The questions Can modes of myth study be applied to film study? and Can structuralism be merged with auteurism? are *not identical.* Both Wollen and Eckert assume this identity, though Eckert strains against the assumption and his text cracks on it. Auteur-structuralism treats the two questions as one; specifically, it reduces the first question to the second. It thereby makes the study of films as myths dependent upon the fusion of auteurism and structuralism and effectively rules out other modes of study. In this way it seeks to take over and occupy this field of study entirely. In English-language studies so far, it has actually done so; the auteur-structuralists have succeeded in identifying their methods and concerns with the very notion of a study of films as myths. Having critiqued auteur-structuralism, we are in a position to reconsider this relationship and to disentangle these questions. When auteur-structuralism is destroyed, it is by no means the case that the study of films as myths is destroyed also. Indeed, it would seem that *only* the destruction of auteur-structuralism *liberates* the other question, that is, allows it to be asked and answered.[12] Since prospects for the merger of auteurism and structuralism are not promising, it seems that film criticism would do better to look for other possibilities. Eckert's aberrant middle section suggests a nonauteurist structuralism, one neither dependent upon auteurist epistemology nor organizing its materials by auteur signature. It also suggests, apparently reinstating Metz, Eco, *et al.,* semiological study of cinematic codes of expression.

But before embarking on such studies, we should consider certain important criticisms of structuralism, which also apply to some practices of semiology. These criticisms derive from the wide-ranging theoretical developments inscribed in the texts of Jacques Derrida, Julia Kristeva, Jacques Lacan, and many others. These criticisms have shaken structuralism to its foundations, or rather, shaken it *at* its foundations (and therefore everywhere), for it is a specifically foundational and epistemological critique. Of course the texts con-

---

12 The problematic of a text is not only the questions that it asks, but the questions that it does not ask. Specifically it is the relationship between these, for a text raises certain questions only at the price of not asking others. The relationship between questions asked and questions suppressed is always ideological.

cerned are far from complete agreement with each other, even in regard to the defects of structuralism. This polyphony, which includes repetition as well as discord, relieves the present text from the need to speak for or from any other particular text, which would in any case be foolhardy. Its list of criticisms of structuralism will therefore be partial, sketchy, and highly general.[13]

The foundational defects of structuralism are interrelated. First of all, it is an empiricism. It takes for its object the text as given. This given, the textual object, is its horizon and absolute. Secondly, structuralism posits the object as other. It is based upon the separation of subject and object, that is, upon empiricist epistemology, which in turn is based upon traditional Western (dualist) metaphysics. This epistemology determines the practice of structuralism as a species of representation, itself locatable as concept and method within the historical ideologies of the West. (Michel Foucault identifies representation as the episteme of the seventeenth and eighteenth centuries.[14]) The structuralist work represents or reproduces the structure of the object; so that the two are related to each other as mirror images. The structuralist text is a similacrum of its object. (See Barthes, "The Structuralist Activity." [15])

The critique of structuralism transforms this model in every respect. On the one hand, the text is no longer seen as an object, given and achieved (essentially a product), but as a process, as itself a production, specifically as a collocation of mechanisms for the production of meaning. Thus it is necessary to speak of the *work* of the text if one is to avoid reifying it à la the consumerist ideology of capitalism. This collocation of mechanisms for producing meaning is itself not a given but is determined by material conditions that

---

13 Of course, *structuralism* refers to a great number of discourses and to a great number of texts combining these discourses in various ways. It is perhaps too early to say that structuralism has been definitively replaced by a subsequent movement, let alone to differentiate the structuralist from the non-structuralist constituents of the new constellation. The critique of structuralism outlined here may even be read as structuralism's critique of itself. The critique is then a purge of the empiricist wing of structuralism and of the empiricist elements that have figured in it more generally. In such a critique-purge, "structuralism"—constituted as a sum of defects, as that which is critiqued—becomes the virtual object of structuralism, the theoretical activity, in the latter's clarification and transformation of itself. Such an object need not have hard edges, still less need it correspond to actual objects. What is important is the theoretical activity that it permits.

14 *The Order of Things* (1966; London: Tavistock, 1970), pp. 46–217.

15 *Collected Essays* (1964; Evanston, Ill.: Northwestern University Press, 1972), pp. 213–220.

must be examined in analyzing the text. Thus the text cannot be understood by examination of the text alone. Similarly, indeed identically, the discourse that studies the text is productive. It does not represent the structure of the text, it does not study an object over a gap that divides subject from object, knower from known. It mixes with the text studied. The productivity of the text studied and that of the discourse that studies merge and interact to form a new text.

Related to the productivity of the text is the principle of intertextuality. This means, oversimply, that no text is isolated, discrete, unique, and that none is self-originating. Every text is a combination of other texts and discourses, which it "knots" in a certain way and from a certain ideological position. (Thus the notion of anthropology, of a universality of studies addressing culture as a whole, disappears. The latter denies its own signifying practice, which is always ideological.) Thus description of the structure of a text impoverishes and distorts it and, indeed, mistakes the nature of textuality itself.

Empiricism is overthrown not only because the productivity of the text replaces the static object, intertextuality replaces structure, and the conjoined productivity of critical practice replaces the subject-object split and representation, but also because inquiry is no longer limited to the object itself, the given, but addresses what is there in light of what is not there. This includes questioning the problematic of the text: not just the answers the text gives, but the questions it asks, and not just the questions it asks, but the questions that it does not ask. Why are certain discourses included in the text and others left out? Why does the text combine these and accent them in a certain way? By subordinating itself to the object and its problematic, empiricism is necessarily ideological in function. It reproduces the ideology of the object and above all its own ideology, by constituting itself as a discourse that does not ask fundamental and foundational questions, above all of itself.

The relation of this theoretical work to film study may not be immediately apparent, except for the immense shadow it throws on the entire project of cine-structuralism, by which we mean here not only auteur-structuralism but other kinds as well. There exists in English, however, a film-critical text that seeks to build itself upon this theoretical foundation, the *Cahiers* collective text, "*Young Mr. Lincoln.*" As mentioned above, the entirety of "*Young Mr. Lincoln*" may be read as a critique of structuralism and as a realization of the theoretical critique of structuralism in the area of film criticism.

▌▌ (1974)

This text is concerned with the *Cahiers du Cinéma* text "John Ford's *Young Mr. Lincoln*"(1939) and with Ben Brewster's notes on this text in the most recent issue of *Screen*.[16] The *Cahiers* study is most interesting for the method of reading films that it proposes and carries out. Brewster's article reads the *Cahiers* reading. It also seeks to provide the *Cahiers* method with an altered or improved theoretical underpinning. In so doing it seems to turn *Screen's* important work on Christian Metz in a distinctly new direction.

The *Cahiers* methodology is set forth clearly at the outset of the *Young Mr. Lincoln* text.

> 1. Object: a certain number of "classic" films, which today are *readable* (and therefore, anticipating our definition of method we will designate this work as one of reading) insofar as we can distinguish the historicity of their inscription: the relation of these films to the codes (social, cultural . . .) for which they are a site of intersection, and to other films, themselves held in an intertextual space; therefore, the relation of these films to the ideology which they convey, a particular "phase" which they represent, and to the events (present, past, historical, mythical, fictional) which they aimed to represent. . . .
>
> 2. Our work will therefore be a *reading* in the sense of a *re-scanning* of these films. That is, to define it negatively first: (*a*) it will not be (yet another) commentary. The function of the commentary is to distill an ideally constituted sense presented as the object's ultimate meaning (which however remains elusive indefinitely, given the infinite possibilities of talking about film): a wandering and prolific pseudo-reading which misses the reality of the inscription, and substitutes for it a discourse consisting of a simple ideological delineation of what appear(s) to be the main statement(s) of the film at a given moment.
>
> (*b*) Nor will it be a new *interpretation*, i.e., the translation of what is supposed to be already in the film into a critical system

---

[16] "John Ford's *Young Mr. Lincoln,* a collective text by the editors of *Cahiers du Cinéma,*" trans. Helene Lackner and Diana Matias, *Screen,* 13, no. 3 (Autumn 1972), p. 5; "Notes on the Text 'John Ford's *Young Mr. Lincoln'* by the editors of *Cahiers du Cinéma"* by Ben Brewster, *Screen,* 14, no. 3 (Autumn 1973), p. 29.

(metalanguage) where the interpreter has the kind of absolute knowledge of the exegetist blind to the (historical) ideological determination of his practice and his object-pretext, when he is not a hermeneute à la Viridiana slotting things into a preordained structure.

(c) Nor will this be a dissection of an object conceived of as a closed structure, the cataloguing of progressively smaller and more "discrete" units; in other words, an inventory of the elements which ignores their predestination for the film-maker's writing project and, having added a portion of intelligibility to the initial object, claims to deconstruct, then reconstruct that object, without taking any account of the dynamic of the inscription. Not, therefore, a mechanistic structural reading.

(d) Nor finally will it be a demystification in the sense where it is enough to re-locate the film within its historical determinations, "reveal" its assumptions, declare its problematic and its aesthetic prejudices and criticize its statement in the name of a mechanically applied materialist knowledge, in order to see it collapse and feel no more needs to be said. . . . (An effective reading can only be such by returning on its own deciphering operation and by integrating its functioning into the text it produces, which is something quite different from brandishing a method—even if it is marxist-leninist—and leaving it at that.) . . . [A] materialist reading of art products which appear to lack any intentional critical dimension concerning capitalist relations of production must do the same thing [consider literary work not as a reflection of the relations of production, but as having a place *within* these relations].[17] . . .

What will be attempted here through a re-scansion of these films in a process of active reading is to make them say what they have to say *within* what they leave unsaid, to reveal their constituent lacks; these are neither faults in the work (since these films, as Jean-Pierre Oudart has clearly demonstrated, are the work of extremely skilled film-makers) nor a deception on the part of the author (for why should he practice deception?); they are *structuring absences,* always displaced—an overdetermination which is the only possible basis from which these discourses could be realised, the unsaid included in the said and necessary to its constitution. In short, to use Althusser's expression—"the internal shadows of exclusion."

The films we will be studying do not need filling out, they do not demand a teleological reading, nor do we require them to account for their *external* shadows (except purely and simply to dismiss them); all that is involved is traversing their statement to locate what sets it in place, to double their writing with an active

---

[17] "John Ford's *Young Mr. Lincoln,*" pp. 5–6.

reading to reveal what is already there, but silent (cf. the notion of *palimpsest* in Barthes and Daney), to make them say not only "what this says, but what it doesn't say because it doesn't want to say it" (J. A. Miller, and we would add: what, while intending to leave unsaid, it is nevertheless obliged to say). . . .

[T]he structuring absences mentioned above and the establishment of an ersatz which this dictates have some connection with the sexual *other scene,* and that "other other scene" which is politics; that the double repression—politics and eroticism—which our reading will bring out (a repression which cannot be indicated once and for all and left at that but rather has to be written into the constantly renewed process of its repression) allows the answer to be deduced; and this is an answer whose very question would not have been possible without the two discourses of overdetermination, the Marxist and the Freudian. This is why we will not choose films for their value as "eternal masterpieces" but rather because the negatory force of their writing provides enough *scope* for a reading—because they can be re-written. (p. 8)

Since the essay "returns on its own deciphering operation" again and again, its methodology discussions are not limited to the introductory section. After sections on Hollywood in 1938/39, the U.S.A. in 1938/39, Fox and Zanuck, and Ford and Lincoln, a section called "Ideological Undertaking" asks, "What is the subject of *Young Mr. Lincoln?*" The previous sections have established economic and political conditions in the U.S. just prior to the film's making. They conclude that the Republican Zanuck wanted to make a film about the Republican Lincoln in order to promote a Republican victory in the presidential election of 1940. This explains politically and economically why and how the film was put into production; these factors determine but are not the same thing as the ideological undertaking of the film. The latter is:

the *reformulation* of the historical figure of Lincoln on the level of the myth and the eternal.

This ideological project may appear to be clear and simple— of the edifying and apologetic type. Of course, if one considers its statements alone, extracting it as a *separable ideological statement* disconnected from the complex network of determinations through which it is realised and inscribed—through which it possibly even criticizes itself—then it is easy to operate an illusory deconstruction of the film through a reading of the demystificatory type (see 1). Our work, on the contrary, will consist in activating this network in its complexity, where philosophical assumptions (idealism, theologism), political determinations (republicanism, capitalism), and the relatively autonomous aesthetic process (characters, cinematic *signifiers*, narrative mode) specific to Ford's writing intervene simultaneously. If our work, which will necessarily be held to the linear sequentiality of the discourse, should isolate the orders of determination interlocking in the film, it will always be in the perspective of their relations: it therefore demands a recurrent reading, on all levels.

7. Methodology

Young Mr. Lincoln, like the vast majority of Hollywood films, follows linear and chronological narrative, in which events appear to follow each other according to a certain "natural" sequence and logic. Thus two options were open to us: either, in discussing each of the determining moments, to simultaneously refer to all the scenes involved; or to present each scene in its fictional chronological *order* and discuss the different determining moments, emphasizing in each case what we believe to be the main determinant (the key signification), and indicating the secondary determinants, which may in turn become the main determinant in other scenes. The first method thus sets up the film as the object of a reading (a text) and then supposedly takes up the totality of its overdetermination networks simultaneously, *without taking account of the repressive operation* which, in each scene, determines the realisation of a key signification; while the second method *bases itself on the key signification of each scene,* in order to understand the scriptural operation (over-determination and repression) which has set it up.

The first method has the drawback of turning the film into a text which is *readable a priori;* the second has the advantage of making the reading itself participate in the *film's process of becoming-a-text,* and of authorizing such a reading only by what authorizes it in each successive moment of the film. We have therefore chosen the latter method. The fact that the course of our reading will be modelled on the "cutting" of the film into sequences is absolutely intentional, but the work will involve breaking down the closures of the individual scenes by setting them in action with each other and *in* each other. (pp. 13–14)

This is the essay's methodological preface. The reading of the film that follows identifies several systems of oppositions and likenesses, somewhat in the manner of Lévi-Strauss. Thus, Lincoln is both the figure of ideal law, which prohibits all violence/desire, and the agent of its inscription, which is achieved only through violence. This doubling complements the film's mass-individual opposition, whereby Lincoln is set apart from others by his sacred relation to law and himself imposes this law on others violently. These systems mutually inscribe the anology between Nature-Law-(River)-Woman and an allied system of debt and exchange, whereby Lincoln is taught to read, led to knowledge, and given the Book of Law by Woman (his mother, Ann Rutledge, and Mrs. Clay respectively), in return for which he owes Her a debt that can only be paid back by his assumption of his mission (to be the Lincoln of myth) and by his incarnation of the Law.

These systems and their interrelations interest us less than the manner of their inscription by the film and of their reading by the *Cahiers* text. A Lévi-Straussian analysis reduces its object to synchrony and then derives its paradigms. The *Cahiers* analysis performs a second operation. It analyzes how these systems present themselves in the film and how the film negotiates the reader's access to them. They are not presented by the film all at once, they are inscribed, trace by trace, in the film's successive scenes, in its "process of becoming-a-text."

> The principal function of this sequence (Scene 2) is to introduce a number of constituent elements of the symbolic scene from which the film is to proceed, by *varying* it and activating it . . . : The Book and the Law, the Family and the Son, exchange and debt, predestination. . . ."
>
> [Third Sequence] Centered on Lincoln, the scene presents the relationship Law-Woman-Nature which will be articulated according to a system of complementarity and of substitution-replacement. (pp. 20–21)

This presentation of the film's systems by its writing is not merely an *ordering*, for that suggests an arrangement of what already exists. *Presenting* is itself a half-wrong term for it suggests a deployment of *presences* and omits the equally important function of absenting. It omits *"the repressive operation* which, in each scene, determines the realization of a key signification . . . [We must study this] in order to understand the scriptural operation (over-determination and repression) which has set it up" (p. 14). This presenting-absenting-conjoining operation is "the dynamic of the inscription." Like the ideological project itself and the selection of discourses which inscribe it, the dynamic of the inscription is overdetermined—"an over-determination which is the only possible basis from which these discourses could be realized, the unsaid included in the said and necessary to its constitution."

The dynamic of the inscription is doubled by a process of active reading, which is necessary to make films say what they have to say within what they leave unsaid. The *Cahiers* concept of active reading involves integrating the reader's knowledge with the film and breaking down the closure between individual scenes. An example is section 18, "The Balcony," which reads the film's dance scene. This follows the lynching scene, the peak of Lincoln's castrating power to date. Mary Todd leads a passive Lincoln from the dance floor to the balcony.

> As soon as he is on the balcony, Lincoln is enchanted by the river. Mary Todd waits for a moment for Lincoln to speak or show some interest in her. Then she draws aside, leaving him alone in front of the river.
>
> (*a*) Dance, balcony, river, moonlight, couple: all these elements create a romantic, intimate, sentimental atmosphere. The scene, however, mercilessly destroys this atmosphere (whose physical signifieds could be already read as more fantastic than romantic) to introduce the dimension of the Sacred.
>
> (*b*) The transfer from one dimension to the other is effected by Lincoln's enchantment with the river: the commonplace accessory of the "romantic scene" is shifted to an other scene and is at the same time the agent of this shift. An other scene (from which Mary Todd, having no place, withdraws) in which a process of displacement-condensation takes place so that the river simultaneously evokes the first woman Lincoln loved (Ann Rutledge)—an evocation here emptied of any nostalgic or sentimental character—and (see 11) the relationship Nature-Woman-Law. The river is here the ratification of Lincoln's contract with Law. Lincoln, faced with his fate accepts it; the classic moment of any mythological story, where the hero sees his future written and accepts its revelation (the balcony, also a typical accessory of romantic love scenes, is here promoted, by Lincoln's gesture and the camera angle, to the anticipated role of the presidential balcony). Correlatively Lincoln's renunciation of pleasure is written here: from now on Ann Rutledge's death must be read as the real origin both of his castration and of his identification with the Law; and the "inversion" of the dance scene as well as its relation to the lynching scene take on their true meaning: Lincoln does not have the phallus, he is the phallus (see Lacan, "La signification du phallus"). (pp. 30–31)

This section "makes the reading itself participate in the film's process of becoming a text" and it "authorizes such a reading only by what authorizes it in each successive moment of the film," while at the same time "breaking down the closures of the individual scenes by setting them in action with each other and *in* each other." The scene and the reading—the film's process of becoming a text and the essay's process of rewriting the text—are one. The reading is constitutive of the text: "We do not hesitate to force the text, even to rewrite it, insofar as the film only constitutes itself as a text by integration of the reader's knowledge.

In this scene-section the operation of writing-reading is transformative: it alters the meaning of what has gone before and of what is to follow. Previous scenes-readings are changed retrospectively, subsequent scenes-readings are changed prospectively. These operations are described precisely by the phrases "is written here," "take on their true meaning," and (especially) "from now on . . . must be read as the origin of." The breakdown of closure may be tested by tracing the effects of this scene in other scenes and of others in it. The meaning of these earlier scenes-readings is here altered: those with Ann Rutledge and her gravestone, the early and later meetings with Mrs. Clay. From this point, the scenes-readings concerning Ann Rutledge are not returned to. Their meaning, which is the basis for the film/reading's subsequent development, is settled. The remainder of the film/reading develops the logic of Lincoln's castration, secured here. This logic reaches full realization in the trial scene, which is in turn the passageway to Lincoln's destiny and the nominal fulfillment of the film's ideological project.

The film's discourses and the inscription that presents-absents-conjoins them are studied not in themselves but in relation to the ideological project that they inscribe. The reading shows in great detail the many kinds and grades of relationship between the film's writing, its "relatively autonomous aesthetic process (characters, cinematic *signifiers*, narrative mode)," and its ideological project. Thus the film's digressive narrative mode permits and covers the film's first repression of politics by morality. The cinematic code for time passing permits another ideological suppression, that of Lincoln's time of reflection concerning what to do, which reinforces its theme of predestination. The Hollywood code of the vigil before an ordeal permits suppression of a scene required by logic but forbidden by the film's hagiographic project. The film's writing also exposes and/or criticizes its ideological project in a number of ways: the excessiveness of Lincoln's violence throughout, Lincoln's own castration, the film's cruel humor (Lincoln's hitting his opponents at their weakest points), Lincoln's lack of control over his destiny, his being the instrument of truth, etc.

"*Young Mr. Lincoln*" may be read as a critique of structuralism and as a realization of the theoretical critique of structuralism in the area of film criticism. So said Part I of this text and it is easy to show that this is true. The critique of interpretation in *Cahiers* 1(*b*) applies to practices of paradigmatic structuralism that claim "the kind of absolute knowledge of the exegetist blind to the (historical) ideological determination of his practice and his object-pretext." Section 1(*c*) critiques that mechanistic structuralism that dissects the object conceived of as a closed structure of discrete units. Section 7 criticizes setting up the film as the object of a reading and turning the film into a text that is readable a priori in favor of its own method of reading.

"*Young Mr. Lincoln*" realizes its theoretical critique of structuralism in its own film-reading practice. Just as defects of structuralism are correlative (see Part I of this text), so are the features of the *Cahiers* reading that overcome them. Proceeding from empiricist epistemology, structuralism constitutes the text as an object and itself as knowing subject vis-à-vis that object. The object-text may then be broken down into discrete units. The *Cahiers* method abolishes the division between the text studied and the discourse that studies. It mixes with the text studied in the ways discussed. As a consequence, it cannot divide the text into closed units, for there is no secure position outside the object-text from which to do so. In mixing itself with the text studied, it necessarily breaks down the closure between the sections of the text studied, and between its own sections also.

Ben Brewster's article in the new *Screen* examines Metz's concept of the "singular textual system" in relation to the *Cahiers* study of *Young Mr. Lincoln*. The article sets out to show that the *Cahiers* analysis is a genuine reading, and not merely a commentary, because it is a motivated reading rather than an arbitrary one. Brewster argues that the codes studied by Metz, produced by study of a large corpus of films and based on the methods of linguistics, are so general that they say very little about any particular film. The large codes analyzed by Metz have a codifying power that is so low as to be almost negligible. "Hence *in themselves* the cinematic codes implied in the film text are not capable of producing an unambiguous reader who would be able to provide an objective reading of a film text."

What Brewster proposes instead, following the later Metz, is the notion of a conjuncture of codes. "However, when we turn from the codes themselves to the singular textual system, that is, to the application of the codes in a single film text, the ambiguity inherent in a secondary modelling system can be drastically reduced by the simple procedure of *doubling* (or trebling, quadrupling . . .) that code or system." Separately the codes have a low encoding value. Combined in a particular film, however, they reinforce each other, largely through redundancy, so that a principle of pertinence is established that regulates or guides the viewer's reading of the film. In this way the reading may be made nonarbitrary. "This codic doubling is by no means an unfamiliar phenomenon. It is what is known in linguistics as *motivation*." Thus the principle of pertinence comes from inside the film, not from outside it. "[T]he motivation of the singular film text marks the pertinent codes, and indeed often first provides these signifying systems with a signified." It is this marking of pertinent codes that defines the implicit reader that Brewster has been seeking.

One problem remains. "The implicit reader is an ideal reader, one who completely conforms to the supposed intentions of the text. Lotman, however, has examined the effects of discrepancy between the text and its (concrete) reader, in particular . . . between the codes employed in the production of a text and those used in its decipherment." A long quotation from Lotman provides a taxonomy of various relations between codes of production and codes of decipherment of artistic texts. From this passage, Brewster concludes:

> It follows that the critical approach to a text is a *reading* in that it both utilizes the codes it has in common with the producer of the text and produces new codes that may or may not have gone into the production of the text with the proviso that the "reading in" of codes is not arbitrary, because it is governed by the rule of pertinence established by the motivations, i.e., multiple codings, that the reading can establish in the text. The authors of *"Young Mr. Lincoln"* are right to insist that "we do not hesitate to force the text, even to rewrite it, insofar as the film only constitutes itself as a text by integration of the reader's knowledge." [18]

We note first that the problems discussed in Brewster's article are generated by the article itself. They are not problems internal to *"Young Mr. Lincoln."* They arise in the attempt to assimilate that

---

[18] Brewster, "Notes on the Text," pp. 36–37.

study to a theoretical position other than its own. Brewster defends the *Cahiers* study through a Metzian analysis of its method of reading films. He thereby shows the compatibility of the two approaches, and, in effect, appropriates the one to the other. Brewster's text specifies its Metzian position in its first paragraph, what might be called its own principle of pertinence in reading *"Young Mr. Lincoln."* It does not, however, justify its proposed reading by showing that it is implicit in the *Cahiers* text. The principle of pertinence is not organized by the text that is read, it is imposed from outside. Hence, in Brewster's own terms, his reading of *"Young Mr. Lincoln"* is arbitrary—it forces and rewrites the *Cahiers* text.

This rewriting is facilitated by Brewster's neglect of *Cahiers*'s own statement of position, a massive omission since the latter is set forth at great length. (The reader can produce his/her own critique of Brewster by actively rereading at this point the long passages from *Cahiers* above.) Because he specifies his own position and skips the *Cahiers* position, Brewster is able to read his position directly into the *Cahiers* study, reduced for this purpose to an unfounded phenomenon in search of a theoretical anchor.

The principal question posed by Brewster asserts his position in the form of a question. Behind it lies a complex of unwritten questions, some asked and answered (the unspoken assumptions on which the question rests), some suppressed (alternative questions that might be asked). Brewster asks: Is the *Cahiers* study a genuine reading, because motivated, or merely a commentary, because unmotivated? The question combines two sets of oppositions. The opposition reading/commentary is taken from the *Cahiers* study. The opposition motivated/unmotivated (arbitrary) is taken from Metz. Brewster conjoins these questions in a way that equates them. This equation imposes a Metzian rewriting on *Cahiers*, for even if the latter's study is arbitrary, that is, nonmotivated by the film itself, it is still not a commentary in the *Cahiers* sense. It does not distill an ideally constituted sense presented as the object's ultimate meaning; above all, it does not miss the reality of the inscription and does not substitute for it a discourse delineating the apparent main statement(s) of the film at a given time. Several passages of *"Young Mr. Lincoln"* make overt admissions of arbitrariness, but this is not the basis on which *Cahiers* distinguishes reading from commentary. Brewster's principal question is entirely systematic, that is, generated by his position. Rather than acknowledge this, however, he presents it as a problem within *"Young Mr. Lincoln"* itself. "[I]t is not so clear

what distinguishes a reading which forces the text from the commentary which restates its meaning in an arbitrarily determined
manner."

The *Cahiers* distinction between reading and commentary rests on
its concepts of an active reading and of making the reading participate in the film's becoming-a-text. In considering the former, Brewster operates a disjuncture that is crucial for the entirety of his argument. "The intention of this 'active reading' is to make the film say
what it has to say within what it leaves unsaid, to reveal its 'structuring absences.' This last theme I shall return to later in this paper:
for the moment I want to discuss the problems of the notion of reading in general and of an 'active' reading in particular." Brewster puts
aside the question of structuring absences in order to consider the notions of reading and active reading. But in so doing he violates the
Cahiers concept, indeed he obliterates it, for you cannot disjoin the
Cahiers active reading from the structuring absences to which it relates what is present in the text, without utterly rewriting the concept. In separating these terms, Brewster opens up a space for the
infusion of Metz—essentially he wants to redefine the concept of
active reading in Metzian terms.

So far we have examined the problematic of Brewster's article and
its strategy, how his posing of terms sets up the transformation of
"Young Mr. Lincoln" under the cover of defending it. The balance
of our analysis concerns the model of reading that Brewster develops
and how this differs from the model proposed in the *Cahiers* study.
The complex of differences between the two models may be grouped
under the heading, empiricism versus antiempiricism, for the principal direction of Brewster's article is that of a regression from the
ambitious, if imperfect, postempiricism of the *Cahiers* analysis. The
latter is no more reducible to an empiricist semiology than to an empiricist structuralism. Not surprisingly, we shall find many of our
criticisms of the latter (see Part I) recurring in new form in relation
to Brewster's semiological model.

Brewster's article moves toward identification of the film's discourses and their interrelations. Thus, on page 38, Brewster arrives
at a formula for *Young Mr. Lincoln:* the generic code of the early
life of a great man is inversely motivated by the Fordian subcode
and the detective story plot (subcode), which are themselves in
parallel motivation. As noted above, the *Cahiers* study does a second
and very important operation. It analyzes progressively how the film's
discourses appear, disappear, join and disjoin, scene by scene. Brew-

ster merely turns the film into a synchrony, identifies the filmwide codes, and expresses their interrelationships as monoliths. He "turns the film into a text which is readable a priori" and, of course, misses the reality of the inscription. But, as *Cahiers* argues, the truth of the film does not consist in the discourses that it speaks, but in the ways in which it presents, absents, hides, delays, transforms, and combines the discourses that speak it. Of course this operation is ideologically determined and is only revealed by an ideological analysis.

We note further that Brewster's method of reading turns the practice of the analyst into mere reproduction and representation, as opposed to the active, constitutive rewriting activity of the *Cahiers* model. Brewster's model of reading finally resembles, despite his disavowals, a semiotics of communication, concerned above all with the transmission of meaning. Hence his equation of reading with "decoding" and his paramount concern with nonarbitrary decoding, that is, with justifying one's reading entirely by the work itself. It is true that, using Lotman, he seems to come round to a more active, constitutive concept of reading. Indeed, he is required to do so by the *Cahiers*'s "integration of the reader's knowledge," toward the naturalization of which within his own system, Brewster's article moves. But his bridging this gap is ambiguous at best and fishy at worst; because, in the last instance as well as in the first, the text controls the reading. Even if the reading involves the production of new codes that have not entered into the production of the text, this production itself is required by and controlled by the text. Thus "the 'reading in' of codes is not arbitrary, because it is governed by a rule of pertinence established by the motivations, i.e., multiple codings, that the reading can establish in the text." Brewster moves from this sentence to affirmation of the *Cahiers* "forcing the text" and "even rewriting it," but he fails to bridge this gap as well. It is evident from the passages quoted above that *Cahiers* does not subject these concepts or that of active reading to the pertinence principle established by the text. The *Cahiers* reading goes beyond the text, relating what is present to what is absent, thereby defining its own principles of pertinence. Brewster is concerned with the empirical reading imposed by the text, the reading to which the spectator is subjected: *Cahiers*'s interest is not limited to this level.

Concerning this point, it is worth taking seriously *Cahiers*'s invocation of Derrida, particularly his concept of inscription. (Though it would be hasty to suppose that the *Cahiers* study has reconciled its diverse theoretical sources—Althusser, Derrida, Lacan, etc.) When the writer or filmmaker is conceived as inscriber, that is, as mark-maker, rather than as encoder of a message, then the problem of an arbitrary versus a nonarbitrary reading recedes. This opposition and the model of encoding-transmission-decoding rest upon that essentialism of the sign that Derrida critiques. No longer does the sign contain or present a meaning or stand in for a meaning that is absent. If a text consists only of marks differed in space and deferred in time, then there can be no reading (and indeed no text) without integration of the reader's knowledge.

As noted before, the *Cahiers* study is based (in part) upon the Althusserian concept of a symptomatic reading, centering on the *absence* of problems and concepts within a problematic as much as their presence and seeking to relate the two. Such a reading leads, through the hole in the structure, to the nonasked questions, to the point where the inscription links the visible structure to the larger structure that encompasses it and determines it. There is a strong tendency in Brewster's article, and in empiricist analyses and models generally, to reduce all absences to presences, and thereby to eliminate all holes and gaps. Of course this is part of the empiricist tendency to reify the text as a static object and then to limit itself to analysis of this object. This is what Brewster does in reducing *Young Mr. Lincoln* to the formula mentioned above. First, all aspects of the film are expressed as positivities; second, the relations among these, and therefore the whole of the film, are expressed as a relation among simple positivities. Thus Brewster's "inverse" and "parallel" motivations, which function as simple plus and minus signs in relating filmwide codes. Aside from other defects, this is an alarming reduction and simplification of complex texts such as films. It also tends to undermine the concept of "singular textual system" as Brewster presents it, for its coding value hardly avoids that generality of extrafilmic codes that the article set out to correct, a result Brewster exploits (see below).

Most alarming of all is Brewster's tendency to reduce ideology itself to a simple positivity, which can be identified and related to other positivities within the film object. Brewster does this, among other ways, by identifying the ideology of *Young Mr. Lincoln* as that of the Hayes-Tilden compromise of 1876. (Peter Wollen also empiricizes ideology in his "Afterword" to the *Young Mr. Lincoln* piece.) Besides committing all the errors of empiricism mentioned above, this removes the sting from ideology by turning it into a simple knowledge that the film merely reproduces and conveniently puts on view for all to see. This turns the film itself into a simple positivity, whose parts may be analyzed and understood perfectly. Like every empirical analysis, however, this leaves the most important questions unanswered. Why was the film itself produced? Why did it include these discourses and leave out others? Why did it combine and inscribe the discourses chosen in the way that it did? If it is ever possible or useful to identify ideology as a simple positivity or text, such as the Hayes-Tilden ideology, then it remains necessary to analyze that *ideological operation* that produces this presence in a particular film, presents it in particular ways, and relates it to other presences. Its specific ideological texts are in truth merely phenomena that are manipulated by the film's ideological operation for its own ends. There can be no adequate analysis based upon such phenomena alone; the ideology that such positivities speak must be uncovered. Thus (need one say it?), the Hayes-Tilden compromise has no permanent or essential meaning. Everything depends upon why, how, and in what context it is spoken. Ideology in the controlling sense is thus the tutor code of the particular ideological texts that speak it. What must be studied is ideology at work in the text, as well as outside it. This is what *"Young Mr. Lincoln"* attempts to do. Thus the film's repression of politics by morality is not a simple fact or datum or positivity. Neither is it a text. It is "a repression which cannot be indicated once and for all and left at that but rather has to be written into the constantly renewed process of its repression."

Brewster's reduction of ideology to a datum has another important consequence, which is culminated in the article's last paragraph. Identification of the film's ideology as that of the Hayes-Tilden compromise reveals at the same time that many films (including Griffith's) share this ideology. The comparison with Griffith reveals also that *Young Mr. Lincoln*'s future anterior structure is not as important as the *Cahiers* analysis supposed, as Griffith's *Abraham Lincoln* carries its hero through political events, yet its ideology is similar to that of *Young Mr. Lincoln*. Brewster concludes:

> It follows from these two points that the generic code (the youth of the hero) and its specific ideological motivation in this film text (the ideology of the Hayes-Tilden compromise) are much less specific to the text and probably to the political conjecture of its production than the *Cahiers* analysis suggests. Inversely, the "cracks"—the inverse motivations—are due to the interaction of these very broad sub-codes with the Fordian sub-code—the textual system constituted by Ford's films—and hence this system/code is of more importance than the *Cahiers* analysis implies. *"Young*

Mr. Lincoln" thus seems to confirm the intuition, if not the theory and method, of author criticism. The authorial system/code remains a crucial element in the analysis of the American cinema. (p. 41)

Brewster's conclusion is a shock. One is astonished that this is what Brewster's analysis has led to, the return of the author. Nothing has prepared one for this. One immediately goes back to determine the steps that led up to this. This conclusion, in relation to which everything before must be reconsidered, requires an entirely different reading of the article. In retrospect it seems that Brewster's analysis has weakened *both* the Metzian position and that of *"Young Mr. Lincoln"* and that the surprise beneficiary of this double collapse is —the author. While apparently pursuing a Metzian inquiry, Brewster has considerably diluted the effective importance of the Metzian system by showing it to be of little use in dealing with particular films. Thus he does not undermine the premises of Metzism or otherwise attack it directly. He affirms his loyalty at the same time as he hollows out its real importance, turns it into a shell. We have seen how Brewster's analysis results in a flattened, denatured *"Young Mr. Lincoln."* The process whereby the latter was systematically reduced to three codes may now be understood as a careful preadapting. The nominal project of integrating Metzism reduced to a shell with a denatured *"Young Mr. Lincoln"* sets up the mutual collapse that Brewster's text has engineered. It remains only, through some historical logical manipulation, to explode two of the three remaining codes to a useless generality, to complete the coup. A carefully built house of cards collapses abruptly; what remains is the author.

Brewster's article must be considered as theoretical and ideological preparation for its eventuation, rearrival of the author, revival of auteur criticism. In this light Brewster's text plays agent provocateur or just plain saboteur. It is the double agent who has entered the capital where two powerful factions contend and, professing loyalty, undermines both groups in order to prepare the way for that personage whom no one expected, the man on the white horse, the man of destiny, the author. Depleted, weakened from battle, both sides capitulate to the strong man who stands ready to relieve them of their duties: a surprising and decidedly premature reappearance of the author.

Sam Rohdie's editorial takes up the chant.

That process makes the generic codes and their motivations appear less specific to *Young Mr. Lincoln* than the Fordian sub-code.

As Ben Brewster points out, this is an affirmation in part of the procedures of author criticism.

Brewster's conclusion gives added relevance to Ed Buscombe's account of author theory and Stephen Heath's comments, particularly Heath's call for a theory of the subject. Ben Brewster indicated the Fordian sub-code as one among a number which intersect within the text and structure the activity of the text. If author criticism is confirmed thereby it is confirmation of an authorial system/code as an element, often crucial, in the work of the text. It is not a confirmation of the ideological construct of the author as punctual source, creator. The concept of text developed by Brewster and Heath in this number is pivotal for a theory of the subject which will displace rather than re-anchor traditional notions.[19]

Fortunately Stephen Heath has not lost his head amid rumors of palace revolution. His "call for a theory of the subject" has nothing to do with the *return* of the subject. It is instead the distinctly different operation of specifying the lowest order of discursive regularity. Discourse produces a subject to speak itself and this production is regulated by ideology. But this has nothing whatever to do with author criticism.[20]

Brewster's "confirmation of the intuition of author criticism" and Rohdie's "affirmation in part of the procedures of author criticism" are misrecognitions based upon and produced by a misreading of the *Cahiers* text. This much the present text has established. But larger issues are involved in these claims, which will require further discussion.

---

[19] *Screen,* 14, no. 3 (Autumn 1973), p. 3.

[20] The evaluations of Part II of this essay concern only the Autumn 1973 *Screen,* not other issues of *Screen* or other work by the writers mentioned.